BLACK-BOX TESTING

Techniques for Functional Testing of Software and Systems

Boris Beizer

WILEY

John Wiley & Sons, Inc.
New York • Chichester • Brisbane • Toronto • Singapore

Publisher: Katherine Schowalter
Senior Editor: Diane D. Cerra
Managing Editor: Robert S. Aronds
Text Design & Composition: Pronto Design and Production, Inc.

Library of Congress Cataloging-in-Publication Data:
Beizer, Boris, 1934–
        Black-box testing : techniques for functional testing of software and systems / Boris Beizer.
                p. cm.
        Includes index.
        ISBN 0-471-12094-4 (pbk. : acid-free paper)
        1. Computer Software—Testing. 2. Computer software—Development.
I. Title.
QA76.76.T48B44   1995
005.1'4—dc20   94-44711
                                                      CIP

Printed in the United States of America

16 15 14 13 12 11 10 9 8 7 6 5 4 2 1

Dedicated to my loyal readers, consulting clients, and seminar students who have continually shown me better ways to present this material, and who have been a source of challenge and delight (as well as income)

CONTENTS

PREFACE

Whose needs is this book intended to satisfy? Software testers and software developers. By "tester" I mean individuals who regularly test other people's software or who are at the moment doing so. By "developer" I mean individuals who regularly develop software but who are currently testing that software. Either of these types of readers will do testing that does not strongly depend on the software's design: the testing you do when you put yourself in the software user's place to verify that it behaves the way it's supposed to, no matter how it may be built. That's what is meant by Black-Box Testing.

When most people first start testing, especially if they do so without formal training in the subject, they rediscover black-box testing (alternatively called **behavioral** or **functional testing**). Without training they may reinvent heuristic versions of methods in the literature for which there may be commercial tools. I wrote this book to make the essential knowledge of tried behavioral testing techniques available to its likeliest users.

Test tool vendors influenced me because they've built sophisticated tools based (in part) on test techniques in this book, but they've been frustrated because testers don't know the techniques that their tools embody. There's a deadlock. You, the testers, are reluctant to invest in learning a technique, especially one that relies on automation, unless there's a commercial tool for it. The vendors can't make the capital investment to develop tools that embody those techniques until they see a market of potential testers who know something about the techniques involved. This book is intended to help break that deadlock. Read it and then go to your favorite test tool vendor and insist that they implement Chapter NNN. Conversely, as I feed back to those vendors the sales figures for this book, we will be sending a clear message to them that the risk is reasonable because there's a demonstrable market for those tools and sophisticated testers who understand the features and the principles on which those features are based.

I must tell you what this book is *not* intended to be. It's not intended to be an entry to the huge literature of testing—as such, it's not a replacement for my *Software Testing Techniques*, 2nd edition [STT2—BEIZ90]. *STT2* is a comprehensive (550 pages) introduction to the literature of testing: a book intended to meet the needs of the broadest possible audience, from developer to tester, to researcher, to graduate or undergraduate student. This book is too small to do that job. The section on software design issues in almost every chapter is a key feature of *STT2:* there's none of that in this book. *STT2* is balanced between structural and behavioral testing. This book deals only with behavioral testing. This book is also not intended to replace *Software System Testing and Quality Assurance* [BEIZ84], or my next book now in progress, *Integration and System Testing* [BEIZ96]. Those books concern system and integration testing; the techniques discussed here are used to create integration and system tests. I will assume in *Integration and System Testing* that you know the appropriate techniques—that you have read *this* book.

This book is also not intended as an introduction to the theoretical literature of software testing. No theorems are proven here and few are mentioned. It's a book for practitioners. However, be assured that everything discussed here, where there is a solid theoretical basis, is based on that foundation. The impact of my attempt to conform to theoretical niceties is that at times the text, especially definitions, might seem to be overly formal, draw seemingly minor distinctions, or seem to be not quite to the direct point of designing tests. If so, I did it to ensure that should you read the advanced literature, you won't have to unlearn anything because this book is consistent with that literature.

Several other things I don't intend to do here. I won't waste your time telling you that testing and quality are important. If you don't know that by now, learning those lessons has a higher priority than reading this book. Also, I don't deal with quality assurance, management, organization, politics, finance, culture, nurturing programmers' egos, comparing scar depth among independent testers, who should test software, should software be tested, do we need laws to force software quality, the infobahn, open systems, freeware, the drug crisis, or the moral decay of today's youth. Interesting though those topics are, I leave them to you to debate and to you to conquer. But if you want to learn behavioral test techniques with a minimum of hassle and prerequisites, then I hope this book won't disappoint you.

THE MISSING MODELS

1. General

This section is for readers familiar with the testing literature, especially readers of Glen Myers' *The Art of Software Testing* [MYER79]: readers who may be puzzled by my omission of several behavioral test techniques. Primary among these are logic-based models.

I set an initial goal of a 175-page book: a good size for a one-semester textbook. This book was also designed to replace Myers' dated little gem, *The Art of Software Testing*. Myers topped out at 191 pages. It became obvious to me as I wrote that examples took more space than I had anticipated. I also set modest technical prerequisites (e.g., sophomore level), which meant that I had to provide more material to make the book self-contained. Meeting the 175-page target was impossible, but throughout, I was under a self-imposed pressure to cut material.

My industrial seminars have been a primary source of feedback for the testing topics about which people want to know. I've taught these over 200 times in the past 10 years, to thousands of testers. My seminar participants fill out an evaluation sheet that asks them which techniques they think will be immediately useful to them and which will be useful to them in the future (say in three to five years). I confirm these responses by continuing contacts with former students and sponsoring organizations to learn which techniques they actually use. This book was guided by that feedback.

2. Myers, *The Art of Software Testing*

The Art of Software Testing covered the scope of testing as then (1979) understood. We've had almost two decades of testing technology development since, so his understandably loyal readers shouldn't be surprised to find that most of the technical material has been superseded. For one thing, we know testing much better now. For another, to do justice to the same scope today requires not one but seven books: Inspections, Test Techniques, Integration Testing, System Testing, Testing Theory, Debugging Methods, Test Organization, and Management. I have a narrower goal in this book: to provide an introduction to test techniques.

Here's a contemporary perspective on the five techniques that Myers discussed.

1. **Logic Coverage Testing.** What Myers called "logic coverage testing" is today called control-flow testing (Chapter 3). This book, however, being concerned with behavioral (black-box) rather than structural (white-box) techniques, deals with behavioral control-flow testing.

2. **Equivalence Partitioning.** All the test techniques in this book are based on the idea of partitioning the set of all possible inputs into equivalence classes (see Chapter 2); that is, they are all examples of **partition testing** methods. Myers essentially asked his reader to examine the specifications and code and from that to create an equivalence class partition for testing the program. He also provided some sage heuristics for doing that. It boils down to creating a specialized test technique for each program. That is a nice idea and impeccably correct, but practicing testers had difficulty defining those elusive (and productive) equivalence classes. Here I present you with ready-made equivalence class partitioning methods (or test techniques) that have proven their utility by practice.

3. **Boundary Value Analysis.** Myers' discussion of boundary value analysis is subsumed under the more general and more powerful domain testing methodology (Chapter 7). Those aspects of boundary value analysis that apply to loops are covered in Chapter 4.

4. **Cause-Effect Graphing** [ELME73, MYER79]. For a more detailed discussion of why cause-effect graphing and related techniques were not included, see section 3, "Logic-based Models." In practice, these techniques proved to be difficult to exploit by would-be testers who did not have the prerequisite knowledge, such as boolean algebra and switching theory. Ostrand [OSTR88] criticized this technique best: "By transforming a written specification into a set of cause-effect graphs, the tester is replacing one complex representation with another."

5. **Error Guessing.** Whenever we select a test technique, we are betting on the kinds of bugs we expect to find because each technique has built-in bug assumptions. Error guessing, then, is not a test technique but an aspect of all test techniques. Error guessing based on programmers' bug statistics is a good idea (but see the "Pesticide Paradox" in Chapter 1). The difference today is that if we have such statistics, we use them as a guide to select specific test methods. There is also a formal theory of error-based testing, which is beyond the scope of this book [HOWD89, MORE90].

3. Logic-based Models

The logic-based models include cause-effect graphing [ELME73, MYER79], decision table models [BEIZ90, GOOD75], and many variants that are used as part of various design methodologies [BEND85, WEYU94B]. They're fine techniques, but they take many pages to explain. Logic-based models, for example, took 42 pages in *Software Testing Techniques*. In this book, because of more modest prerequisites and examples, the draft was over 75 pages. That's another two long (and too-long) chapters that would put the book beyond the bounds of a one-semester undergraduate course.

I can't teach logic-based models without boolean algebra; and there's no point in teaching boolean algebra if you don't teach Karnaugh-Veitch charts [BEIZ90] because people won't use boolean algebra without this vital tool. I found that the audience was sharply polarized. Those who knew boolean algebra and Karnaugh maps could learn the techniques on their own, say from *STT2*. Those who didn't have the prerequisites couldn't learn it in the four hours I devoted to the topic. As a result logic-based testing has always been at the bottom of the list of desirable topics in the feedback from my students and sponsors. I eventually removed the topic from my seminars altogether.

There shouldn't be only one course on testing. An intermediate course, in the junior or senior year, after students have had the prerequisites, would be a good place to deal with logic-based models and others not included here.

4. Language-based Models

There are many models based on specialized test design languages and associated tools. Primary example of this type are Ostrand's category partition method [LAYC92, OSTR88] and Poston's "T" [POST94]. Other methods of this type are reported in BALC89, BELF76, DAVI88, KEMM85, and RICH89.

These methods are based on a test specification language. The languages vary in the degree of formality and expressive power, ranging from rudimentary to full-blown formal languages. The tester expresses the required behavior in this language. A language processor checks the specification for ambiguities and contradictions. A subsequent processor then automatically generates test cases (positive and negative) from the specification by a wide variety of formal and heuristic test techniques.

What's wrong with this approach? Nothing. I love it. I believe that, eventually, much of test design will be done with such tools. But these tools are complex, and there's no understanding them without understanding the test techniques on which the test generators are based. This book is intended to provide the understanding of many of the underlying test techniques.

A second problem is fundamental to any programming language. One of the most important lessons I've learned in almost four decades of observing the software scene is not to bet on a programming language until it's in dominant use; and even then, hedge your bets. People have predicted the demise of COBOL for decades—but like an immortal vampire, it is still with us. Who could have guessed that C would usurp assembly languages, much of FORTRAN, and even COBOL? What happened to PL/1 and Algol? The operational success of programming languages seems to bear no relation to their inherent merit. Test languages, because they have a narrower audience, will have even more capricious future histories. I hope that eventually one or two of these languages and their associated test generators will emerge as commonly used tools. Then will be the time to write books about them, probably at the intermediate level.

README.DOC!

Why Readme. Doc

Will I have more success getting you to read this section before you start the book than shrink-wrapped software vendors have with similar sections? This section is an instruction manual for the book. I'm no different than you are. I get a new package, I run to the stuff that interests me, start playing around, and then when I inevitably get into trouble, I go back and read the README.DOC file to find out what I did wrong. So if you're reading this section, you've probably tried a chapter whose techniques seemed to be germane to your situation and found it confusing. So let's do it right this time.

The Book's Strategy

This book has a strategy. Chapter 1 sets the stage and tells you what I assume about your situation—the context in which you do your testing. It may seem an idealistic context to some of you, but it is real, variations of it are in place in many software development organizations, and it is a context toward which you should strive. Comparing your situation with Chapter 1 gives you some insight on where you are and where you have to go. For those of you familiar with the idea, my standards are SEI maturity level 5 and then some [SCAC94].

Chapter 2 is prerequisite to Chapters 3, 4, 5, 6, 8, and 9. Chapter 4 is prerequisite to 5, 6, and 8. Most of you are pragmatic testers who work under pressure, so I don't blame you for trying to skip over a chapter that seems abstract and only vaguely related to the substantive problems you face. Sorry about that. Chapter 2 is essential. If you don't understand it, the subsequent chapters could be incomprehensible. At best, you won't get as much out of them as you might had you taken the time to read the chapter.

Chapter 2 is a knowledge subroutine. Instead of repeating the same basic ideas over and over again in a different context for each chapter, I develop the ideas of testing once, in abstract form, which I then use in each chapter. Once you understand the abstractions of Chapter 2, I can teach the techniques of each subsequent chapter in a few pages. This makes the book shorter and cheaper; and your knowledge acquisition more efficient.

Chapters 3 to 9 deal with specific techniques. One technique and its variations is discussed in each chapter. I have tried to make these chapters as independent of one another as possible. With Chapter 2 under your belt, you should have no trouble reading these chapters in almost any order.

The **graph** on the right shows the book's prerequisite structure. A solid line means that you must understand the material in the chapter at the arrow's tail to get the full benefit of the chapter at the arrow's head. A dashed lines means that the prerequisite chapter contains some definitions that will be used in the subsequent chapter, but

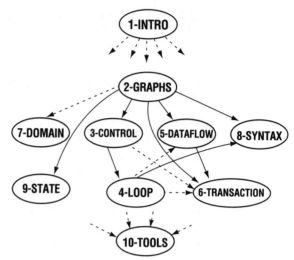

otherwise you can understand the material without mastering the content of the prerequisite chapter. Chapter 1 is a weak prerequisite to the other chapters. The last chapter assumes definitions from all the other chapters and therefore assumes them as weak prerequisites.

The last chapter concerns tools and automation. Although the techniques in this book can be used without automation, they won't be effective if done that way. I hope you'll forgive me for not being overly specific about tools—that is, for not providing you with an up-to-date comprehensive guide of commercially available tools. Such information can be found in DAIC93, GRAH93, SQET94, and similar periodic guides. The field is changing too quickly to provide such data in a static book.

Chapter Structure

Chapters 3 through 9, which contain the meat of this book, have similar structures although the order may vary from chapter to chapter.

Synopsis: What the chapter is about expressed in terms that don't depend on the chapter's content.

Vocabulary—External Prerequisite Terms: Technical terms I expect you to know; they won't be explained in this book. English-speaking readers may find the inclusion of many very basic software terms surprising. About half the terms in the external vocabulary should be understood in their technical sense by any software professional or student. My purpose in including these basic terms is to help my many readers for whom English is not a mother tongue. These terms will, I also hope, materially ease the translator's burden.

Some of the external prerequisite terms are not basic to understanding the book because they are used in one of several illustrations of an idea or in a comment not central to the topic. If you don't understand terms used in an illustration, don't be overly concerned because that shouldn't get in the way of understanding the test technique. All such terms are in the index, so you can look it up in context to see if you do or don't really need to understand the term to understand the topic.

Vocabulary—Internal Prerequisite Terms: Technical terms that I expect you to know but that are explained in a previous chapter.

Vocabulary—New Definitions: These are definitions that will be used within the chapter. Definitions appear in bold-face type when introduced. They may appear in bold again when expanded or refined. Definitions are presented in a logical order in which subsequent definitions depend on the previous—You should read them in the order presented. Definitions are highlighted in the index by putting the page number on which they first appear in bold. Study the new definitions and be sure you understand them before going on.

Vocabulary Conflicts: Sometimes you'll see a term both in the external and internal prerequisites or also in the new definitions. If a term appears both in the external and internal prerequisites, it means that if you understood the term before reading this book, you'll be okay with the chapter, but there is a more precise definition in the context of testing in that you should know. Similarly, if a term appears both in the internal prerequisites and in the first (vocabulary) problem, then it means that there's a more precise or expanded (re-)definition in the chapter.

Terms may appear in the text in bold (which means that you are not expected to understand them), but there is no definition of that term and the term doesn't appear in the chapter new vocabulary. That means that the term is a forward reference to something that will be defined in a future chapter. I've kept forward references to an absolute minimum and put them in only when I felt that it was beneficial. You might want to glance at the appropriate chapter to get the gist of it, but if you don't, don't worry because understanding the present chapter *never* depends on understanding forward references.

The Model: The model on which the technique is based. It includes what we take into account about the software's behavior, what we ignore, and how we represent that behavior.

Bug Assumptions: Every test technique is based on assumptions about the software, the design, the users, and the kind of bugs and the likeliest symptoms of those bugs. This section will give you insight into the effectiveness of the technique in your case.

Typical Applications: A discussion of applications for which the technique is likeliest to be effective.

The Technique: The technique; what it is, how it works; why it works.

Examples: Worked examples of the technique—from requirements to sample test cases. Wherever possible, I've created examples based on standard IRS tax forms. I picked the income tax forms because: they're in the public domain; they have an amazing amount of complicated logic; they can be used to illustrate most black-box test techniques; despite the sweat we put into trying to do our income taxes and understand these seemingly incomprehensible forms, they are reasonable complete specifications and bug-free; and finally, we *should* all know them.

Caveats and Limitations: What the technique can and can't do and the kind of bugs to which it's likely to be blind.

Automation and Tools: Comments on automated test case generation and tools based on the technique.

Summary: A summary of the chapter's content using the vocabulary introduced in the chapter. By comparing the synopsis with the summary, you'll get a good idea of what the chapter has to offer.

Self-Evaluation Quiz and Exercises: Exercises and question appropriate to the chapter. You won't master testing without effort. Also, you must know the terminology introduced in that chapter if it is expected for a later chapter. Be your own QA. Test yourself.

I also chose the IRS tax forms because there's a convenient test engine. Check your work by running the tests against an off-the-shelf personal tax package. You can assume that such packages are correct with respect to implementing the sometimes-arcane IRS rules. They also check if you have filled out all the essential boxes. Also, if you put in values that are deliberately out of bounds, the program should catch it and warn you. I'm sorry that I had to freeze the tax returns at 1994, but if the tax laws change (as they inevitably will), you'll gain useful experience in test suite maintenance.

If you've been out of school for a while, then these exercises will give you additional practice with doing your income taxes. If you're a student and have never done your own taxes, it's time you learned. As for the complexity of the tax forms, don't blame me—contact your senators and representative. Besides, real testing problems are much more complicated than these exercises.

Income Tax Forms and Reference to Them

I illustrated as many techniques as possible by using US Federal Income Tax Form 1040 and associated schedules for 1994. Copies of the forms used in this book are provided in Appendix A. These forms define the requirements we're testing. I've assumed throughout this book that as you look at the example, you are also looking at a copy of the appropriate form.

I refer to various lines on the tax forms, such as "1040 Line 23." Unless otherwise noted, if the form name (e.g., Schedule-C) is not given, reference is to Form 1040. Also, in order to create useful models, we may add "lines" to our model that are not in the real form. For example, a single complicated line such as Line 34 can become Lines 34.1, 34.2, and so on.

Reader Prerequisites

I've assumed some things about your knowledge or experience. Any of the following should be sufficient: one or more years of undergraduate study in a computer science or software engineering curriculum, a two-year associate degree in computer science or software development, an intensive one-year course of study at a certified commercial data processing school or the equivalent, a complete course of study in software at a U.S. military service school, three or more years of working experience as a programmer. Whether you are currently doing programming is not important. What counts is that you know the basic principles of programming and how it is done.

Readers with experience in testing from an application point of view but without experience in programming will be at a disadvantage. You'll have to work harder to understand and to be able to exploit Chapter 2. The external prerequisite terms section of each chapter tell you what you need to know for each technique. Most people tend to underestimate their knowledge rather than overestimate it. If you understand the prerequisite terms, then however you got that knowledge, it is sufficient to the needs of the chapter.

A Note on Footnotes

I don't expect all readers to understand all footnotes. There are two types. The first, and most common, is a comment that doesn't properly fit in the text. The second type is intended for teachers and theorists. These are also comments, but of a technical nature that may help teachers who know testing theory who wish to expand the course with additional theoretical material. Such footnotes are always in italics.

Not Just Software

From the above it may seem that this book is addressed only to software developers and testers. Not so. The prerequisites are relatively modest and common to almost all engineering, science, business, and accounting training today. After all, who doesn't take Programming 101? "Black-box testing" means that we don't really care how a programlike process is implemented. It could be software, of course, but it could also be the logic of chemical reactions, the physics of an electromechanical system, or the mysterious workings of the legal mind when it drafts tax laws. Such systems also must be tested. Every technique in this book can be exploited to test things that are not implemented by software. So if you're a biochemist who wants to optimize testing of the reactions you use in a blood analyzer, you may find something useful in this book because it's unlikely that there will be a book published on testing blood chemistry; and would that the members of our legislatures and Congress think to apply formal analysis and testing techniques to the insane tax laws (and especially all the loopholes) that they draft. They certainly could use this book—but that, of course, is too much to ask.

Using the Index

The index is comprehensive. Every page number in the index has something on the subject, although the index term may not always appear on that page explicitly. Bold face entries mean that the referenced page has a definition of the term. The index also extends to the reference section: References are included in the index so that if an index entry refers to a reference section page number, then there is a paper on that page that deals with the subject. You'll know that from the title or from the comments associated with reach entry.

References

The references are not intended to meet the researchers' needs. They are intended for the book's users—as resources where you can learn more about the subject or sometimes find contradictory points of view, or examples of successful applications that you can use as ammunition in your fight to get the technique implemented in your organization. I also have limited the bibliography to papers, that, although they may contain advanced material, are not substantially beyond the expected readers' grasp. Many excellent papers, especially theoretical treatments, were not included because they were too far beyond the scope of this book.

The references are keyed by the ACM reference convention. The first four characters of the first author's name are used, followed by the publication year and a capital letter (starting) with "A" if there are more than one such author in that year. For example, BEIZ90 is a paper or book by Beizer published in 1990, while BEIZ91C would be the third paper by Beizer in 1991. Often there is a short summary, abstract, or review of the paper if the subject is not obvious from the title.

Quality Control

Quality control is *your* job. I'm depending on you to bring substantive errors, gripes, and comments to my attention so that I can correct them for the next printing. Technology has made the job easy. FAX or E-mail your comments to me at the following numbers. Please provide the following information:

Your name, affiliation (company, university, department)

Your title

Snail mail address

Telephone number, FAX number, E-mail address

Book Title, Edition and Printing number (see below)

Page number and comment or correction.

If you use a FAX, then you can make a copy of the page, write your comments directly on the copy, and FAX it me.

In publishing we use the equivalent of version and release numbers. The "version number" is the **edition number,** and that always appears with the title. For example *Software Testing Techniques*, 2nd edition. The "release number" is provided by the **printing number.** You'll find the printing number on the back of the title page, just above the section that starts with "Library of Congress. . ." You'll see count-down numbers: 16 15 14 . . . 4 3 2. The lowest number in the series is the printing number. So the second edition, third printing is denoted as 2.3.

Please send your QC feedback to:

Boris Beizer

FAX: 215-886-0144, Group 3 FAX, answers on first ring.

E-mail: BBEIZER@MCIMAIL.COM

Acknowledgments

I undertook this book at the urging of Bob Posten of Programming Environments Inc., with nudges by Ginger Houston-Ludlum of Frontier Technologies, Edward Miller of Software Research Associates, Bill Perry of The Quality Assurance Institute, Richard Bender of Bender Associates, and too many academic colleagues to name. There were many others who prompted me to write this book—industrial colleagues, readers of my other books, my seminar students, consulting clients—but it's difficult to say who urged what at which time. The above persons are probably not aware that they are in part responsible for this book because their urging was rarely conscious. Their motivation, conscious or otherwise, is sincerely appreciated.

I also want to thank everyone who responded to my Internet call for guidance, too many to mention. Finally, I want to thank Lee White for his cogent and useful critique of Chapter 7.

Disclaimer

Examples in this book have been based, to the maximum extent possible, on U.S. Internal Revenue Service tax forms. These are used to illustrate software testing problems and should not be interpreted as conveying any substantive information whatsoever on how to file tax returns or how to interpret the IRS code. I have freely abridged, modified, or extracted from various forms, if that suited my pedagogical objectives. Do not use the forms in this book for any real tax purposes whatsoever. Do not submit any of these forms, copies thereof, or material contained therein to the IRS for any purpose whatsoever. I disclaim all responsibility for any usage other than the specific pedagogical objectives of this book.

These disclaimers aside, the tax forms, their complexity, and their associated instructions are all taken from US Internal Revenue Service tax forms with no substantive changes. Tax laws, I am told by my non-American colleagues, are comparably complex the world over. I am not responsible for that. The laws and forms, however, do give us something for which to be grateful. If you can write tests for your nation's tax forms, then you're probably ready to tackle any testing task of something that's simple by comparison, such as the control software for a nuclear reactor.

1
Introduction

1.1 SYNOPSIS

This chapter introduces the vocabulary of testing and puts testing in perspective with respect to the software development process.

1.2 VOCABULARY

Software testing has an established vocabulary. The definitions in this book are the mainstream usages; study them. You're likelier to err by using them in an overly narrow sense than you are by applying them too broadly.

External prerequisite terms: aggregate, algorithm, analysis, beta test, branch, by-product, call, called, calling, call parameter, code, coding, communication, compare, compilable segment, compiler, complete, complexity, computation, consistent, control, crash, data, data base, data corruption, data integrity, debug, delay, design, deterministic, development environment, development stage, disk, document, execute, experiment, file, flowchart, formal analysis, function, global data, hardware, hypothesis, implementable, independent testing, inspection, installation, interaction, keystroke, keyword, library, macro, maintenance, management, mapping, message, metric, model, module, multitasking, multiuser, object instruction, object-oriented programming, one-one mapping, operating system, output, performance, (software development) process, processing, program, program segment, program statement, programmable, programmer, programming, protocol, quality, quality assurance, RAM, random, range, reliability, resource, reusable, screen, security, set, sequence, shared data, simulator, software, software logic, source code, space, statement, statistical, store, storage management, subroutine, subprogram, subsystem, test tool, table, throughput, truth, user, value, variable.

Object: A generic term that includes both data and software.

State: The set of all values of all objects in a given set of objects at any given moment. The word "state" is particularized by specifying the set of objects and/or their condition: for example, unit state, system state, object state, initial state.

Initial state: The state of an object before a test.

Final state: The state of an object after a test.

Input: Any means by which data can be supplied to an object. Examples: stored data, generated data, keystrokes, message.

Observable: Any demonstrable change of state of an object when a change is expected, or the lack of change of state when a change is not expected. Examples: a new screen, wrong output, an unchanged screen.

Outcome: That which is observable as a result of a test. Examples: a changed data object, a message, a new screen, a state change, an unchanged object, the absence of a message, a blank screen. We are concerned with *outcomes*, not just *outputs*, in testing. This isn't semantic bickering. The fact that the screen did not change as a result of a test is a tangible *outcome* although there is no *output*. If you assume that all tests must result in *output*, you will miss many useful tests. All tests, however, must have an outcome.

Oracle: Any means used to predict the outcome of a test [HOWD86].

Test design: The process of specifying the object, initial state, and input and predicting the outcome and/or final state for that object, initial state, and input.

Testing: The act of designing, debugging, and executing tests.

Subtest: The smallest part of testing consisting of an object, initial state, input, and predicted outcome.

Test: A sequence of one or more subtests executed as a sequence because the outcome and/or final state of one subtest is the input and/or initial state of the next. The word "test" is used to include subtests, tests proper, and test suites.

Test suite: A set of one or more tests, usually aimed at a single object, with a common purpose and data base, usually run as a set.

Falsifiable: A statement is falsifiable if you can design an experiment that will either demonstrate or disprove the statement's truth.

Requirements: That which an object should do and/or characteristics that it should have. Requirements are arbitrary but they must still be consistent, reasonably complete, implementable, and most important of all, falsifiable.

Feature: A desirable behavior of an object; a computation or value produced by an object. Requirements are aggregates of features.

Case: Features are aggregates of cases.

Specification: A tangible, usually partial expression of requirements. Examples: document, list of features, prototype, test suite. Specifications are usually incomplete because many requirements are understood. For example, "the software will not crash or corrupt data." *The biggest mistake a tester can make is to assume that all requirements are expressed by the specifications.*

Validation: The process of evaluating an object to demonstrate that it meets requirements. Testing is not the only validation method you should use, but it is the only method discussed in this book [WALL94].

Falsification: The process of evaluating an object to demonstrate that it does not meet requirements.

Validation criteria: The means used to demonstrate that a requirement has been validated or falsified. Examples: strict comparison with predicted values, comparison within specified ranges of values, observed sequence of events.

Outcome matching: An actual and a predicted outcome are matched only with respect to specified validation criteria.

Test script: A document, program, or object that specifies for every test and subtest in a test suite: object to be tested, requirement (usually a case), initial state, inputs, expected outcome, and validation criteria.

Symptom (IEEE94 failure): Any observable misbehavior of any object (not just the object under test), such as the falsification of a requirement or an unexpected processing by-product.

Bug (IEEE94 fault): A design flaw that will result in symptoms exhibited by some object (the object under test or some other object) when an object is subjected to an appropriate test.

A test is **passed** if it is executed, the validation criteria are correctly applied, the actual outcome matches the predicted outcome, and there are no symptoms.

A test is **failed** if it is executed and the actual and predicted outcomes do not match and/or there are symptoms. This could be caused by: wrong object, wrong input, wrong predicted outcome, wrong initial state, wrong validation criteria, incorrect application of the validation criteria, a bug in the test design, a bug in the test execution, a bug in the validation process, or perhaps as strange as it may seem, even a bug in the object being tested.

Tested: An object has been (successfully) tested when all planned tests have been run and no symptoms have been observed; that is, all tests have been passed. Unless stated otherwise, "tested" means successfully tested.

Bug-free: We say that an object is "bug-free" when we believe that the likelihood that it exhibits symptoms or causes other objects to exhibit symptoms while in use is low enough to warrant the object's use. The idea of absolutely "bug-free" is unfalsifiable, and, therefore, it cannot be a requirement.

Coincidental correctness: Successfully passing all tests doesn't mean that an object is bug-free. Actual and predicted outcomes can match but there are bugs in the software because outcomes matched by coincidence. For example, if a program is to calculate $y:=x^2$ but is incorrectly programmed as $y:=2x$ and the test input value for x happens to be 2, the outcome will be $y=4$, despite the bug. The program, under this test, is said to be **coincidentally correct**.

Blindness: Every test method (short of testing all possible inputs in all possible initial states) is **blind** to bugs specific to that technique. For example, many techniques are blind to coincidental correctness.

Unit: The smallest thing that can be tested conveniently. It (usually) begins as the work of one programmer and corresponds to the smallest compilable program segment, such as a subroutine. A unit, as a tested object, does not usually include the subroutines or functions that it calls, fixed tables, and so on.

Unit testing: Testing of units. In unit testing, called subroutine and function calls are treated as if they are language parts (e.g., keywords). Called and calling components are either assumed to work correctly or are replaced by simulators. Unit testing usually is done by the unit's originator.

Unit bug: A bug likeliest to be caught by good unit testing.

A unit is a **component**. A **component** is an aggregate of one or more components that can be tested as an aggregate. Examples: unit, subroutine, function, macro, program and the subroutines it calls, communicating routines, an entire software system.

The **interface** between components is any means by which data can be passed between or shared by them. Examples: subroutine call, shared data object, global data, physical interface, message.

Integration tests: Tests that explore the interaction and consistency of successfully tested components. That is, components A and B have both passed their component tests. They are aggregated to create a new component C = (A, B). Integration testing is done to explore the self-consistency of the aggregate. The aggregate behavior of interest in integration testing is usually observed at the interface between the components.

Integration bug: A bug likeliest to be caught by good integration testing.

Integration: The process of integration testing, interface debugging, and integration bug repair. Integration can bring new behavior and therefore new bugs. Integration usually is done by the components' originator if the components to be integrated are that originator's responsibility. It is often done by a separate integrator if the components have several originators.

Component testing: Component testing differs from unit testing because called components and data objects are included in component tests. Examples: testing a routine aggregated with the subroutines it calls, testing a routine and a fixed table of data. Sane component testing presumes prior, successful, integration of subsidiary components, and unit and integration testing of such components. Component testing is not the same as unit testing because in unit testing, the component has yet to be integrated with its associated components.

Component bug: A bug likeliest to be caught by component testing.

Software system: An aggregate of components such that some requirements can still be tested even if some components are missing or are yet untested.

System testing is done to explore system behaviors that can't be done by unit, component, or integration testing. Examples, testing: performance, installation, data integrity, storage management, security, reliability. Ideal system testing presumes that all components have been previously, successfully, integrated. System testing is often done by independent testers.

Performance bug: A bug whose main symptoms are inadequate or reduced performance (e.g., reduced throughput, increased delay).

Security bug: A bug that enhances the ability of unauthorized persons to access a system; which allows unauthorized viewing or manipulation of files.

Resource-loss bug: A bug that results in the loss of dynamically allocated resources, such as RAM or disk space.

System bug: A bug unlikely to be caught by unit testing, component testing, or integration testing. A bug that concerns behavior that cannot be attributed to individual components but only to the entire system. Examples: performance bugs, security bugs, resource-loss bug.

Module, subprogram, program, subsystem: Imprecise designations for components of roughly increasing size.

Environment: The combination of hardware, software, and data in which and through which a component is created, tested, and used. It includes (but is not restricted to) the calling components, called components, operating system, hardware, compiler, your test tools (of course), and whatever else may affect or be affected by the component's execution.

1.3 ABOUT TESTING

1.3.1 The Tester and the Programmer

You'll see, throughout this book, references to, and contrasts between, "the tester" and "the programmer" as if they are separate persons. Such distinctions might lead you to believe that black-box testing is only for independent testers, not for programmers. Another possible misconception is that I advocate that testing and programming should be done by different people (e.g., independent testing). I want to prevent and/or correct such misconceptions.

Programmers must wear two hats: a programmer's hat and a tester's hat. When they are testing, they should wear the tester's hat and think like testers. That's the "tester" for which I wrote this book. So, the tester may or may not be the same person who wrote the program. It's a good idea to talk about the two roles as if they are done by different people because test thinking and programming thinking are very different. Programming thinking is very old, and there are many good books on the subject, so there's no point in making a special note of it. Tester thinking, however, is relatively new, and it pays to emphasize the difference. The test techniques taught here are both for independent testers and for programmers who are at the moment testing their own or someone else's software.

1.3.2 Why We Test Software

We test software in order to:

1. Give programmers information they can use to prevent bugs.
2. Give management information it needs to rationally evaluate the risk of using an object.
3. Achieve an object as bug-free as warranted by the situation.
4. Achieve a **testable design**; a design that can be easily validated, falsified, and maintained.
5. Falsify the object with respect to stated and unstated requirements [MYER79]; also called, "breaking the software."
6. Validate the object; that is, show that it works.

The information needed to achieve the second objective is measured by the extent (e.g., number of subtests passed and failed) to which the object has been validated and the extent to which it has not been possible to falsify it. That is, the extent to which it has not been broken and the extent to which it works. The extent to which an object is believed to be bug-free also is measured by the extent to which it has been validated and not falsified. Therefore, we are left with three central objectives: a good design, falsification, and validation.

Anything written by people has bugs. Not testing something is equivalent to asserting that it's bug-free. Programmers can't think of everything—especially of all the possible interactions between features and between different pieces of software. We try to break software because that's the only practical way we know of to be confident about the product's fitness for use.

The penultimate objective of testing is to gather management information. Given enough history and enough testing, we can make reasonably comfortable predictions about the software's fitness for use. Ultimately, that's what testers are paid for—to help create useful software.

The highest goal of testing is to support quality assurance: to gather information that, when fed back to programmers, results in avoidance of past mistakes and in better future software.

Dirty test (also **negative test**): A test whose primary purpose is falsification; that is, tests designed to break the software.

Clean test (also **positive test**): A test whose primary purpose is validation; that is, tests designed to demonstrate the software's correct working.

A test is **revealing** if its execution results in symptoms if there are bugs.

Specifications usually address only requirements that must be validated (that which the object is to do) and not the unstated requirements that we must attempt to falsify (that which the object is not supposed to do). Because the number of things that an object should do is finite and the number of things that it should not do is infinite, common sense suggests that dirty tests should far outnumber clean tests. That is, in fact, the case. In mature test suites, dirty tests typically outnumber clean tests in a ratio of 4:1 or 5:1.

1.3.3 TEST STRATEGIES

A **test strategy** or **test technique** is a systematic method used to select and/or generate tests to be included in a test suite. Examples: random inputs, tests based on my hunches, tests based on your hunches, tests intended to validate requirements, tests intended to falsify requirements, the tests we ran the last time, the tests that differ from the tests we ran the last time. We ask of a strategy that there be rules by which we can determine if a given test does or does not satisfy the strategy. In principle, a strategy should be programmable.

A strategy is **effective** if the tests included by that strategy are likely to reveal bugs in the tested object. That a strategy is effective results from the combination of the nature of the tests and the nature of the bugs to which those tests are applied. As in war and business, there are effective and ineffectual strategies. Furthermore, because objects are modified in order to correct their bugs or to enhance their features, the kinds of bugs found in an object change with time, and, therefore, the effectiveness of a strategy changes. While it is theoretically possible that a strategy against a specific object improves with time, realistically, the effectiveness of most strategies degrades with time.

Behavioral test strategies are based on requirements. For example: Test all features mentioned in the specification, do all dirty tests implied by requirements. Testing done under a behavioral test strategy is called **behavioral testing**. Behavioral testing is also called **black-box testing**. The term **functional testing** is also used for behavioral testing.* Behavioral testing can, in principle but not in practice, be done in total ignorance of how the object is constructed. The subject of this book is behavioral (black-box) testing.

Structural test strategies are derived from the structure of the tested object [BASI87, BEIZ90, NTAF88, OSTR94]. Examples: execute every statement at least once, execute every branch at least once, test the use of all data objects, execute every object instruction produced by the compiler. Testing done under a structural testing strategy is also called **glass-box testing** or **white-box testing**. Structural test strategies require complete access to the object's structure—that is, the source code. This book is only peripherally concerned with structural testing techniques.

---

* "Functional testing" is the term most commonly used in the literature, but practitioners prefer "black-box testing." There is an older and better term in computer science, "behavioral testing." The trouble with "functional testing" is that the term is also used to mean some specific test strategies, such as those used to test mathematical functions. In this book, the three terms "functional testing," "black-box testing," and "behavioral testing," will be used interchangeably, with a distinct bias toward "behavioral testing."

Hybrid test strategies combine behavioral and structural strategies [CLAR76, RICH81]. There is no conflict among behavioral, structural, and hybrid strategies; and none of these families of strategies can be said to be superior to any other. Unit and low-level components often are tested by structural strategies. Big components and system testing is dominated by behavioral strategies. Hybrid strategies are useful at all levels. No strategy is clearly superior because a strategy's utility depends on the nature of the object tested, the nature of the bugs in the object, and the state of our knowledge.

1.3.4 The Pesticide Paradox* [BEIZ90]

Most of us like to achieve closure: to know that the job is done, done right, and now it's time to go on to the next thing. Software and software testing are not like that. If you, the testers, do a good job of exposing bugs, and if quality assurance does a good job of feeding your discoveries back to the programmers, then they are unlikely to repeat those mistakes. Good programmers, if given the time and resources needed, usually look at the problems the testers (or they themselves) have exposed, generalize the idea, and then search their software to find and remove all other instances of the same or similar bugs.

All test techniques have built-in assumptions about the nature of bugs. Every test technique targets a different set of bugs. If programmers respond to testing and bug information by reducing or eliminating such bugs, it follows that as their software improves, the effectiveness of previous tests is eroded. That is, your tests wear out and you'll have to learn, create, and use new tests based on new techniques to catch their new bugs.

1.3.5 The Nature of Bugs and Why

See BEIZ90 and ANSI94 for an extensive discussion of bugs and bug categories. The main reason I use "bug" rather than the official term "fault" is because "fault" implies that someone is to blame. It implies lack of conscientiousness by programmers, laziness, or incompetence. The bugs produced by competent programmers working on contemporary cooperative software in a proper software development environment are not anybody's fault—unless, of course, you want to blame our humanity.

In good, mature software, bugs are caused by complexity and the limited ability of humans to handle complexity, not duplicity. The better the software process, the less likely it is that the bugs that persist to behavioral testing are caused by mistakes of individual programmers. In good software developed under a good process, most of the bugs we find during behavioral testing are a consequence of unpredictable interactions between compo-

---

* It's called the "pesticide paradox" after the agricultural phenomenon, where bugs such as the boll weevil build up tolerance to pesticides, leaving you with the choice of ever-more powerful pesticides followed by ever-more powerful bugs or an altogether different approach.

nents or between objects, or result from unpredicted side effects of seemingly innocent processes.

If the bugs we find by behavioral testing are simple and easily categorized, it indicates an inadequate process, not inadequate programmers. We assume, as an article of faith, that the programmers are well trained, well supplied with the proper tools, and competent.* This is called the "**competent programmer hypothesis**". Because the person who does behavioral testing may not be the person who wrote the software, it's important to keep this hypothesis in mind so that personal issues and rancor don't intrude into the programming process.

Three broad classifications of bugs are useful: **unit/component bugs**, **integration bugs**, and **system bugs**—named after the phase in development process at which the bug is likeliest to be found.

Unit/component bugs are the easiest to find and avoid. When we're testing a system and a test is failed, we can't tell if the failure is caused by a unit, integration, or system bug. It's only after the bug is resolved that we know. Because system testing is much more expensive than unit/component testing [BOEH81], any unit bug remaining during system testing represents wasted effort. An objective of unit/component testing, then, is to reduce bugs that remain in subsequent process stages.

Integration bugs are more difficult to detect and prevent because they arise from interactions between otherwise correct components. Component interactions are **combinatoric**— that is, they grow as n^2 (the square of the number of components involved) or worse (e.g., $n!$— that number factorial). An objective of integration testing is to assure that few, if any, harmful component interactions remain when we get to system testing.

System testing is a qualitative change. Even if every feature had been tested during unit/component and integration testing, we would have to redo behavioral testing as part of system testing. During unit/component and integration testing, that which we are testing has deterministic behavior. In system testing, however, we have the additional complexity of multitasking. Consequently, the order in which things happen can no longer be predicted with certitude. This uncertainty and the issue of timing is an even richer soil for even more complex bugs. A central objective of system testing is to confirm that the predictable behavior of the deterministic software world is repeated in the nondeterministic world.

1.3.6 When Will It Be Done?

Testing is potentially endless, both theoretically and pragmatically. Yet we must stop testing, knowing that bugs remain, because if we don't stop, the effort is pointless. If we have historical data, then it is possible to concoct sta-

---

* If incompetent programmers can't be trained to competence, get rid of them; if the process is faulty, fix it; and no one can be expected to be fully productive with inadequate tools.

tistical models that can give us insight into the risk of not testing further and putting the software to gainful use [HAML94, MUSA90]. If you detect a hint of caution in my wording, take it to heart because the validity of such models is no simple nor settled matter. However, progress continues, and most useful models need the information we gather during testing, especially during system testing, as part of the data used to determine when to stop testing.

1.3.7 Black-box Testing Isn't Everything
[BEIZ90, WHIT87]

Behavioral testing isn't all the testing we should do. No single testing approach is enough. If we consider all the testing that can and should be done to software, from the time it is first conceived to the time (if ever) it is finished, behavioral testing represents 35 to 65 percent of all testing.* The relative utility of behavioral testing depends on the design. When design is wholly done by hard-coding of features with a lot of ad hoc logic, then structural techniques dominate. When design is based on the use of generic algorithms whose specific behavior is determined by data in tables or by call parameters, then behavioral techniques dominate. The importance of behavioral testing is like the importance of various nagivational techniques. What is useful depends on the weather, how close the shore is, what tools you have, and so on. We would do well to emulate one of my favorite authors, Nathaniel Bowditch [BOWD77]: *"The wise navigator never relies solely on one technique."*

1.3.8 Testing Isn't Everything [POWE82, WALL94]

We should celebrate when our testing discovers bugs, but we also should mourn. Be glad because that's one less to worry about; be sad because our software development process failed. But be glad because we've learned how to improve the process and prevent a future recurrence. We've been developing software for over 40 years, and one of the most important lessons we've learned is: *Do it early* [BOEH81]!

The earlier in the process a bug is discovered and corrected, the cheaper the correction. Effort spent prior to design is better than effort spent during design. Effort spent prior to coding is better than effort spent after coding. Effort spent in unit testing is better than effort spent in system testing, which is far better than effort spent after the software is installed. Here are some effective nontesting activities, in roughly the order in which they should occur.

Prototyping: A prototype of software is an incomplete implementation of software that mimics the behavior we think the users need [STAK89]. The

---

Object-oriented programming increases the importance of behavioral testing. It is clear that behavioral testing techniques will be more important for software constructed over a dependable library of reusable objects whose internal workings and structure are deliberately hidden from us; but we also may have to do a lot more testing to achieve reliable objects [BERA94, NORT94].

objective of prototyping is to get something into the users' hands so that they can tell us if what we intend to build is or is not useful to them—will they buy it if we build it? The prototype doesn't really have to work, and it often doesn't. We build software for users. Getting them involved as early as possible is an effective way of avoiding product blunders.

Requirements Analysis: Requirements drive design [YEHR80]. If requirements are inconsistent, no design can be correct. Requirements analysis means checking the requirements for logical self–consistency, for testability, for feasibility. Users can't be expected to provide us with valid requirements because they're not trained to do so. We'd all like a car that gets 100 kilometers to the liter of water, doesn't pollute, carries 12 adults, and fits into a 2m by 3m parking space. We'd all like a Mercedes for the price of a Yugo. As software builders it's not our objective to do the impossible or to satisfy the users' every whim: Our objective is to provide value for money.

Formal Analysis [ANDE79, BABE94, HANT76, WING94]: We can't and shouldn't test everything. That's especially true for behavioral testing. Among the things we can't practically test today (if ever) is all the possible ways that features can interact with one another. Testing the behavior of software in every possible installation is another impossible task. So are the interaction of our package with other packages, whether software is secure, some communications protocols, and many algorithms. Whenever it is the combination of things that makes testing complexity grow faster than the complexity of the tested object, formal analysis, possibly mathematical, is preferable to testing. We still need some testing to assure us that our analysis itself is reasonably bug-free.*

Design: Good designs have fewer bugs and are easier to test. It is much easier to design something that can't be tested than to design something that can. It is much easier to design something that can't be maintained than to design something that can. The best requirements are destroyed by ill-considered designs that no amount of testing can fix.

Formal Inspections [FAGA76, GILB93, WEIN90] have been repeatedly confirmed as a primary bug-prevention method. A software development process that does not include formal inspections is seriously flawed and depends too much on testing to eliminate bugs.

Self-testing: A programmer's own testing is more efficient than someone else's testing. Similarly for a group testing the software it produces. Similarly, a software development organization's testing is better than an external (e.g., beta testing) test of the same software. This does not contra-

---

* Everything we do in the software development process is prone to bugs. A formal (e.g., mathematical) proof of an algorithm's correctness is as vulnerable to bugs as any other human process. That's easily proved: Think of all the articles in math journals entitled: "A counterexample to a theorem by . . ."

dict the idea that independent testing can be effective because efficiency is not the sole criterion for deciding who does what kind of testing.

If an independent tester repeats the tests previously done by the developer, or merely does the testing that should have been done by the developer, then nothing is learned from independent testing and it is of little value. Such testing (independent repetition of the developers' tests) can be useful only if the developers are incompetent or malicious. That contradicts our competent programmer hypothesis.

The purpose of independent testing is to provide a different perspective and, therefore, different tests; furthermore, to conduct those tests in a richer (and, therefore, more complex and expensive) environment than is possible for the developer. The purpose of self-testing is to eliminate those bugs that can be found at lower cost in the simpler, deterministic, environment of the unit/component or low-level system test.

Tools: We once counted source code syntax errors as bugs—not anymore, because we have a tool (the compiler) that finds such bugs far better than we can. Our programming languages and compilers have progressed to ever more sophisticated bug detection, relegating what were once difficult tasks for humans to an automated activity. If a bug can be detected (and/or corrected) automatically, it should be. Don't try to justify automation and tools; what must be justified is the continued use of error-prone manual processes when automation is available. There's a widening gap between the tools that programmers and testers actually use and the tools developed for their use by researchers. Close the gap! It pays. It's profitable.

Our unachievable objective as testers should be to get out of testing. Testing is **quality** *control*. **Quality** *assurance* means preventing bugs. It's always more profitable to prevent bugs than to fix them. But this objective is unachievable because history shows us that automating aspects of our process and preventing previous bugs is prerequisite to meeting the challenge of increased complexity that our users want. Our current process (however imperfect it may be) is far better than our process of a decade ago. We are no longer programming the software of a decade ago, but new software that brings much more complex bugs to the fore. Also, our users keep escalating their quality expectations, thereby stretching our testing ability and techniques.

1.4 SOFTWARE DEVELOPMENT PROCESS

1.4.1 What's Really Important

The most important things about a software development process are (1) there is a process, (2) it is understood, (3) it is followed.

There is a process: I suppose that there is always a process because even chaos is a process of sorts. Having a process means that it's possible to predict what will next happen to a piece of software. That predictability starts when the need is conceived and ends when the software is retired.

Having a process doesn't mean elaborate process documents. Some of the best projects I've seen had few formal process documents. Conversely, the process document I always point to when someone asks me what is needed came from one of the worst fiascos I've ever seen. Formal process documents are an inevitable consequence of project size. Documents (if they are read) are a more efficient way to transmit process details to individuals unfamiliar with the process and the culture. Also, process control, which is the key to quality, usually is easier when the process steps are documented.

It is understood: If the process isn't understood by those who must understand it, it won't be followed. Understanding can be gained from reading documents, if people are given the time to absorb and integrate what they've read. Videos also can do the job. General training in a process is inadequate because what messes things up are the specifics, not the generics. Some kind of specific process training is essential.

It is followed: Having an understood process doesn't mean that it will be followed. A key indicator of a process in trouble is a disparity between the official process (e.g., the documented process) and what people actually do. In this respect, I'll side with programmers and testers who don't follow the process rather than with the putatively wiser heads who created the process. If the process isn't followed, it's probably because it doesn't work, not because the programmers are hide-bound and reluctant to change. Most, but not all, people who are given a demonstrably better way to do something and the tools and training with which to master the new technique will do it the new way. If the process isn't being followed, then it is flawed, there are barriers to its use, or proper resources (e.g., training, time, tools) haven't been provided.

1.4.2 Ten₍₁₆₎ Process Commandments Plus One

This is the place in many books where you'll find an elaborate set of process flowcharts with cryptically labeled boxes and arrows of different types and styles connecting those boxes every which way. I'm not going to do that here because I've learned the heretical notion that process flowcharts and models don't matter. They don't matter because process models don't determine the success or failure of a software development process. Cultural, ethnic, application, and national specifics have a greater influence on process than do grandiose process theories. Saying that "process X is better than process Y" is like saying that Japanese is a better language than Tagalog. Saying that a preliminary design review must come before coding is like saying that verbs in a sentence must come before nouns. The specifics of a language and the order in which things must occur are very important to the speakers of that language or to one who would translate from that language to another, but in and of themselves, they do not determine the speaker's ability to communicate.

So it's not going to be the waterfall model [ROYC70] or the spiral model [BOEH86], stepwise refinements, top-down, bottom-up, and all that jazz. Without worrying about how they're to be put together to form a meaningful process, here are the ingredients you should look for in any effective process, just as you look for nouns, verbs, and other parts of speech in a language.

process road map: Everybody must know where they and their software are in the process at all times. If you like process flowcharts, good—some people prefer narratives and checklists. A useful process road map divides the process into simple steps that are easy to understand and control. Enough detail so that you and everybody else can find their way around, but not so much detail that individuality and creativity are stifled.

process control: "Process control" doesn't imply rigid adherence to minutely detailed activities, and it doesn't mean totalitarianism and suppression of individuality. "Process control" means that there are effective mechanisms by which the participants in the process can learn how to improve those parts of the process with which they are most directly concerned. Process control means feedback, education, and opportunity, aimed at providing a climate in which people can strive to make themselves, their product, and the world better.

quantification and metrics: We're not dealing with art but with engineering, and, therefore, objectivity is a prerequisite to process control. In engineering, quantification is the key to objectivity. In software, metrics are the primary arm of quantification [BERL94, FENT91, GRAD87, GRAD92, MOLL93, ZUSE90, ZUSE94].

configuration control is as old as Imhotep, the great pyramid architect. It means that at any instant of time, we can examine the product of our labor (a program, requirements, or test suite, say) and know: who, what, when, where, why, and how. Everything intended to last must be configuration controlled, and anything that isn't just doesn't exist as part of the product.

requirements: What are we building? Does everybody know? Does everybody understand the same thing? Here I have to insist on documents because human memory is too fallible.

requirements traceability: Where did these requirements come from? If, as often happens, requirements change during the course of software development, what other requirements are affected? Traceability means that requirements can be mapped onto software components and vice versa. But don't ask for, or expect, a one-to-one mapping, because software and requirements don't map onto one another that way.

strategic mores: For whom is this software being developed? What do they expect to get out of it, beyond mere utility? Will this software *not* kill the user? Will it crush the competition? Will it enhance our reputation for quality? Will it make lots of money? Will it be the fastest? There are hundreds of such strategic objectives, and management establishes the relative importance of each. Without such guidance (given, it is hoped, in quantitative form), no one can know the true objectives of the design or when those objectives are met.

requirement validation criteria: How will we know that a requirement is satisfied? What are the objective satisfaction criteria associated with each and every requirement?

responsibility: Who is responsible for what and when.

exit criteria: How do we know that a given piece of software is ready to go to the next stage of the development process? What are the tangible, objective signs of completion?

entry criteria: How do we know that a given piece of software is ready to be accepted by the next stage of the development process? This is not a redundant specification. A component can be passed to many different stages or be used by many different other components, each of which may have different entry criteria. Typically, the exit criteria for a component are the union of all the entry criteria for that component.

analysis: Analysis is the engineering process by which a design evolves that fulfills requirements. It may be wholly intuitive or wholly formal. Intuitive analysis, while often effective, cannot be communicated to others easily and, consequently, some kind of formal, often mathematical, analysis is needed, even if only retroactively.

design: That's what its all about it, isn't it? Design should precede programming or at least be coincident with it. Engineers first design then build, because it is less risky to do it that way. Design errors are paper errors and much cheaper than welded steel and concrete or congealed code.

design validation: How do we know that a design will work if we haven't designed something like this before? Validating the design is not the same as validating the implementation of the design. Bridges that collapse usually do so because of poor designs that were not validated—rarely because the material and workmanship was poor. The newer the design, the more important that it be validated prior to construction. Validation is done by models, by prototypes, by design inspection.

programming: The act of coding a design and testing it to see to it that what we built is what we intended to build. The bricklayer checks her courses with a level and the programmer with a test.

integration: The whole is far greater than the sum of its parts. Only trivial, toy software has a system complexity equal to the sum of its component complexities. An architect spends as much or more time defining the steps by which his building will be erected as he does on the final form of the building. There is no integration worthy of the name without an integration plan and associated integration tests—whether it is the integration of two low-level subroutines or several hundred quasiautonomous systems.

testing: Testing is required whenever people are involved. Testing is a key ingredient to self-esteem and pride in craftsmanship. A machinist who does not check her work with a micrometer is either a thief or a fool. A programmer who depends on the subsequent actions of others to catch his bugs has no pride, except, perhaps, the fleeting pride of cranking out vast quantities of untested and buggy software in a short time.

1.5 SELF-EVALUATION QUIZ

Define: analysis, behavioral testing, black-box testing, blind, bug, bug-free, case, clean test, coincidental correctness, combinatoric, competent programmer hypothesis, component, component bug, component testing, configuration control, design validation, dirty test, effective strategy, effective test, entry criteria, environment, exit criteria, failed test, failure, falsifiable, falsification, fault, feature, final state, functional testing, glass-box testing, hybrid strategy, initial state, input, integration, integration bug, integration testing, interface, negative test, object, observable, oracle, outcome, outcome matching, passed test, pesticide paradox, performance bug, positive test, process control, programming, prototype, purpose of testing, quality assurance, quality control, requirement, requirement analysis, requirement traceability, requirement validation criteria, resource loss bug, revealing test, security bug, software system, specification, state, structural testing, subtest, symptom, system, system bug, system testing, test, test design, test script, test strategy, test suite, testable design, tested, testing, test technique, unit, unit bug, unit testing, validation, validation criteria, white-box testing.

2
Graphs and Relations

2.1 SYNOPSIS

Graphs are introduced as the central conceptual tool of testing.

2.2 VOCABULARY

External prerequisite terms: application, array, arrowhead, arrowtail, automatic teller machine (ATM), bilateral, branch, bug, bug statistics, calculate, **CASE**, code, data, denote, **DO...WHILE, END**, dynamic binding, execution time, fetch, file, **FOR...DO**, function, **IF–THEN–ELSE**, input value, inspection, list, loop, menu, menu choice, model, mouse, natural language, object–oriented programming, path, payroll, **PRINT**, probability, processing step, program, program branch, program control, program entry, program exit, program path, program statement, programmer, programming language, **READ, RETURN**, screen, software, specification, spreadsheet, statement, statement label, storage limit, straight-line statement, subroutine, table, template, test inspection, toy program, transaction, **TRANSMIT, UNDO**, value, variable, word processor.

Internal prerequisite terms: behavioral testing, bug, input, object, revealing test, specification, state, testing.

Graphs are the central conceptual tool of testing. Many different graph models are used in testing: **control-flow graphs, data-flow graphs, call trees, finite-state machine graphs, transaction-flow graphs.** We first discuss graphs in the abstract in order to introduce a vocabulary that will be useful and consistent, whatever the graph we're talking about.

Relation: An association of interest between objects. If A and B are objects and $\mathfrak{R}$ is a relation, A$\mathfrak{R}$B denotes that A has the relation $\mathfrak{R}$ to B. Using italics to denote relations, here are some examples: A *is connected to* B; Sam *is the father of* Bill; A *calls* B; data object A *is used to calculate a value for* data object B; action A *is followed by* action B. **Verifying that all objects have the expected relation to one another is an objective of testing.**

A **graph** is a collection of objects, a relation over those objects, and a specification (by a list, say) of which objects are related and how.

Node: The objects of a graph are called **nodes.** Nodes are depicted by circles. Verifying that graphs have all the nodes we expect them to have and no more is an objective of testing.

Node name: Every node has a unique identity or name. If the objects are files, the node names can be file names; if the objects are programs or program statements, the node names can be program names or statement labels, respectively. The properties of a graph and the objects it represents are not affected by the way we name the nodes.

Node weights: Nodes can have properties. Such properties are called **node weights.** Examples of node weights used in this book are: the state of a program, the value of a variable, a function that describes which of several values will be used to calculate something, the name of another object. **Verifying that weighted nodes (i.e., nodes that have weights) have the weights they are supposed to have is an objective of testing.**

Link: An arrow or line that joins two nodes is used to show that the relation of interest holds between those nodes. For example, if the relation is A and B *are siblings*, we join A to B by a line to denote that fact. If there is only one relation of interest in our model and that relation is understood, we don't have to label every link with the phrase that denotes the relation. If there can be several relations between the objects, then we can annotate the links with all the specified relations. In the graph on the side, A and B have two relations: ☎, A and B *are siblings*, and ✿, A and B *are friends*. **Verifying that the links are where we expect them to be and that the specified relation(s) hold for every link is an objective of testing.**

Parallel links: Two or more links between a pair of nodes. Parallel links are used when several different relations hold between a pair of nodes.

Link name: Every link has a unique identity or name. There are several ways to name links. Often we'll use numbers for node names, so we use lowercase letters for link names.

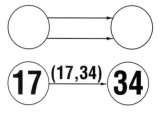

Another way to name a link is to use the node names between which that link lies. For example, if there is a link from node 17 to node 34, we can name it as (17, 34). This doesn't work for graphs with several links between a pair of nodes. We don't always need to use link names, in which case we just leave them out. The properties of a graph and the objects and relations that it represents are not affected by the way we name links.

Link weights: Links can have properties. Such properties are called **link weights.** The simplest possible link weight is the fact that the link exists. Labeling a link with a relation or all the relations that hold is an example of a

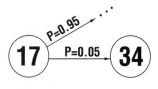

link weight. If the nodes denote processing steps and the links denote which steps follow which, the link weight could be, for example: the execution time of that program along the specified path, the probability of that path's execution, the fact that a specific data object is fetched. The properties of a model depicted by a graph very much depend on the link weights. **Verifying that weighted links have the proper weights is an objective of testing.**

Directed link: A **directed link** is denoted by an arrow—that is, a line with a direction. Directed links are used for **asymmetric relations:** relations that go only in one direction.

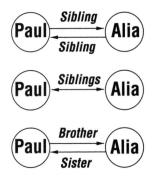

Examples of asymmetric relations: A *is the father of* B; A *is followed by* B; A *is used by* B; A *calls* B. Most relations in testing are asymmetric so most testing models use directed links. If $\Re$ is an asymmetric relation and A $\Re$ B, it does *not* follow that B $\Re$ A. **Verifying that all directed links have the expected direction is an objective of testing.**

Undirected link: A link that designates a **symmetric relation**—that is, a bilateral relation. More formally, a relation $\Re$ such that if A $\Re$ B then it follows (by the nature of the relation) that B $\Re$ A. Symmetric relations have an arrow in both directions, so we usually leave the arrowheads out because both directions are understood. In the first example on the right, the two arrows in opposite directions can be replaced by either a double–headed arrow or just a straight line because the relation *(sibling)* is symmetric. Conversely, in the third example, even though there is a relation in both directions, they are different relations and are not symmetric. Symmetric relations are not common in testing, but here are some (nontesting) examples: A and B *are relatives*; A and B *are married*; A and B *are roommates*. **Verifying that all symmetric relations are indeed symmetric is an objective of testing.**

Graph: A graph is a collection of nodes, node names, node weights, links, link names, link weights, and a relation over the nodes. If the relation holds between two nodes, there is a link between them.

QUESTION: *What do you do when you see a graph?*

ANSWER: *Cover it!*

Directed graph: A graph *all* of whose links are directed. Most graphs in testing are directed. **Showing that links are directed as we expect them to be is an objective of testing.**

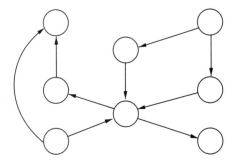

Undirected graph: A graph all of whose links are undirected. That is, a graph *none* of whose links are directed. **Showing that all undirected links indeed go in both directions is an objective of testing.**

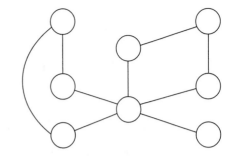

Inlink: A link that comes into a node—that is, the arrowhead.

Entry node: A node with no inlinks. While programs usually have entry points (e.g., BEGIN), graph models of the behavior of programs do not necessarily have entry nodes.

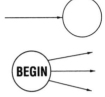

Outlink: The links that leave a node—that is, the arrow tails. A link can both be an inlink and outlink. It just means that it leaves and enters the same node (i.e., a loop).

Branch node: A node with two or more outlinks. A **CASE** statement or an **IF–THEN–ELSE** statement in a programming language are examples of branch nodes. The node on the right represents a three-way branch. Note that these are branch nodes in a graph model of a program's behavior, and there need not be corresponding branches in the program.

Exit node: A node with no outlink. The graphs on the right are exit nodes because no arrows leave them. While programs usually have exit points (e.g., END, RETURN), models of the behavior of programs do not necessarily have exit nodes.

Path: Put your pencil on any node (14, say) and follow links to any other node (17, say); that's a **path** from node 14 to node 17. If you can draw a path on a graph, however, it doesn't mean that you actually can make software follow that path. A path in this

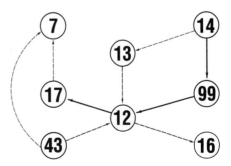

context is not necessarily a path through the code. In behavioral testing we consider paths through *models* that describe the behavior of software. Such paths may or may not correspond to paths through the program.

Achievable path: A path for which it is possible to find input values that will cause the program to follow the path specified in the model.

Unachievable path: A path for which there is no set of inputs that will cause that path (in the graph model) to be traversed.

Entry-exit path: A path from an entry node to an exit node. When context is clear, "path" means "entry-exit path."

Path segment: Usually a path that is not an entry-exit path.

Path name: There are two ways to name a path: (1) by the node names along that path or (2) by the link names along that path. Naming the indicated path in the figure on the right by node names, we have "14, 99, 12, 17" for the name, while naming it by link names it is "krm."

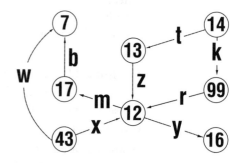

Path length: There are two ways to measure path length: (1) by the number of nodes along the path or (2) by the number of links along the path. In this book, we usually measure path lengths by link counts. The preceding path is three links and four nodes long.

Loop: Any path in which at least one node is visited more than once. Alternatively a path whose node-based (link-based) path name contains the same node (link) name more than once. In the example on the right, the marked looping path is akrmbakrmb, or 7, 14, 99, 12, 17, 7, 14. See if you can find all the looping paths in the drawing on the right.

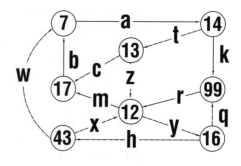

Loop-free path: A path that doesn't have a loop in it; that is, no node name or link name is repeated in the path name.

2.3 EXAMPLES OF GRAPHS USED IN TESTING

2.3.1 General [DAVI88, DEON74, EBER94, PETE76, TRIP88]

The graph is the generic model of testing. Graphs describe relations of interest between objects of interest. If you can identify the objects and relations that exist between those objects, then you can describe the whole by a graph. To build a model (graph), you must specify:

1. The objects of interest (nodes).
2. The relations that should exist between nodes.
3. Which objects are related to which (links).
4. Properties that may be associated with links: that is, the link weights.

Whether a graph (model) inspires you to design a revealing test is another matter. Models are in your head. What inspires you may not inspire me and vice versa. But here are some models most people have found useful.

2.3.2 Transaction-Flow Model (Chapter 6)

objects: Steps in processing a transaction, such as a payroll check or getting money out of an automatic teller machine. There is one node for each step in the transaction process.

relation: *"Is followed by*–the next step." For example, **wage_calculation** *is followed by* **tax_deduction_calculation.**

links: Connects steps that follow one another. That is, the *is followed by* relation holds between the two nodes.

2.3.3 Finite-State Model of Menus (Chapter 9)

object: Menus that appear on the screen of a word processing package, say. There is one node for each menu that can appear on the screen.

relation: *"Can directly reach."* That is, there is a choice in the menu that if selected will cause the program to display the new menu appropriate to that choice.

links: There is one link between nodes for every choice. For example,

if menu A can (by choosing an option) invoke menus B, C, and D, then there is a link between A and B, A and C, and A and D.

2.3.4 Data-Flow Model (Chapter 5)

objects: Data objects of interest. There is one node for every instance (potentially different value) of every data object.

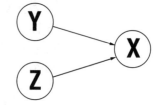

relation: *"Is used to calculate a value of."* In $X = 2Y + Z$, Y and Z are used to calculate a value of X.

links: Draw an arrow (link) from A to B if A's value is used to calculate B's value. In the last example, there is an arrow from Y to X and from Z to X.

2.3.5 Timing Model [BEIZ90]

objects: Sequences of straight-line statements in a program.

relation: *"Is followed by*—the statement." For example, **READ filename** *is followed by* **FOR**....

links: Connects statements that follow one another. That is, the *is followed by* relation holds between the two nodes. Note that **branching statements** (e.g., **IF, CASE**) have one outgoing link for every branch.

properties: (1) The expected execution time (say microseconds) of links, (2) For branch statements, (e.g., **IF...THEN...ELSE, CASE,**), the probability that the program will take that branch for each branch (outlink).

2.4 LIVING AND WORKING WITH RELATIONS

2.4.1 General

Relations have properties and therefore can be categorized. If you can say "Oh! This is such-and-such a kind of relation," then whatever you know about that kind of relation in general applies to the specific case. We won't explore all properties of all relations—just those that are most useful in testing.

2.4.2 Transitive and Intransitive Relations

A relation $\mathfrak{R}$ is **transitive** if A $\mathfrak{R}$ B and B $\mathfrak{R}$ C implies A $\mathfrak{R}$ C. For example, the relation *is faster than* is

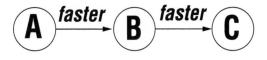

transitive. If A *is faster than* B and B *is faster than* C, then it follows that A *is faster than* C. Examples of transitive relations: *can reach by a path, is greater than, is less than, is greater than or equal to, is less than or equal to, is equal to, is a relative of, is a subset of, is in the shadow of.*

A relation that is not transitive is **intransitive.** Examples of intransitive relations: *is a friend of, is a neighbor of, has lied to, is (directly) connected to.* For example, if A *has lied to* B and B *has lied to* C, it does not follow that A *has lied to* C. It could be that A *has* lied to C, but it does not follow from A's lie to B and B's lie to C. For all we know, A has never spoken to C.

While most relations are either clearly transitive or intransitive, this is not always so. The children's game "Paper, Scissor, Rock" is an example of a game that plays on transitivity. It goes: Scissor *cuts* paper, paper *covers* rock, rock *blunts* scissor. Although three different relations are involved (*cuts, covers,* and *blunts*), the implication of the game is that each of these relations are equivalent to *is stronger than.* Many other children's and adult games hinge on confused transitivity.

It is in our interest (as an objective of testing) to confirm that all transitive relations specified are indeed transitive and, conversely, if transitivity is not a property of the relation, to confirm that the relation is intransitive. Natural languages are not always clear about this, and therefore specifications can be misleading. For example, the very common relation *connected* as described in a natural language often is confusing. Does it mean that A *can reach* B by a path, or does it mean that A is *directly connected* to B by a link? The first case requires that *can reach (by a path)* be transitive. That is, if A *can reach (by a path)* B and B *can reach (by a path)* C, then A *can reach (by a path)* C. But *can reach* need not be transitive. Suppose I leave out "by a path"? For example, if I *can touch my neighbor by reaching with my arm* and my neighbor *can touch her neighbor by reaching with her arm*, it does not follow that *I can touch her neighbor by reaching with my arm*, unless, of course, I am an orangutan or we are very close neighbors.

Always note and then check the transitivity or intransitivity of all relations in a specification. Then check the programmer's notion of transitivity or intransitivity. If either (specification or programmer) is confused or confusing about transitivity, then you have a fertile ground for testing.

2.4.3 Symmetric and Asymmetric Relation

A relation is **symmetric** if it goes both ways. That is, every arrow in the graph goes both ways. Examples: *is a neighbor of, is married to* (usually). The relation *is a neighbor of* is symmetric but not transitive.

The common English usage for symmetric relations is to say "A AND B are 𝕽elated," rather than "A *is* 𝕽elated to B." Thus we have: A and B *are married*, A and B *are neighbors*, A and B are *adjacent*, and so on.

A relation that is not symmetric is **asymmetric.** That a relation is asymmetric does not mean that there are *no* links in both directions between a pair of nodes; it means that it is not necessarily so.

Symmetry is a very important characteristic of relations, and we would do well to test it. For example, if you are testing the menus of a **menu-driven package** (i.e., a package whose primary controls are initiated by selecting choices from a menu), then checking for symmetry means checking that it always possible to back out of any menu and return to a previous menu. Similarly, a program (word processor or spreadsheet, say) that provides an **UNDO** feature advertises itself as providing symmetry for most operations because usually it is possible to reverse the action of the operation. But even the best **UNDO** can't be totally symmetric because some things, such as **PRINT** or **SEND**, are impossible to **UNDO**.

Symmetry, like transitivity, often is confused in specifications and by programmers. Natural languages, as always, create problems for us, but in the case of symmetry, the problem usually arises because it (to some extent or another) is implied rather than explicitly stated.

Always note and then check the symmetry or asymmetry of all relations in a specification. Then check the programmer's notion of symmetry or asymmetry. If either (specification or programmer) is confused or confusing about symmetry, then you have a fertile ground for testing.

2.4.4 Reflexive and Irreflexive Relations

A relation 𝕽 is **reflexive** if it holds for every node in a graph—that is, if every node in the graph has a link leading back to itself (called a **self-loop**). Examples of reflexive relations: *is acquainted with* (because, unless I have amnesia, I am acquainted with myself), *is a relative of, can be reached from, connected, equal, equivalent.*

If reflexivity does not hold for *every* node in a graph, the relation is said to be **irreflexive.** The following relations are irreflexive: *friend* (how often have you heard "She's her own worst enemy?"), *over, under.*

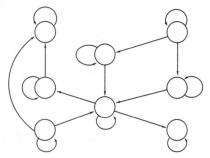

Reflexivity is the ability to do nothing. Reflexivity is an important property of our models (if it holds).

I once used an unfortunate word processing package in which you had to make a choice at every menu. This could be done either by using a mouse (which I didn't have at the time) or by tapping the letter key corresponding to the first letter of the choice's description. Every menu should have been reflexive with respect to invalid choices. That is, if I struck a wrong key, I should have stayed in that menu; this arrogant program made a choice for me—usually wrong. Using menus was not reflexive in this sorry package.

Reflexivity usually is also implied rather than explicitly stated and is therefore another good place to look for bugs. Because reflexivity should be a property of every node, every node in the graph should be checked. *Test reflexivity as for transitivity and symmetry.*

2.4.5 Equivalence Classes and Partitions (Optional) [JENG89, MYER79]

An **equivalence relation** is: symmetric, transitive, and reflexive. If a set of objects satisfy an equivalence relation, then that set is an **equivalence class.** Every member of an equivalence class is said to be equivalent (with respect to the specified relation) to every other member of that class or set of objects.

All the techniques in this book are examples of **partition testing** [HAML88, OSTR88, RICH81, RICH89, WHIT94], that is, strategies based on dividing the set of all possible inputs into equivalence classes under an appropriately defined equivalence relation. I don't tell you how to find or create such relations in this book—I present you with a ready–made set of useful relations and, therefore, useful equivalence class partitions.

If you have a transitive relation, then there's a completely mechanical way of converting it into a corresponding equivalence relation and therefore to partition the input set into equivalence classes. However, the method is beyond the scope of this book. For more information, see BEIZ90, chapter 12.

2.4.6 How Not to Draw Graphs

2.4.6.1 A GRAPH IS HOW YOU SEE IT

The pictorial representation of graphs, as used here, is a convenient teaching tool because most people find such visual presentations less abstract. In practice, however, except for toy problems such as those presented in this book, the graphical representation of graphs is too cumbersome. Instead of drawing pictures and using templates (or their software equivalent), we represent graphs as tables or lists. These are probably the representations that you will find most useful eventually. When you are first learning about graphs, though, it is a good idea to go through the exercise of drawing or displaying them.

2.4.6.2 THE TABLE OR MATRIX REPRESENTATION

Graphs can be conveniently represented in table or **matrix** form. Here's how.

1. Draw a square array whose size is equal to the number of nodes.

2. If there is a link from node i, say, to node j, put a "1" at the ijth position of the table; otherwise leave it blank or put in a zero or a dot.

3. If there are more than one links between a pair of nodes, put in the number of such links.

4. If there are any link weights, put in the appropriate weight.

Usually it is convenient to label the rows and columns of the matrix with the node names. Using this convention, the penultimate graph on page 21 is:

Similarly, the last graph on page 23 is represented as:

	17	34
17	.	1
34	.	.

2.4.6.3 THE LIST REPRESENTATION

The matrix at the right is mostly empty—that's typical because most graphs have relatively few links per node. Although a matrix is compact and easier to draw than the graphical form, the format is cumbersome and error-prone for large matrixes. A more convenient form is to use a list of links. This is easier to show than to explain. The **link list representation** for the last graph is:

	7	13	14	17	12	99	43	16
7	.	.	.	.	.	.	.	.
13	.	.	.	.	1	.	.	.
14	.	1	.	.	.	1	.	.
17	1	.	.	.	.	.	.	.
12	.	.	.	1.	.	.	.	1
99	.	.	.	.	1	.	.	.
43	1	.	.	.	1	.	.	.
16	.	.	.	.	.	.	.	.

7:		12:	17, 16
13:	12	99:	12
14:	13, 99	43:	7
17:	7	16:	

If there are any link weights, you just annotate the list entries with the appropriate weights. For example, using the link names as weights, the second graph on page 24 has the following list:

7:	14(a)	12:	17(m), 16(y)
14:	99(k), 13(t)	17:	7(b)
13:	12(z), 17(c)	16:	99(q), 43(h)
99:	12(r)	43:	12(x), 7(w)

You can vary this notation as you wish, adding properties, comments, and whatever is convenient to make the list comprehensible to you—as long as you use a consistent format that clearly designates:

1. The origin node of the link

2. The destination node of the link

3. Any properties associated with that link

4. Any properties associated with the node

For really big graphs, it's convenient to put each link on a separate line, leaving room for comments and other annotations associated with the links. You also may find it convenient to write in narrative descriptions or references to specification paragraphs, as I've done here.

```
 7:   14(a)  {restart process; see section 3.1.4.1.5.9}
14:   99(k)  {boot–up entry point; see section 3.2.4.5}
      13(t)  {installation entry point; see section 3.3.1.7.5}
      . . . . . . .
43:   12(x)  {recoverable error; section 6.4.5}
       7(w)  {unrecoverable error; spec section 6.4.6}
```

2.5 GENERIC TESTING PRINCIPLES

2.5.1 General

These are the steps to use a graph model to design test cases:

1. Define the graph.
2. Define the relation.
3. Design **node-cover** tests (tests that confirm that the nodes are there).
4. Design **link-cover** tests (that confirm all required links and no more).
5. Test all weights
6. Design loop tests.

QUESTION: *What do you do when you see a graph?*
ANSWER: *Cover it!*

2.5.2 Define the Graph

1. Define the nodes.

    a. What objects (nodes) does this graph represent? There is one node for each object of interest.

    b. Name the nodes. How you name the nodes is arbitrary, but every node must have a unique name or identifier. I like to use numbers, but you might prefer names that are meaningful for your application.

    c. Nodes also can have properties (weights). Annotate every node with properties (values) as appropriate.

2. Define the links.

    a. Every link must start and end at a node. (They can be the same node.) You may want to add an entry and/or an exit node to your model because these are often implied. If a link **dangles** (i.e., comes out of nowhere or points to no node), you have a model error.

    b. Name the links. If there can be more than one link between a pair of nodes, then it is wise to name each link by a unique name. If only one link can **span** (i.e., lie between) a pair of nodes, you don't have to name the links.

    c. Annotate every link with weights as appropriate.

3. Find entry and exit nodes. A graph model doesn't have to have entry or exit nodes, but they often have both. If a graph does have entry and/or exit nodes, then those nodes are likely to be important. Mark all entry and exit nodes appropriately. For example: 14(ENTRY):... or 44(EXIT). Remember, if a node is an entry node, then no link enters it, and if it is an exit node, then no links leave it.

4. Find all loops. A graph model doesn't have to have loops, but if it does have them, they are important. We'll use some special testing methods for loops, so you want to find all the loops in the graph. There are mechanical (i.e., algorithmic) ways to do this, but they are beyond the scope of this book; see BEIZ90.

2.5.3 Define the Relation

1. Start by writing the relation in English (or your native language).

2. Answer the following questions with a YES or NO.

    a. Is it reflexive?

    b. Is it symmetric?

    c. Is it transitive?

If it's reflexive, then *every* node must have a self-loop. If it's symmetric, then *every* link must go in both directions. A graph's relation need not have any of these properties, and, furthermore, there are other properties they might have that are not discussed in this book (see BEIZ90, Chapter 12). Whatever the relation's properties, they must be verified by testing.

2.5.4 Node Cover

The least you can do is enough tests to ensure that all nodes are as they should be. This is called **node cover.** Node cover, however, itself has gradations in terms of increasingly more thorough tests. Here is a priority-ordered list of tests you can run to achieve node cover.

1. Enough tests to ensure that every node that should be there is there—no nodes missing.

2. Enough tests to ensure that there are no extra nodes. (This could take an infinite number of tests and therefore not be possible.)

3. Enough tests to confirm the correctness of the node weights, if any.

4. If there are both entry and exit nodes, then the preceding steps usually can be accomplished by selecting paths that go from entries to exits, with input values selected that will force the software to go down the selected path(s) of the model. Typically, it will take several ENTRY/EXIT paths (test cases) to do this.

While node cover is offered here as a (very) weak testing option, in practice it is so weak that it is essentially useless. All the techniques discussed in this book assume that you will do at least link cover. (See below.) Link cover, as defined, assumes that you have done all the tests demanded by node cover.

2.5.5 Link Cover

The next strongest thing you can do is to run enough tests to ensure that all links are as they should be. This is called **link cover.** Here is a priority-ordered list of tests you can run to achieve link cover.

1. Enough tests to ensure that every link that should be there is there—no links missing.

2. Enough tests to ensure that there are no extra links. (This could take an infinite number of tests and therefore not be possible).

3. Test the relation.
   a. If the relation is symmetric, then test to ensure that every link goes both ways: for example, **DO/UNDO**.
   b. If the relation is reflexive, then test to ensure that every node has a link leading back to itself: for example, **DO NOTHING**.

c. If the relation is transitive, then you must test transitivity wherever it can occur. This is done as follows. Consider three objects, A, B, and C, where there is a link from A to B and also a link from B to C. That is, A 𝕽 B and B 𝕽 C. Having shown that A 𝕽 B is true and B 𝕽 C is true (by testing), also show by testing that A 𝕽 C is true. Do this for *every* triplet of nodes for which the condition holds.

4. If there are both entry and exit nodes, then steps 1 to 3 above usually can be accomplished by selecting paths that go from entries to exits, with input values selected that will force the software to traverse the selected path(s). Typically, it will take several **ENTRY/EXIT** paths (test cases) to do this. Note that usually if you provide a link-covering set of tests, you will also have provided a node-covering set of tests. Also note, however, that it usually takes more tests to provide link cover than node cover.

In black-box testing practice, except for pathological cases, if you design link covering tests, you also will achieve node cover. However, you might not be able to confirm that there are no extra nodes and that node weights, if any, are correct. It's a good idea to add the node cover requirements from section 2.5.4 to your test design and test inspection checklists.

2.5.6 Test the Weights

If the links have weights, then run enough tests to confirm the weight's value for each and every link. Similarly for node weights if they are part of the model.

2.5.7 Loop Testing

We pay special attention to loops in testing because bug statistics show that programmers have trouble with loops. That's why there's a whole chapter on the subject. (See Chapter 4.) This section is intended to cover only the basics.

We don't look at the code to see if it does or does not have a loop. We do loop testing if our *model* of the software's behavior shows loops.

A **loop** is a sequence of node names in which at least one node name is repeated. If a different repeating sequence of node names appears or is possible, then you have a different loop. You must test *every* loop.

Loop testing is based on how many times around the loop you will go. You can bypass the loop altogether, go around once, twice, . . . a maximum number of times, which we will designate by "n." The following example has a node that enters the loop (A) and two nodes that exit the loop (X and Y).

1. Bypass the loop: **AXE** or **AXYZE**. (I would use both).

2. Go around once: **AXYVWXE** or **AXYVWXYZE**.

3. Go around twice: **AXYVWXYVWXE** or **AXYWXYVWXYZE**.

4. Go around a typical number of times: **A(XYVW)^{typical}XE**.

5. Go around the maximum number (n): **A(XYVW)^{n}XE** and **A(XYVW)^{n}XYZE**.

6. Go around one less than the maximum: **A(XYVW)$^{n-1}$XE** and **A(XYVW)$^{n-1}$XYZE**.

7. Attempt one more than the maximum: **A(XYVW)$^{n+1}$XE** and **A(XYVW)$^{n+1}$XYZE**.

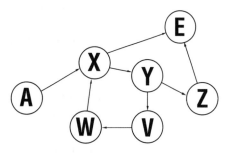

Consider any two nodes in the model, say A and B. If there is a path from A to B (not necessarily a direct link) and another path from B to A and this is true for *every* A and B, then it is possible to start at any node, go to any other node by some path, and come back to the node you started with. Such graphs are said to be **strongly connected.** Exhaustive loop testing as just specified is usually a waste of time for strongly connected graphs. It is obvious that the graph of a symmetric relation (or undirected graph) is strongly connected because all arrows go both ways. Consequently, loop testing is *not* effective for graphs of symmetric relations.

2.6 SUMMARY

You now have the vocabulary and central ideas of behavioral testing. The lesson may be less concrete than some of you like. As I said in the README.DOC, this chapter is a knowledge subroutine that you will use in subsequent chapters to create concrete tests. Think of this chapter as an object in an object-oriented program that will be dynamically bound in subsequent chapters. OOP by my reckoning is far more abstract than this chapter. Alternatively, think of this chapter as a game that you must master. Use the following self-evaluation quiz to find out how well you have absorbed the lesson.

2.7 SELF-EVALUATION QUIZ

1. **Define:** achievable path, asymmetric relation, binary relation, branch node, branching statement, call tree, comment, control-flow graph, cover, dangling link, data-flow graph, directed graph, directed link, entry node, entry-exit path, equivalence class, equivalence relation, exit

node, graph, graph matrix, inlink, intransitive relation, irreflexive relation, link, link cover, link list reprentation, link name, link weight, loop, loop-free path, menu-driven software, node, node cover, node name, node weight, outlink, parallel links, partition testing strategy, path, path length, path name, path segment, reflexive relation, relation, self-loop, span, strongly connected graph, symmetric relation, transaction-flow graph, transitive relation, unachievable path, undirected graph, undirected link.

2. Relations can be: symmetric or asymmetric, reflexive or irreflexive, transitive or intransitive, for a total of eight different combinations. The following table shows examples of each kind of relation. Find three more examples for each type. Prove (e.g., test) each example to show that it is correct. Hint: Try *Roget's Thesaurus*.

SYMMETRIC	REFLEXIVE	TRANSITIVE	EXAMPLES
NO	NO	NO	love, abuse, argue, assault, own
NO	NO	YES	above, taller
NO	YES	NO	is acquainted with
NO	YES	YES	greater than or equal to
YES	NO	NO	first cousin, affianced, married
YES	NO	YES	abreast of, adjacent,
YES	YES	NO	near,
YES	YES	YES	equal

3. Is the relation *in the shadow of* always transitive? Find a situation, meaning, or ways of illuminating in which this relation is not transitive.

4. Consider the relation *has been integrated with* from the point of view of whether it is symmetric, reflexive, or transitive. Find examples or counterexamples to substantiate your beliefs.

5. Classify the following relations (as to symmetric, reflexive, and transitive) and prove your classification by showing that no counterexample can exist: A *calls* B, A *not equal to* B, A *agrees with* B, A *is equivalent to* B, A *is consistent with* B, A *is compatible with* B, A *is incompatible with* B, A *is a part of* B, A *is apart from* B, A *is a part from* B, A *is better than* B, A *dominates* B, A *is subject to* B.

3

Control-Flow
Testing

3.1 SYNOPSIS

The control-flow graph is introduced as the basic model for test design. We apply the control-flow graph to create models of various parts of IRS Form 1040, which is about as complicated a piece of work to test as there is. The model is then used to design a link covering set of tests.

3.2 VOCABULARY

External Prerequisite Terms: algebra, algebraic, **AND** (logical), application, assembly language, boolean branch, bug, **CASE** statement, COBOL, code, complete, complexity, computation, consistent, constraint, contradiction, control, control flow, copy, equation solver, **EXCLUSIVE-OR** (logical), execute, expression, extreme values, formal model, **IF** statement, **IF-THEN-ELSE** statement, **FALSE**, **GOTO** statement, implementation, **INCLUSIVE-OR** (logical), increment, inequality, instance, jump, logic, logical expression, logical value, LOTUS-123, maintenance, matrix, missing requirements, model, model bug, modeling, name, natural language, nested, **NOT** (logical), numerical, operator, **OR** (logical), paste, processing, processing step, program, programmer, programming, pseudocode, realism, rehost, release, requirement, rewrite, sales demonstration, sentence, simultaneous equation, software, specification, specification bug, spreadsheet, structured programs, symbolic substitution, table, test bug, test design, tester, tree, **TRUE**, truth table, truth value, unstructured software, value, version, word processor.

Internal Prerequisite Terms: achievable path, behavior, behavioral testing, black-box testing, blind, branch cover, bug, coincidental correctness, configuration control, covering paths, entry node, exit node, feature, graph, graph model, inlink, input, input value, link, link cover, link weight, link list representation of a graph, loop, missing feature, missing path, node, node name, object, oracle, outcome, output, outlink, parallel links, path, path segment, prototype, relation, requirement, specification, subpath, test case, test suite, test technique, test tool, unachievable path, unit testing, validation criteria.

logical predicate: A sentence or expression that takes on the logical values of TRUE or FALSE. Examples: *"The sky is blue," "This sentence is FALSE," "Your parent can claim you as a dependent on his or her income tax return," "Your child is claimed as your dependent under a pre-1985 agreement."*

selector predicate: An expression that takes on more than two values used to select one of several alternatives. Example: *"Check only one box—(1) single, (2) married filing joint return, (3) married filing separate return, (4) head of household, (5) qualifying widower."* The term "**predicate**" often is used to mean both logical and selector predicates.

logical AND: In logic and formal models, "AND" is precisely defined: Both A and B must be true for A&B to be true. However, for informal documents and nonlogical documents such as income tax forms, words and phrases such as "but," "also," "in-addition to," and even "or" may actually mean logical AND.

logical OR: In logic and formal models, "OR" always means INCLUSIVE-OR, that is, "AND/OR." Informal usage varies and caution is advised.

logical NOT: In logic and formal models, you should place the **NOT** operator first and enclose the sentence in parentheses, as in "**NOT** *(your child lived with you)*," rather than *"Your child did* **NOT** *live with you."* For informal writing, the **NOT** can appear almost anyplace within a sentence and care is advised.

compound predicate: A logical expression involving two or more predicates connected by **AND, OR,** or **NOT.** Examples: (1) "Your child did **NOT** live with you **AND** is claimed as your dependent under a pre-1985 agreement;" (2) (You received wages in 1994 **AND/OR** you received tips in 1994) **AND** your wages combined with tips was **NOT** greater than $60,600 AND you did **NOT** receive tips subject to Social Security or Medicare tax that you did **NOT** report to your employer **AND** you are a minister who received IRS approval **NOT** to be taxed on earnings from these sources **AND** you owe self-employment taxes on other earnings."*

independent predicates: Two or more predicates on a path are **independent** if their truth values (TRUE/FALSE) can be chosen independently.

correlated predicates: Two or more predicates on a path are **correlated** if selecting the truth value of one constrains the truth values of other predicates on that path. Example: If a predicate appears twice on a path, selecting the truth value for the first instance of the predicate forces the value of the next instance of that predicate *on that path*.

complementary path segments: Two path segments that traverse the same predicates such that if the predicate value is TRUE on one path it will be FALSE on the other and vice-versa.

3.3 THE RELATIONS AND THE MODEL

3.3.1 General [ALLE72, CLAR76, EBER94, HOWD76, HOWD87, KRAU73, PETE76]

---

* I didn't make this one up. This specification is a path through IRS Form SE, 1994. See for yourself. Income Tax 101 is surely a tougher course than Programming 101 or Testing 101.

objects (nodes): A sequence of processing steps such that if any part of the sequence is executed, all will be executed (if there are no bugs).

Example: Form 1040. The following lines can be modeled by a single node that includes lines 7 through 14, by several nodes, such as "7-8a-8b, 9-10-11, 12, 13-14," or even by a sequence of 9 separate nodes, one for each line.

7.   (enter) wages, salaries, tips.
8a. (enter) taxable interest income.
8b. (enter) tax-exempt interest income.
9.   (enter) dividend income.
10. (enter) taxable refunds, credits, or offsets of state and local income taxes.
11. (enter) alimony received.
12. (enter) business income or loss.
13. (enter) capital gain or loss.
14. (enter) other gains and losses.

Here are some possible graph models for this specification:

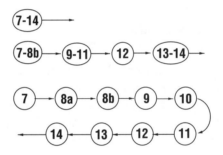

relation (links): *is directly followed by.* In the previous example, assuming that we used one node for each step, node 9 *is directly followed by* node 10, node 10 *is directly followed by* node 11, and so on.

predicate node: A node with two or more outlinks each of which is weighted by a predicate value. That means TRUE/FALSE for a logical predicate and one of several alternatives for a selector predicate. A predicate node selects one of two or more alternative paths that the process can take.

Example: Lines 33b to 34, Form 1040.

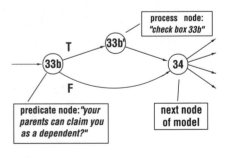

33b. If your parents can claim you as a dependent then check box 33b, otherwise do not check box 33b.

This sentence can be modeled as shown in the above graph.

selector node: A node with more than two outlinks with each link weighted by a selector value. Example: Line 34, Form 1040: Enter the larger of your itemized deduction from Schedule A line 29 **OR** the standard deduction show below for your filing status. But if you checked any box on line 33a or b, see instructions to find your standard deduction. If you checked box 33c, your standard deduction is zero. (a) single =$3,800, (b) married filing jointly=$6,350, (c) qualifying widower=$6,350, (d) married filing separately=$3,175, (e) head of household = $5,600. The following graph models most of this sentence. Node 34.5 is a selector node.

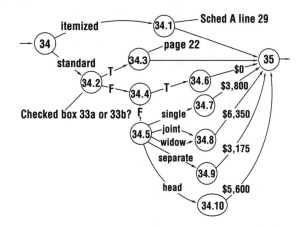

The link list representation is more convenient and shows more detail:

34	"Standard or Itemized Deduction?"		34.1	Itemized
			34.2	Standard
34.1	GOTO Schedule A, line 29		35	
34.2	"Checked box 33a or 33b?"		34.3	TRUE
			34.4	FALSE
34.3	GOTO Page 22		35	
34.4	"Checked box 33c?"		34.6	TRUE
			34.5	FALSE
34.5	Select Alternatives		34.7	Single
			34.8	Joint return
			34.8	Qualified Widower
			34.9	Separate returns
			34.10	Head of household
34.6	Deduction = $0		35	
34.7	Deduction = $3,800		35	
34.8	Deduction = $6,350		35	
34.9	Deduction = $3,175		35	
34.10	Deduction = $5,600		35	
35	Continue with rest of the model			

junction node: A node with two or more inlinks. In the previous example, nodes 34.8 and 35 are junction nodes.

Some comments on this model.

1. Node 34 is a predicate node. Note the usage of the word "or" here. It isn't a logical **OR**; it's a way of signaling a predicate.*

2. The predicate for node 34.2 is a compound predicate and the **OR** is an inclusive **OR** because either or both boxes can be checked. The predicate, written out formally, is: *"You checked box 33a* **OR** *you checked box 33b (or both)."* This predicate is also interesting because of the use of the word "but" to start a predicate. The key is not the "but" but the following "if."

A more detailed model for this node is:

34.2	Checked box 33a?		34.3	TRUE
			34.2.1.	FALSE
34.2.1	Checked box 33b?		34.3	TRUE
			34.4	FALSE

An even more detailed model is:

34.2	Checked box 33a?		34.2.2	TRUE
			34.2.1.	FALSE
34.2.1	Checked box 33b?		34.3	TRUE
			34.4	FALSE
34.2.2	Checked box 33b?		34.3	FALSE

The model improves the original because the complexity of the compound predicate has been exposed and we'll probably catch more bugs with it [MYER79]. The first improved model could be blind to some bugs because it favors the predicate at node 34.2. The second model is more balanced and makes fewer implementation assumptions. Therefore, even though it is more complicated, I prefer it because it will be a better bug catcher.

3. The predicate for line 33c is compound: *"(You are married filing separately* **AND** *your spouse itemizes deductions)* **OR** *you are a dual-status alien."* The **OR** is inclusive because you could be a dual-status alien (whatever that is) and your spouse could be filing separately and itemizing deductions. Note, however, that if you are not a dual-status alien, three conditions must be satisfied: (1) you are married, (2) you are filing separately, and (3) your spouse itemizes deductions.

---

* Actually not a predicate node, but something else to be treated in Chapter 6 on transaction flow testing. It isn't a true predicate because a careful examination of the tax form shows that you could take both alternatives.

4. One of the selected values at node 34.5 is hidden under an "or." It is not a logical OR. It's a way of signaling parallel links and additional selector values: *married filing jointly* versus *qualifying widower.*

5. Nodes 34.1 and 34.3 need models in their own rights. I could have included the details here but didn't because for node 34.1, we are directed to go to Schedule A, which might be entered from several different places. Prudence dictates that we model it separately. I chose to model node 34.3 separately for the same reason.

6. Nodes 34.1, 34.3, 34.6, 34.7, 34.8, 34.9, and 34.10 are not essential. I could have associated the processing with the outlinks of node 34.5 and included them in the weights for those links, as in the following:

34	"Standard or Itemized Deduction?"	35	Itemized/GOTO Sched A, L29
		34.2	Standard
34.2	"Checked box 33a or 33b?"	35	TRUE/GOTO page 22
		34.4	FALSE
34.4	"Checked box 33c?"	35	TRUE/Ded = $0
		34.5	FALSE
34.5	Select alternatives	35	Single/Ded = $3,800
		35	Joint return/Ded =$6,350
		35	Widower/ded = $6,350
		35	Separate returns/Ded = $3,175
		35	Head household /Ded =$5,600
35	Continue with rest of the model		

This model is equivalent but not as useful because it's harder to understand and because links are overloaded with information. It's better to use more nodes and links in the interest of clarity.

7. These models don't assume anything about the software that implements this processing. Although the use of IF-THEN statements for nodes 34, 34.2, and 34.4 and a CASE statement for node 34.5 are obvious, there are ways to implement this that don't use CASE or IF statements. In behavioral testing we shouldn't be too concerned with implementation details.

3.3.2 Modeling Compound Predicates

Compound predicates are deceptive because they hide complexity. They are also good to test because programmers mess them up. You can always expand a compound predicate to reveal the hidden complexity, and you can model one by a graph or by a table. Here's the graph model. Suppose you have a compound predicate that consists of several subsidiary **simple predicates** (i.e., not compound) that we'll call A, B, and C. For example: "**A&B OR C.**" You build a predicate tree with as many branches as there are possibilities. For two predicates, that's four branches; for three predicates, eight branches; and for n subsidiary predicates, 2^n branches. The graph on the right shows the first step.

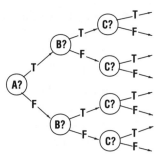

The order in which you put the predicates doesn't matter. What matters is that all 2^n cases (eight for this example) are considered. The next step is to gather the outlinks for the TRUE cases to a TRUE node and the outlinks for the FALSE cases to a FALSE node, as in the next graph.

The single node with the compound predicate **A&B OR C** is replaced by a more detailed model that shows all the predicate parts. You might think that the top C predicate node is redundant because the flow will go to the TRUE node no matter the value of this predicate. However, it is not redundant because it will work that way if and only if

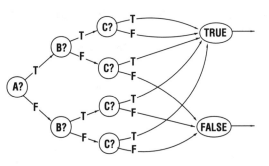

there are no bugs in the implementation. Only by testing all eight (2^n, in general) cases explicitly can we be reasonably sure that the logic, however it is implemented, is not buggy. You *can* back off from testing all possible 2^n conditions explicitly; that's okay as long as you accept the fact that your testing is weaker and may miss more bugs.

Another way to model this is to use a **truth table** instead of the explicit graph tree. You use a single node for the compound predicate and make a notation that all the cases in the truth table must be tested. You'll recall that a **truth table** lists the conditions for the component predicates and states whether the whole predicate is TRUE or FALSE for that condition.

I use truth tables for compound predicates with more

A	B	C	A&B or C
TRUE	TRUE	TRUE	TRUE
TRUE	TRUE	FALSE	TRUE
TRUE	FALSE	TRUE	TRUE
TRUE	FALSE	FALSE	FALSE
FALSE	TRUE	TRUE	TRUE
FALSE	TRUE	FALSE	FALSE
FALSE	FALSE	TRUE	TRUE
FALSE	FALSE	FALSE	FALSE

than three predicates. Adding four nodes to the graph for a compound predicate with two terms doesn't clutter the model up too much. But just three component predicates makes the graph much busier, and four is almost impossible. Remember, you can't discount the possibility that your model has bugs!

3.4 THE TECHNIQUE

3.4.1 General

Test design and execution consists of the following steps:

1. Examine the requirements and analyze them for operationally satisfactory completeness and self-consistency. Confirm that the specification correctly reflects the requirements, and correct the specification if it doesn't.

2. Rewrite the specification as a sequence of short sentences. Pay special attention to predicates. Break up compound predicates to equivalent sequences of simple predicates. Watch for selector nodes and document them as simple lists. Remove any "ANDs" that are not part of predicates—break the sentence in half instead.

3. Number sentence uniquely. These will be your node names later.

4. Build the model.

5. Verify the model—your work is as bug prone as the programmers'.

6. Select test paths.

7. **Sensitize** the test paths you picked. That is, select input values that would cause the software to do the equivalent of traversing your selected paths if there were no bugs.

8. Predict and record the expected outcome for each test.

9. Define the validation criterion(ia) for each test.

10. Run the tests.

11. Confirm the outcomes.

12. Confirm the path.

3.4.2 Building the Model

As an example to illustrate the process, we'll use lines 32 through 40 of IRS Form 1040. The original specification is in appendix A. The easiest way to demonstrate this is to work the exercise and comment as we go, in a stream of consciousness. My comments are in italics.

Step 1: **Examine the requirements and validate.** Not much to do because we hope that the IRS has done this for us. Is that a vain hope?

Step 2: **Rewrite the specification.** Personally, I rewrite the specification using my own brand of pseudocode. The use of a semiformal language (e.g., pseudocode) helps to assure that things will be stated unambiguously. Although this looks like programming, it is not programming—it is modeling.

I use the link list notation because it's easier; however, as I worked, I drew little graphs to make sure I had the flow correct around the various predicates. I've included some of my sketches to help you see what I was thinking. Although drawing and using the full graph in graphical form is cumbersome, these intermediate sketches for small graph segments help you to get the logic correct.

input AGI   cnt=0   (33a3) cnt +1

(32)——(33a1)——(33a2)–T——————(33a4)—
                        F
        65 or older?

32:	33a1	input adjusted_gross_income	*Must keep track of number of*
33a1	33a2	set checkmark_count to zero	*check marks we make on the*
			form.
33a2	33a3	If 65 or older	*This is a predicate node, so there will be at least two outlinks.*
	33a4	if NOT 65 or older	*Jump around the increment if not 65 or older.*
33a3	33a4	increment checkmark_count	*We'll need the total number of check marks later, so this is as good a way to model it as any.*
33a4	33a5	If blind	*Another predicate node.*
	33a6	If NOT blind	*Skip around if NOT blind*
33a5	33a6	increment checkmark_count	*Increment the checkmark counter if blind.*
33a6	33a7	If spouse is 65 or older	

*Note that the logic here is really much more complicated. If our model was for the entire 1040, then we would have to correlate this with lines 1–5 to take into account the filing status. Only filing status (2) Married and (5) qualifying widow(er) can have this and the next box checked. You would, in a real model, precede this and the next predicate node with another predicate node that asks "Married filing joint return **OR** qualifying widower with dependent child?" If the*

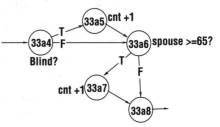

predicate is TRUE, you execute nodes 33a6 through 33a9, otherwise you skip to node 33a10. However, in order to keep this model to a reasonable size, we'll ignore reality and assume that this segment does not depend on any previous segments and logic.

	33a8	if spouse is NOT 65 or older
33a7	33a8	increment checkmark_count
33a8	33a9	if spouse is blind
	33a10	if spouse is NOT blind
33a9	33a10	increment checkmark_count

Node 33a10 is superfluous because we've been "calculating" the **checkmark_count** as we go; however, I like to make sure that there is at least one node (at first) for every statement in the specification.

33b	33b1	If your parents can claim you—Predicate node.
	33c	Parents can't claim you.
33b1	33c	Check box 33b.
33c	33c1	Married file separately.

Compound predicate. If you were to look at the IRS instructions, you would find even more logic to model. In order to keep things reasonable, we'll ignore the instruction to look at the instructions—but in a real problem, you wouldn't have that option. I've broken the predicate down to its component parts in order not to have hidden complexity. My model for this section is on the right. Other, equivalent, models are possible.

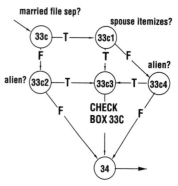

I messed this one up. The first time I did it, I forgot the possibility of married filing separately with a spouse who did not itemize but in which I was a dual-status alien. Therefore, I had to go back and add the predicate node at 33c4. Here again, the sketch helped me.

33c	33c2	Not married file separately
33c1	33c4	Spouse does not itemize
	33c3	Spouse itemizes
33c2	33c3	Dual-status alien
	34	Not dual-status alien
33c3	34	check box 33c
33c4	34	Not dual-status alien
	33c3	Dual-status alien
34	34.1	Did you itemize?
	34.2	Did not itemize

This isn't redundant.

*Node 34 is a very interesting situation. It looks like a predicate node but it really isn't. It's an example of what we call a **transaction split**. (See Chapter 6.) In order to follow the instructions as stated (see node 34.13 below) – that is, to take the larger of itemized or standard deductions – you must do both calculations: for the standard deductions and for the itemized deductions. We must actually take both paths in parallel, otherwise there's nothing to compare against at node 34.13. But you knew that from filling out your tax return.*

34.1	**34.12**	**Use schedule A line 26**	*Another whole model buried here.*
34.2	**34.3**	**Did NOT check box 33a**	
	34.4.	**Did check box 33a**	
34.3	**34.4**	**Checked box 33b**	
	34.5	**Did NOT check box 33b**	

Wait a minute! What about a person who is 65 or older AND/OR blind AND whose parents or someone else can claim as a dependent? Is this case covered by the model?

34.4	**34.12**	**Standard deduction from instructions**	
34.5	**34.6**	**Checked box 33c?**	
	34.7	**Did not check box 33c**	
34.6	**34.12**	**Standard deduction = 0**	
34.7	**34.8**	**Single**	*Selector predicate.*
	34.9	**Head of household**	
	34.10	**Married filing joint return**	
	34.11	**Married filing separately**	
34.8	**34.12**	**Standard deduction = $3,800**	
34.9	**34.12**	**Standard deduction = $5,600**	
34.10	**34.12**	**Standard deduction = $6,350**	
34.11	**34.12**	**Standard deduction = $3,175**	

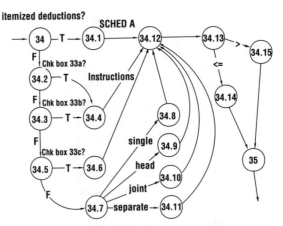

34.12	34.13	**Dummy node for clarity**
34.13	34.14	**Standard greater than itemized?**
	34.15	**Standard NOT greater than itemized**
34.14	35	**Use standard**
34.15	35	**Use itemized**
35	36	**Subtract line 34 from line 32**
36	36.1	**Line 32 <= $83,850**
	36.2	**Line 32 > $83,850**
36.1	37	**$2,450 exemptions**
36.2	37	**From instructions**
~~37~~	~~38~~	~~**Max (0, Line_35 - Line_36)**~~ *Saves another predicate but hides a path segment. So let's do it right.*
37	37.1	**Line_35 − Line_36**
37.1	38	**Greater than zero**
	37.2	**<= zero**
37.2	38	**Enter zero on line 37**
38	38.1	**tax table**

This one is cute. On the surface it looks as if there are five mutually exclusive possibilities: (a) tax table, (b) tax rate schedule, (c) schedule D, (d) Form 8615, or (e)Form 8814. However, on looking at forms 8615 and 8814, it seemed to me that these could be two additional entries over and above the first three options. I tried to get a clarification from the IRS but couldn't get through. I called my accountant and he asked if this was a "special consultation," so I said: "Never mind, Charley." This is the kind of research you may have to do to create useful models, but for this example, I'll treat it as five separate options.

38	38.2	**tax rate schedule**
	38.3	**Schedule C**
	38.4	**Form 8615**
	38.5	**Form(s) 8814**

Note that there could be several Form 8814s, but we're not told to put in the sum of these forms. That kind of stuff should be researched. Here we should put in the sum of the 8814 forms, because one must be filled out for each child whose interest and dividends you elect to report on your return. So there's a loop here.

38.1	39	**tax from tax table**
38.2	39	**tax from tax rate schedule**
38.3	39	**tax from schedule C**
38.4	39	**tax from Form 8615**
38.5	39	**tax from Form(s) 8814**

39	39.1	Additional taxes from Form 4970
	39.2	NO additional taxes from Form 4970
39.1	39.3	Enter Form 4970 tax
39.2	39.3	Enter zero additional taxes for line 39
39.3	39.4	Additional taxes from Form 4972
	39.5	NO additional taxes from Form 4972
39.4	40	Add taxes from Form 4972 to line 39

I modeled it this way because it seemed to me from the tax forms that one could have taxes from either Form 4970 or 4972 or both. Such things are never obvious, and you must research them.

39.5	40	Do nothing
40	41	Add lines 39 and 40

Gruesome? Building this model of a seemingly simple specification was a lot of work. It took me five hours, including the time to do nice versions of the graph sketches and the explanatory comments that I wouldn't make if I were doing actual test design. But all those comments and the stream of consciousness isn't a bad idea. Someone (such as yourself) might be grateful for them later.

With practice and experience, two or three hours is all that the preceding model should take. If you must do a lot of research, it will probably take much longer. Note that my graphical models got simpler as I went along. The last one, for example, has very little detail other than the control flow. That's deliberate. You use the graphical form to make sure that you have the logic right, but you depend on the narrative list form to document the details.

I changed the notation as I went. The graph on page 41 has the format **node_name / action / node_name / predicate value**, while the later format is **node_name / node_name / action or predicate value / comment**. Links are easier to mark and check with the latter notation, but the earlier notation is closer to the original narrative form. It doesn't matter what format you use. Pick any one that has all the needed data and that you can live with and stick to it.

Another reason this isn't programming. I didn't try to use structured constructs so my models are full of GOTOs and stuff like that. Today, if implemented as explicit logic, it would most likely be restricted to strictly structured constructs. I like the GOTOs and other unstructured stuff here because it doesn't force me to divert too far from the natural language of the specification. Most natural-language specifications are unstructured. If you divert too much from the original wording by forcing the use of, say, nested trees of IF-THEN-ELSES, then you're increasing the likelihood of modeling bugs, which in turn lead to test bugs or undiscovered program bugs.

3.4.3 Select Test Paths

3.4.3.1 GENERAL

There's nothing to be gained by reducing the number of tests. It's better to use several simple, obvious tests than to do the job with fewer, but grander, tests. The previous example could probably be done with 10 tests, but we should use more if doing so makes the tests clearer and more directly related to the requirements.

Path selection and sensitization are often done simultaneously because correlated predicates can prevent the software from traversing arbitrarily chosen paths. Although that's good practice, it's bad pedagogy so we'll do the path selection and then sensitize the paths in the next section.

We do path building segment by segment, starting with the entry node and continuing to the exit node. We pick our segments to start at points where the control flow diverges from a single node and continue until the control flow once again pinches down to a single node. Examples: 32–33a4, 33a4–33a6, 33c–34. We do it this way in order to build paths by combinations of previously selected segments. You can combine paths segments only at such single-node pinch points. At each predicate, we make choices (e.g., TRUE/FALSE) that split the paths we've built up to that point.

There's no choice for nodes 32 and 33a1; all our tests must begin with 32, 33a1.

The first predicate is at 33a2. This can be selected as either TRUE or FALSE, leading to the following two families of tests:

A1:   32, 33a1, 33a2(T), 33a3, 33a4.
A2:   32, 33a1, 33a2(F), 33a4.

The next predicate is at 33a4 (*blind?*). This is clearly independent of the previous predicate at 33a2 (*65 or over?*). So although the paths split again, there's no need to add to the tests. For now, I'll hold the TRUE cases to A1 and the FALSE cases to A2, to yield:

A1:   32, 33a1, 33a2(T), 33a3, 33a4(T), 33a5, 33a6.
A2:   32, 33a1, 33a2(F), 33a4(F), 33a6.

At node 33a6 we ask if the spouse is 65 or older, and at 33a8 we ask if the spouse is blind. Looking at these first four predicates, we can see that there are a total of 16 possible paths through this segment of the specification. We could, if we wanted to, set up 16 tests just to this point, to check out all 16 combinations of these first four predicates, but that would be a bad bet. That is, we would be trying to test for unlikely bugs. Only two path segments are needed to achieve link cover from node 32 to 33b; which should we take? Any two complementary paths will do. The paths from 32 to 33b can result in a count of zero to four. We know from experience that programmers tend to mess up the extreme value cases (zero and four), so we might as well select those cases—besides, I like the idea of testing this logic with tests in which the filer and spouse are both blind and over 65.

A1:   32, 33a1, 33a2(T), 33a3, 33a4(T), 33a5, 33a6(T), 33a7, 33a8(T), 33a9, 33a10, 33b

A2:   32, 33a1, 33a2(F), 33a4(F), 33a6(F), 33a8(F), 33a10, 33b

The next predicate is at 33b. I made a mistake the first time I did this and had sensitization trouble. I didn't look far enough ahead to see that this predicate would block paths farther down in the 34–35 segment. The two possibilities for this segment are: **B1: 33b(T), 33b1, 33c** and **B2: 33b(F), 33c.**

I can't be sure which combinations will be blocked later on, so I'll combine the A and B sets to create four possibilities at this point. Later we'll eliminate tests that can't be executed. Doing this yields:

B1A1:   32, 33a1, 33a2(T), 33a3, 33a4(T), 33a5, 33a6(T), 33a7, 33a8(T), 33a9, 33a10, 33b(T), 33b1, 33c

B2A1:   32, 33a1, 33a2(T), 33a3, 33a4(T), 33a5, 33a6(T), 33a7, 33a8(T), 33a9, 33a10, 33b(F), 33c.

B1A2:   32, 33a1, 33a2(F), 33a4(F), 33a6(F), 33a8(F), 33a10, 33b(T), 33b1, 33c

B2A2:   32, 33a1, 33a2(F), 33a4(F), 33a6(F), 33a8(F), 33a10, 33b(F), 33c.

The next segment is 33c–34. There are five possible paths through this segment, and all five are needed to achieve link cover. The five segments are:

C1:   33c(F), 33c2(T), 33c3, 34

C2:   33c(T), 33c1(T), 33c3, 34

C3:   33c(T), 33c1(F), 33c4(T), 33c3, 34

C4:   33c(F), 33c2(F), 34

C5:   33c(T), 33c1(F), 33c4(F), 34

A quick check here is advisable. I looked at the four predicates (33c, 33c1, 33c2, and 33c4) in the preceding list to make sure that each predicate appeared both with a TRUE and FALSE in some test segment.

C1B1A1:   32, 33a1, 33a2(T), 33a3, 33a4(T), 33a5, 33a6(T), 33a7, 33a8(T), 33a9, 33a10, 33b(T), 33b1, 33c(F), 33c2(T), 33c3, 34

C2B1A1:   32, 33a1, 33a2(T), 33a3, 33a4(T), 33a5, 33a6(T), 33a7, 33a8(T), 33a9, 33a10, 33b(T), 33b1, 33c(T), 33c1(T), 33c3, 34

C3B1A1: 32, 33a1, 33a2(T), 33a3, 33a4(T), 33a5, 33a6(T), 33a7, 33a8(T), 33a9, 33a10, 33b(T), 33b1, 33c(T), 33c1(F), 33c4(T), 33c3, 34

C4B1A1: 32, 33a1, 33a2(T), 33a3, 33a4(T), 33a5, 33a6(T), 33a7, 33a8(T), 33a9, 33a10, 33b(T), 33b1, 33c(F), 33c2(F), 34

C5B1A1: 32, 33a1, 33a2(T), 33a3, 33a4(T), 33a5, 33a6(T), 33a7, 33a8(T), 33a9, 33a10, 33b(T), 33b1, 33c(T), 33c1(F), 33c4(F), 34

C1B2A1: 32, 33a1, 33a2(T), 33a3, 33a4(T), 33a5, 33a6(T), 33a7, 33a8(T), 33a9, 33a10, 33b(F), 3c(F), 33c2(T), 33c3, 34

C2B2A1: 32, 33a1, 33a2(T), 33a3, 33a4(T), 33a5, 33a6(T), 33a7, 33a8(T), 33a9, 33a10, 33b(F), 33c(T), 33c1(T), 33c3, 34

C3B2A1: 32, 33a1, 33a2(T), 33a3, 33a4(T), 33a5, 33a6(T), 33a7, 33a8(T), 33a9, 33a10, 33b(F), 33c(T), 33c1(F), 33c4(T), 33c3, 34

C4B2A1: 32, 33a1, 33a2(T), 33a3, 33a4(T), 33a5, 33a6(T), 33a7, 33a8(T), 33a9, 33a10, 33b(F), 33c(F), 33c2(F), 34

C5B2A1: 32, 33a1, 33a2(T), 33a3, 33a4(T), 33a5, 33a6(T), 33a7, 33a8(T), 33a9, 33a10, 33b(F), 33c(T), 33c1(F), 33c4(F), 34

C1B1A2: 32, 33a1, 33a2(F), 33a4(F), 33a6(F), 33a8(F), 33a10, 33b(T), 33b1, 33c(F), 33c2(T), 33c3, 34

C2B1A2: 32, 33a1, 33a2(F), 33a4(F), 33a6(F), 33a8(F), 33a10, 33b(T), 33b1, 33c(T), 33c1(T), 33c3, 34

C3B1A2: 32, 33a1, 33a2(F), 33a4(F), 33a6(F), 33a8(F), 33a10, 33b(T), 33b1, 33c(T), 33c1(F), 33c4(T), 33c3, 34

C4B1A2: 32, 33a1, 33a2(F), 33a4(F), 33a6(F), 33a8(F), 33a10, 33b(T), 33b1, 33c(F), 33c2(F), 34

C5B1A2: 32, 33a1, 33a2(F), 33a4(F), 33a6(F), 33a8(F), 33a10, 33b(T), 33b1, 33c(T), 33c1(F), 33c4(F), 34

C1B2A2: 32, 33a1, 33a2(F), 33a4(F), 33a6(F), 33a8(F), 33a10, 33b(F),33c(F), 33c2(T), 33c3, 34

C2B2A2: 32, 33a1, 33a2(F), 33a4(F), 33a6(F), 33a8(F), 33a10, 33b(F),33c(T), 33c1(T), 33c3, 34

C3B2A2: 32, 33a1, 33a2(F), 33a4(F), 33a6(F), 33a8(F), 33a10, 33b(F),33c(T), 33c1(F), 33c4(T), 33c3, 34

C4B2A2: 32, 33a1, 33a2(F), 33a4(F), 33a6(F), 33a8(F), 33a10, 33b(F),33c(F), 33c2(F), 34

C5B2A2: 32, 33a1, 33a2(F), 33a4(F), 33a6(F), 33a8(F), 33a10, 33b(F),33c(T), 33c1(F), 33c4(F), 34

A hint here. Exploit your word processor's features to prevent test design bugs. I did this by first copying the C1 to C5 segments, and then I used the copy and paste to paste-in the previous segments (B1A2 to B2A2) before C1 through C5. By not including node 33c in the copy block, I didn't have to remove its duplicate appearance. This way of doing it is both easier and more reliable.

There are eight possible path segments from nodes 34 through 34.12.

D1:	**34(T), 34.1, 34.12**
D2:	**34(F), 34.2(T), 34.4, 34.12**
D3:	**34(F), 34.2(F), 34.3(T), 34.4, 34.12**
D4:	**34(F), 34.2(F), 34.3(F), 34.5(T), 34.6, 34.12**
D5:	**34(F), 34.2(F), 34.3(F), 34.5(F), 34.7(SINGLE), 34.8, 34.12**
D6:	**34(F), 34.2(F), 34.3(F), 34.5(F), 34.7(HEAD), 34.9, 34.12**
D7:	**34(F), 34.2(F), 34.3(F), 34.5(F), 34.7(JOINT), 34.10, 34.12**
D8:	**34(F), 34.2(F), 34.3(F), 34.5(F), 34.7(SEPARATE), 34.11, 34.12**

If we continue with combinations, we'll have 20 cases combined with eight cases for a total of 160 cases to consider, so it's time to eliminate some cases as we go. This is another reason why sensitization and path selection usually go together.

We eliminate paths by removing combinations that cannot be executed because predicates block one another. I created a table with 20 rows and eight columns. The row headings were segments C1B1A1 through C5B2A2, and the column headings were segments D1 to D8.

1a. A FALSE at node 34.5 means that box 33c was not checked, therefore the path could not have gone through node 33c3, which was where this box was checked. I used the word processor search to find which segments had a 33c3 in them. Those are cases with C1, C2, and C3. They can't be combined with D5 to D8 because box 33c3 must be checked for these cases. So cross them off the table.

1b. Conversely, a TRUE at node 34.5 means that box 33c was checked, so the path had to go through node 33c3. Therefore, D4 can't be combined with C4 and C5.

2a. If box 33b is checked, the logic can't take the false path at node 34.3. Therefore, if node 33b1 is executed, segments D4 to D8 can't be executed. Using the search for node 33b1 (where box 33b is checked), we see that any segment with a B1 in it can't be combined with a D4 to D8 segment.

2b. Conversely, if box 33b (B2) is not checked, the logic can't take the TRUE path at node 34.3 (D3) and can't combine with any path that took 33b(F). These are the paths with a B2 in them. So any segment with a B2 can't be combined with a D3.

3a. If box 33a is checked, then segments D3 to D8 can be eliminated. Box 33a is checked at nodes 33a3, 33a5, 33a7, and 33a9. Searching our segments again we see that it is any segment with an A1. So A1 can't be combined with D3 to D8.

SEGMENT	D1	D2	D3	D4	D5	D6	D7	D8
C1B1A1	XXXX	XXXX	XXXX	XXXX	XXXX	XXXX		
C2B1A1		XXXX	XXXX	XXXX	XXXX	XXXX	XXXX	XXXX
C3B1A1	XXXX		XXXX	XXXX	XXXX	XXXX	XXXX	XXXX
C4B1A1			XXXX	XXXX	XXXX	XXXX	XXXX	XXXX
C5B1A1	XXXX		XXXX	XXXX	XXXX	XXXX	XXXX	XXXX
C1B2A1			XXXX	XXXX	XXXX	XXXX	XXXX	XXXX
C2B2A1		XXXX	XXXX	XXXX	XXXX	XXXX	XXXX	XXXX
C3B2A1	XXXX		XXXX	XXXX	XXXX	XXXX	XXXX	XXXX
C4B2A1			XXXX	XXXX	XXXX	XXXX	XXXX	XXXX
C5B2A1	XXXX		XXXX	XXXX	XXXX	XXXX	XXXX	XXXX
C1B1A2		XXXX		XXXX	XXXX	XXXX	XXXX	XXXX
C2B1A2		XXXX		XXXX	XXXX	XXXX	XXXX	XXXX
C3B1A2	XXXX	XXXX		XXXX	XXXX	XXXX	XXXX	XXXX
C4B1A2		XXXX		XXXX	XXXX	XXXX	XXXX	XXXX
C5B1A2	XXXX	XXXX		XXXX	XXXX	XXXX	XXXX	XXXX
C1B2A2		XXXX	XXXX		XXXX	XXXX	XXXX	XXXX
C2B2A2		XXXX	XXXX		XXXX	XXXX	XXXX	XXXX
C3B2A2	XXXX	XXXX	XXXX		XXXX	XXXX	XXXX	XXXX
C4B2A2		XXXX	XXXX	XXXX				XXXX
C5B2A2	XXXX	XXXX	XXXX	XXXX	XXXX	XXXX	XXXX	

3b. Conversely, if box 33a is not checked (A2), then D2 can't be taken.

4a. If you're married, filing separately (checked at 33c), then you can't be filing jointly at 34.7. Therefore, any C1B1A1 to C5B2A2 segment with a 33c(T) can't be combined with D7. That's anything with a C2, C3, or C5.

4b. Conversely, anything with a C1 or C4 can't be combined with D8. Because 33c(F) is not filing a separate return and 34.7 (SEPARATE) contradicts it.

5. If you're single (34.7(SINGLE)-D5) or a head of household (34.7(HEAD)-D6), your spouse can't itemize. Therefore, 33c1(T)-C2 segments can't combine with D5 or D6 segments. That didn't buy us anything but, incidentally, we've already eliminated 116 out of the 160 possibilities.

6a. We know from years of filling out joint returns that if you itemize, your spouse must itemize and vice-versa. Therefore, any case with 33c1(F)-C3 and C5 can't be combined 34(T)-D1, and eight more cases are eliminated.

6b. By the converse reasoning, C2 cannot be combined with D2 to D8.

7. If you're married, filing separate returns, and your spouse doesn't itemize and is not an alien (C5), you can't be single (D5) or a head of household (D6).

We can now continue generating paths. Looking at the unmarked boxes in the table, there's no choices for D5, D6, D7, and D8. They must be combined respectively with C4B2A2, C4B2A2, C4B2A2, and C5B2A2.

D5C4B2A2: 32, 33a1, 33a2(F), 33a4(F), 33a6(F), 33a8(F), 33a10, 33b(F), 33c(F), 33c2(F), 34(F), 34.2(F), 34.3(F), 34.5(F), 34.7(SINGLE), 34.8, 34.12

D6C4B2A2: 32, 33a1, 33a2(F), 33a4(F), 33a6(F), 33a8(F), 33a10, 33b(F), 33c(F), 33c2(F), 34(F), 34.2(F), 34.3(F), 34.5(F), 34.7(HEAD), 34.9, 34.12

D7C4B2A2: 32, 33a1, 33a2(F), 33a4(F), 33a6(F), 33a8(F), 33a10, 33b(F), 33c(F), 33c2(F), 34(F), 34.2(F), 34.3(F), 34.5(F), 34.7(JOINT), 34.10, 34.12

D8C5B2A2: 32, 33a1, 33a2(F), 33a4(F), 33a6(F), 33a8(F), 33a10, 33b(F), 33c(T), 33c1(F), 33c4(F), 34(F), 34.2(F), 34.3(F), 34.5(F), 34.7(SEPARATE), 34.11, 34.12

We have three choices for D4. I'll take the C1 case for now, leading to D4C1B2A2.

D4C1B2A2: 32, 33a1, 33a2(F), 33a4(F), 33a6(F), 33a8(F), 33a10, 33b(F),33c(F), 33c2(T), 33c3, 34(F), 34.2(F), 34.3(F), 34.5(T), 34.6, 34.12

At this point, we have yet to include A1, B1, C2, C3, D1, D2, and D3. D3 can combine only with the B1A2 combination, so let's do it with the C3 case to combine C3B1A2 with D3:

D3C3B1A2: 32, 33a1, 33a2(F), 33a4(F), 33a6(F), 33a8(F), 33a10, 33b(T), 33b1, 33c(T), 33c1(F), 33c4(T), 33c3, 34(F), 34.2(F), 34.3(T), 34.4, 34.12

We now must include A1, C2, D1, and D2. D2 can't combine with C2, so let's combine it with C3B2A1.

D2C3B2A1: 32, 33a1, 33a2(T), 33a3, 33a4(T), 33a5, 33a6(T), 33a7, 33a8(T), 33a9, 33a10, 33b(F), 33c(T), 33c1(F), 33c4(T), 33c3, 34(F), 34.2(T), 34.4, 34.12

And finally, we end with:

D1C1B1A1: 32, 33a1, 33a2(T), 33a3, 33a4(T), 33a5, 33a6(T), 33a7, 33a8(T), 33a9, 33a10, 33b(T), 33b1, 33c(F), 33c2(T), 33c3, 34(T), 34.1, 34.12

There were no choices for D5 to D8. Where you have choices, such as for D1 to D4, pick the combinations based on one or more of the following criteria: past bug history, how difficult it is to analyze the combination (take the tough one because if you have trouble, so might the programmer), how much research you had to do to clarify issues (pick the high research combinations), your hunches, your knowledge of the responsible programmer.

Finish the path selection from node 34.12 to 40 as an exercise. We have eight tests up to node 34.12. Node 34.13 will add only one test. Node 36 doesn't add any tests (why?). Node 38 adds two tests. The rest of the predicates need not add to our test load. So it looks as if we can achieve link cover with 11 tests. I haven't worked it through, so I could be wrong. However, we may have to backtrack and add other tests when we attempt to sensitize these tests.

My time for the path selection exercise above was seven hours. I may be more experienced than you, but I also had to explain it. The preceding example is as tough as it gets. You should be able to do it in about the same time.

3.4.4 Sensitization

3.4.4.1 GENERAL

Sensitization: Finding input values that will cause (if there are no bugs in the implementation) a selected path in the model to be traversed.

Much of what we did in the previous section was sensitizing the model's logic. The sensitizing procedure depends on the predicates along the path. If the predicates are mostly logical, as they were in the previous section, then sensitization and path selection are done simultaneously. If the predicates are mostly numerical (e.g., algebraic), the procedure is different, as discussed in "Algebraic Sensitization" below.

Application knowledge is more important than sensitization algorithms. Knowing what the application is expected to do is usually sufficient to select a set of covering paths and their sensitization values. I'm sure that had we been tax experts, we would not have had to work so hard to find a set of covering paths for the previous example. Before you invest heavy labor in sensitization, run the obvious tests through your model and see if that provides link cover. You'll then probably have only a few tricky paths to sensitize by formal methods.

If you have great trouble sensitizing a path, the odds are that one of the following holds: (1) the path is unachievable, (2) your model has bugs, (3) the specification has bugs. Check these possibilities before you do hours of useless work.

3.4.4.2 LOGIC SENSITIZATION

This is a review of what we did to select (and sensitize) paths.

1. Divide the model into segments that start and end with one node. In the example given in the 3.4.3section "Select Test Paths," these segments are: 32–33a4, 33a4–33a6, 33a6–33a8, 33a8–33b, 33b–33c, 33c–34, 34–34.12, 34.13–35, 35–37, 37–38, 39–39.3, 39.3–40.

2. Examine the segments and the predicates in them to see which have correlated predicates. Do this two segments at a time. Make a list of the segments whose predicates are correlated. In the example, some of the correlated segments are: 32–33a4/34–34.12, 33a4-33a6/34–34.12,

33a6–33a8/34–34.12, 33a8–33a10/34–34.12, 33b–33c/33c–34, 33c–34/34–34.12.

3. For every segment, list all the possible subpaths through that segment that do not contain loops.

4. Take any two segments with correlated predicates, even if they are not directly connected, starting especially with pairs of segments that have identical predicates. You want strong correlation. For example, a segment in which a condition is set with a subsequent segment in which that condition is checked. 33b–33c marks box 33b, which is subsequently checked in 34–34.12 at node 34.3.

5. Eliminate unachievable paths by contradiction. Assume that the predicate in the first segment is TRUE, thereby eliminating the subpaths in the second segment in which the correlated predicate is FALSE. Then assume that the first predicate is FALSE and eliminate the subpaths in the second segment in which the predicate is TRUE. Be careful, though, because the contradiction of a sequence of predicates in the form A&B&C&D...is the logical sum of their denials: that is, NOTA OR NOTB OR NOTC OR NOTD.... Use boolean algebra to be sure.

6. Continue step 5 above merging path segments and eliminating combinations as you go. You build ever longer paths this way through the correlated segments. As you merge the segments (e.g., 33c–34/34–34.12) you are creating ever larger segments, albeit with fewer possible paths in each segment.

7. You now have a set of bigger segments that are uncorrelated with one another, which means that you can pick the subpaths within each segment as you wish, independent of other segments. Pick enough paths through each segment to assure link cover within that segment.

8. Merge the segments by combining the paths and selecting sensible combinations. Note that the number of tests need not increase as you do this. For example, segment A has six paths and segment B has 10; that doesn't lead to 60 paths through the pair of segments, but only 10 paths. Because the two segments are uncorrelated, you can match any segment A subpath with any segment B subpath.

9. Continue until you have a covering path set.

10. Sensitization should now be straightforward. Go along the path and, as you reach a predicate, specify the input condition that will make that predicate TRUE or FALSE as required by the path. You may have to use some of the techniques of the next section to accomplish this, but in general, for mostly logical and selector predicates, this should be straightforward because you are assured that there are no contradictions along the paths.

3.4.4.3 ALGEBRAIC SENSITIZATION

Predicate interpretation: A predicate is interpreted when it is expressed in terms of input values. Predicate interpretation is specific to a path. That is, it is the equivalent predicate we obtain by following through the computation along a specific path leading to that predicate.

The example for this section is the itemized deduction worksheet for Schedule A line 29. See appendix A. A model for this worksheet follows. This is not a complete model—it includes only the nodes along the path we will sensitize. Variables starting with the letter A refer to schedule A or Form 1040 lines. Variables starting with the letter W refer to the worksheet lines.

1	1.1	input AL4
1.1	1.2	input AL9
1.2	1.3	input AL14
1.3	1.4	input AL18
1.4	1.5	input AL19
1.5	1.6	input AL26
1.6	1.7	input AL27
1.7	1.8	input AL28
1.8	2	W1 = AL4 + AL9 + AL14 + AL18 + AL19 + AL26 + AL27 + AL28
2	2.1	input AL13
2.1	2.2	input AL28g
2.2	3	W2 = AL4 + AL13 + AL19 + AL28g
3	3.1	W3 = W2−W1
		W3 = AL4 + AL9 +AL14 + AL18 + AL19 + AL26 + AL27 + AL28 − (AL4 + AL13 + AL19 + AL28g)
		W3 = AL8 + AL14 + AL18 + AL26 + AL27 + AL28 − AL13 − AL28g
~~3.1.~~	~~10.5~~	~~IF W3 <= 0~~
		~~IF AL9 + AL14 + AL18 + AL26 + AL27 + AL28 − AL13 − AL28g <=0~~

The second form of the predicate on the last uncrossed line is the interpreted predicate. We have substituted input values and expressed the predicate in terms of those values by successive symbolic substitution as we went.

As a side issues, the specification is wrong. It says *"if the result is zero ..."* but it should have said *"if the result is less than or equal to zero ..."*

I crossed out the last line because sensitization is done along a specific path. We'll take the path that exits at line 10. Continuing with the model:

3.1	4	IF AL9 + AL14 + AL18 + AL26 + AL27 + AL28 − AL13 − AL28g > 0	
4	5	0.8 * W3 = 0.8 * (AL9 + AL14 + AL18 + AL26 + AL27 + AL28 − AL13 − AL28g)	
5	6	input AL32	
6	6.5	If separate	*This is the path I've decided to take for this test.*
	~~6.6~~	~~If joint~~	

6.5	7	W6 = $55,900
~~6.6~~	~~7~~	~~W6 = $111,800~~
7	7.1	W7 = W5 − W6 = AL32 − 55,900
~~7.1~~	~~10.6~~	~~if W7 <= 0~~
	8	if W7> 0; if AL32 − 55,900 > 0
8	9	W7* 0.03 = AL32* 0.03 −1,667.00
9	~~9.1~~	~~if AL32* 0.03 −1,667.00 <= 0.8 * (AL9 + AL14 + AL18 + AL26 + AL27 + AL28 − AL13 − AL28g)~~
	9.2	if AL32* 0.03 −1,667.00 > 0.8 * (AL9 + AL14 + AL18 + AL26 + AL27 +
+		AL28 − AL13 − AL28g)
9.2	9.5	WL9 = 0.8 * (AL9 + AL14 + AL18 + AL26 + AL27 + AL28 − AL13 − AL28g)
9.5	10	WL10 = AL4 + AL9 + AL14 + AL18 + AL19 + AL26 + AL27 + AL28 − 0.8*(AL9 + AL14 + AL18 + AL26 + AL27 + AL28 − AL11 − AL28g)

The interpreted forms of the predicates along this path are:

AL9 + AL14 + AL18 + AL26 + AL27 + AL28 − AL13 − AL28g > 0
SEPARATE RETURNS
AL32 − 55,900 > 0

This case is easy because the three predicates are totally independent. In general, that's unusual. Usually you'll see various input values appearing in more than one interpreted predicate. Another point to note is that there are actually more conditions than shown here. The additional conditions are that all input variables should be greater than or equal to zero. You really should put that information down so that you don't forget it in the next phase of sensitization.

The next step in sensitization is to find a set of input values that satisfies all the interpreted predicates for the selected path. In the last example, this is easy:

AL9 + AL14 + AL18 + AL26 + AL27 + AL28 > AL13 + AL28g
SEPARATE RETURNS
AL32 > 55,900

If we're very unlucky, we may have to solve a set of simultaneous equations to get sensitizing values. The simultaneous equations are the interpreted predicates. Usually, however, it is just a question of picking input values for the first interpreted predicate, substituting those values in subsequent predicates, and simplifying as you go along. For example, suppose the set of interpreted predicates (not for this model, however) for the selected path had been:

$$\text{AL9} + \text{AL14} + \text{AL18} + \text{AL26} + \text{AL27} + \text{AL32} > \text{AL13} + \text{AL28}$$
$$\text{AL9} + 0.05 \ast \text{AL14} > \text{AL32}$$
$$\text{AL32} > 55{,}900$$
$$\text{AL14} > \text{AL18}$$

Note that I've arranged the inequalities so that they all go in the same direction. First pick values for any input variables that will directly get rid of an equation. In this case, the value of **AL 32**, which I'll pick as $55,905, say. Then substitute that in the other expressions, to yield the following:

$$\text{AL9} + \text{AL14} + \text{AL18} + \text{AL26} + \text{AL27} + 55{,}905 > \text{AL13} + \text{AL28}$$
$$\text{AL9} + 0.05 \ast \text{AL14} > 55{,}905$$
$$55{,}905 > 55{,}900$$
$$\text{AL14} > \text{AL18}$$

We can force **AL14** to be bigger than **AL18** by substituting $\text{AL14} = \text{AL18} + 10$, say.

$$\text{AL9} + \text{AL18} + 10 + \text{AL18} + \text{AL26} + \text{AL27} + 55{,}905 > \text{AL13} + \text{AL28}$$
$$\text{AL9} + 0.05 \ast (\text{AL18} + 10) > 55{,}905$$
$$55{,}905 > 55{,}900$$
$$\text{AL14} = \text{AL18} + 10 > \text{AL18}$$

Simplifying and gathering terms:

$$\text{AL9} + 2 \ast \text{AL18} + \text{AL26} + \text{AL27} + 55{,}915 > \text{AL13} + \text{AL28}$$
$$\text{AL9} + 0.05 \ast \text{AL18} - 55{,}904.50 > 0$$

Adding these two expression yields:

$$2 \ast \text{AL9} + 2.05 \ast \text{AL18} + \text{AL26} + \text{AL27} + 10.5 - \text{AL13} - \text{AL28} > 0$$

We've boiled all our constraints down to a single expression whose values we can pick at will. We do that, and substitute back for expressions we've previously eliminated (**AL14**, for example), resulting in a set of consistent input values that will go down the selected path. Here's my set of values:

AL9	=	10	
AL18	=	15	
AL26	=	30	
AL27	=	40	
AL13	=	5	
AL28	=	10	
AL14	=	AL18 + 10	= 25
AL32	=	55,900	

You can usually do sensitization without formal equation solving using matrices, even though that's what you're actually doing. Start with the simplest inequalities that have the greatest freedom and pick values for them. Then substitute those values in the other inequalities and simplify. Use ordinary algebraic techniques to eliminate variables by combining the remaining expressions by addition and subtraction.

If you can't do it by simple intuitive substitutions and simplification and you find yourself inverting matrices, before you invest in that labor, check your previous work and the specification. Usually the reason you think you have a matrix to invert is that you've made an error and/or the specification is buggy.

Another approach to this problem is to set up the inequalities as expressions in a spreadsheet and use the spreadsheet's equation solver to get the answers for you. For example, LOTUS 1-2-3's equation solver will do the job nicely, and furthermore, it allows you to mix logical and algebraic predicates in the same set of inequalities.

3.4.5 Outcome Prediction

The next step in the test design process is to predict the outcome for every selected path. While your first notion might be to try playing computer and work through the paths manually, don't do it! First of all, it can be very hard work. Second, you're trying to simulate a computer, and that's something none of us humans are very good at: You're likelier to make an error in your manual outcome prediction than the programmer is in programming. Here are several, more attractive, alternatives.

Existing Tests: About 80 percent of software development labor today is spent in maintenance. Most testers and programmers work on modifications to a base of existing software. That means that more than 95 percent of your tests don't change from release to release. If you keep tests under the same meticulous configuration control that you use for software, then you'll have an oracle for most of your tests.

Old Program: A major rewrite need not entail a corresponding change to the test suite and the old program may therefore serve as an oracle. For example, the original program was written for MS-DOS. It is now to be ported to various mainframes. Though such rehosting efforts may entail a complete rewrite, the old program is an excellent oracle. Run it on your tests to find the expected outcome.

Previous Version: Even if the code you're testing has been rewritten, the previous version will often have the correct outcome for most test paths. At worst, only a few paths are affected and the difference between the outcome of the previous and the new versions are easily analyzed. Use the outcomes from the previous version as a starting point for finding the outcome of the present version on the corresponding paths.

Prototypes and Model Programs: You can build a prototype in enough detail to provide the correct expected outcome [STAK89]. Good prototypes often don't lack functionality. The reason that they're not operationally useful is that they may be too slow, too big, or can't run in the target environment.

If you don't have a detailed prototype, you can get an oracle by building a **model program.** For example, if I were to write an income tax package, I would start by programming each form on a spreadsheet or program the algebra and logic in an easy language, such as BASIC. This isn't the same as programming the actual software because you don't worry about things the programmer worries about, such as: access to data structures, operating system interfaces, input and output. Most of typical software deals with things that are not directly related to the application. I don't have reliable figures, but I think that less than 10 percent of most programs' code is specific to the application. Furthermore, that 10 percent is often the easiest 10 percent. Therefore, it is not unreasonable to build a model program to use as an oracle.

Forced Easy Cases: Sometimes it's possible to select input values that force a selected path but that are trivial to calculate, such as setting all but a few inputs to zero. In our earlier example, we could have satisfied all the constraints by picking values for **AL9**, **AL18**, and **AL13**. The rest of the inputs could have been set to zero.

You might argue that so many zero inputs aren't realistic, but your argument is incorrect. There's an unfortunate unwritten rule in testing that input values should be realistic. *Realism is a hangup that prevents good testing.* Realism is essential to a demonstration, but that's not the purpose of testing. Realistic tests tend to be weak, albeit falsely convincing, precisely because they are the tests that programmers are likeliest to try. Realism isn't very good at revealing bugs—and revealing bugs, not making people falsely confident, is what testing's about.

If you expand your allowable input domain to include unrealistic values such as zero, you'll often find that outcome prediction, predicate interpretation, and therefore sensitization are easier. Because unrealistic tests often differ from the programmers' tests, they also tend to find more bugs.

The Actual Program: You can use the actual program under test as an oracle if you're honest about it. Usually it's easier to verify the correctness of an outcome than it is to calculate the outcome by manually simulating the computer . This is especially so if there are intermediate values printed out that you can verify. By being honest I mean that you do the analysis needed to verify the outcome. If you just accept the outcome as is, without verification, you might as well not have bothered.

3.4.6 Path Verification

You need path verification because of the possibility of coincidental correctness. But path verification in black-box testing is difficult because in black-box testing we're working with *models* of behavior. The test paths are paths through a specification of behavior, and there's no assurance (or even need) that any such paths exist in the actual software. The only way you can verify behavioral control-flow paths is to verify that intermediate calculations are correctly done, especially those calculations that end up in control-flow predicates. If those values are not available as a normal by-product of processing, the only way you'll get them is with the programmers' cooperation to install **assertions**, say [ANDR81, CHEN78B].

You don't need to verify *every* computation. Recall our definition of node at the beginning of this chapter: "one or more processing steps. . . ." In most of these models, I've been generous with adding links and nodes in the interest of clarity. For example, in the model on page 48, nodes 34.1, 34.6, 34.8, 34.9, 34.10, 34.11, 34.14, and 34.15 are not essential. The following graph conveys the same information.

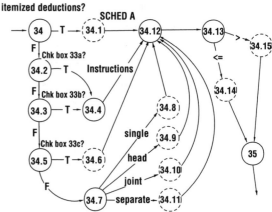

Any sequence of nodes that are neither junction nodes nor predicate (or selector) nodes can be replaced by a single node with one outlink. This reduced model is simpler. All you need to verify is one value for each link on the selected path that uniquely identifies that link. For example, there could be a lot of computation between 34.7–34.11–34.12, but all we need verify to confirm that that link has been traversed is a single value, 3,175, the deduction for married filing separate returns.

Let's keep the issue of path verification in perspective: It is needed because of the possibility of coincidental correctness. Furthermore, control-flow behavioral testing is not the only test technique that you'll be using. At this point, verify as much as you can of the path if you can do so conveniently. For example: Because intermediate processing values are easily accessible, you have test tools that provide path verification, programmers are happy to accommodate you and can do so without introducing yet more bugs.

Another viable alternative is to guard against coincidental correctness by testing several cases along each path. That will happen as a natural outcome of other test techniques discussed later, especially **domain testing.**

3.5 APPLICATION CONSIDERATION

3.5.1 Application Indicators

Control-flow behavioral testing applies to almost all software and is effective for most software. It is a fundamental technique. Its applicability is mostly to relatively small programs or segments of larger programs. As you saw in the foregoing examples, it would probably work for individual IRS forms, but to test an entire tax package this way would be too difficult. It would be difficult because the models would be very big and, as a consequence, path selection and sensitization would be much too complicated to justify the effort.

3.5.2 Bug Assumptions

Most bugs can result in control-flow errors and therefore misbehavior that could be caught by control-flow testing. However, the primary assumption about the bugs targeted by control-flow testing is that they directly affect control-flow predicates or that the control flow itself is wrong. An example of the former is a computational error in a term that is later used as part of a control-flow predicate, such as using $>=$ when $<$ was intended. A raw control-flow error example is if node 34.4 above was linked (by error) to 34.14 instead of 34.12. Such gross control-flow bugs are not as common as they used to be because structured programming languages minimize them. For old software, written in COBOL or assembly language, say, such bugs are more common.

Computational bugs that do not affect the control flow may be caught by this technique, but it is not the best technique to use. **Domain testing** (Chapter 7) and **data flow testing** (Chapter 5) are better at finding such bugs.

3.5.3 Limitations and Caveats

Here are some limitations and warnings.

1. You won't find missing requirements unless, of course, your model included such requirements and the programmer didn't.

2. You're unlikely to find spurious or gratuitous features that were included in the software but were not in the requirements.

3. The better the job the programmers have done with unit testing, the less likely it is that this technique will find new bugs—for example, this was the technique used in unit testing (not a bad idea).

4. It's unlikely to find missing paths and features if the program and the model on which the tests are based are done by the same person. If

you're a programmer using this technique to test your own software, the odds are that the misconceptions that led you to leaving paths and features out of your program will still be in your head when you design the tests. If the tests are designed by someone else, this likelihood is reduced, albeit at the cost of more labor.

5. Coincidental correctness, however improbable, defeats this technique unless you can verify all intermediate calculations and predicate values.

6. Your tests are no better than your oracle.

3.5.4 Automation and Tools

As of this writing, no commercial tools directly supported behavioral control-flow testing, but many tools support structural control-flow testing. You can exploit these tools by actually programming your models in a supported programming language, such as C, Pascal, or Basic [DAIC93, GERH88, SCHI69, WARN64]. This is not a waste, nor is it redundant programming. If you have done all the work needed to create a properly detailed graph model, then you have done most of the work required to express that semiformal model as a program.

The reason programming the model isn't redundant, and certainly not the same as programming the real thing, is that you don't have to be concerned with all the realistic stuff, such as data base access, I/O, operating system interfaces, environment issues, and all the rest of the stuff where the real bugs are born. The model program need not include the details, it doesn't have to work on the target platform, it doesn't have to be efficient, and most important of all, it doesn't have to be integrated with the rest of the software.

Of what use is the model? It isn't at all the same as running tests on the actual program. It's the program that must be tested and not some tester's toy! That's true. Testing a model is not the same as testing the real software, and, ultimately, that's what you must do. But how did you propose to debug your tests? The model is used as a tool to help you design a covering set of tests, to help pick and sensitize paths, and to act as an oracle for the real software. If you build a running model, then you can use commercial test tools on it. And that could make your job much easier.

3.6 SUMMARY

Behavioral control-flow testing was introduced as the fundamental model of black-box testing. It is basic to all other test techniques discussed in this book, and it will be assumed in the sequel that you understand it.

Test design begins by creating a behavioral control-flow graph model from requirements documents such as specifications. The list notation is generally more convenient than graphical graphs, but small graphs are an aid to model design.

Compound predicates should be avoided in the model and spelled out (e.g., replaced by equivalent graphs) so as not to hide essential complexity. Use a truth table instead of a graph to model compound predicates with more than three component predicates.

Segment your model into pieces that start and end with a single node and note which predicates are correlated with which in all other segments. Build your test paths as combinations of paths in the segments, eliminating unachievable paths as you go. Use contradictions between correlated predicates to rule out combinations wholesale. This procedure is unlikely to lead to unachievable paths that can't be sensitized.

Pick enough paths through the model to assure 100 percent link cover. Don't worry about having too many tests. Start by picking the obvious paths that relate directly to the requirements and see if you can achieve cover that way. They may not be the most effective tests you can use, but it is politic. Augment these tests by however many paths you need to guarantee 100 percent link cover.

Sensitize the selected paths by first interpreting the predicates along the path in terms of input values. The interpreted predicates yield a set of conditions or equations (actually, inequalities) such that any solution to that set of inequalities will cause the selected path to be traversed. If sensitization is not obvious, check your work for a specification or model bug before you invest big time in equation solving. If the conditions are necessarily complicated, consider using a commercial solver such as in LOTUS 1-2-3 to solve the sensitization inequalities. An algebraic package may help with predicate interpretation.

Don't forget the possibility of coincidental correctness and work with the programmers to get the intermediate computational outputs you'll need to verify the path. Give predicate expressions a high priority but don't push for more than one value on each link of the graph.

Consider programming your model in an actual programming language and using the programmed model as an aid to test design.

3.7 SELF-EVALUATION QUIZ

1. **Define:** AND, complementary path segment, compound predicate, control-flow graph, correlated predicates, independent predicates, junction node, logical model program, logical predicate, NOT, OR, predicate, predicate interpretation, predicate node, selector node, selector predicate, sensitize, simple predicate, transaction split, truth table.

In all of the following examples, do not model any subsidiary forms or sheets specified in the IRS instructions.

2. For schedule SE, 1994 and the graph shown there, model this as a control-flow graph with the predicates as shown in the boxes.

3. For schedule SE, 1994, remodel this graph replacing all single compound predicates with equivalent sequences of simple predicates.

4. For schedule SE, 1994, write out a single compound predicate that gives all the conditions under which the short schedule can be used and all the conditions under which the long schedule must be used.

5. Do a control-flow graph model for Form 1040. Treat data that come from other forms or other parts as if they are inputs. For each case, do the model, select the test paths, and design the tests using the following criteria: (i) node cover, (ii) link cover. Check your work with a tax package or a spreadsheet model to use as an oracle. If you use a tax package, you may have to override and insert values from other forms as inputs. (a) lines 1–5, (b) lines 6–22, (c) lines 32–40, (d) lines 41–46, (e) lines 47–53, (f) lines 54–60, (g) lines 61–65.

6. As for problem 5 Form 1040, Schedule SE, short form, lines 1–6, but include the logic to determine if the short form can or can't be used.

7. Form 1040, Line 10 Worksheet. Entire form.

8. Form 1040, Line 20a Worksheet, social security income. Entire form.

9. Form 1040, Line 34 Worksheet, dependent deductions. Entire form.

10. Model lines 1-5 of Form 1040 Line 26 worksheet (1994 Self-Employed Health Insurance Deduction Worksheet).

11. Find all the pairs of correlated path segments for the example of section 3.4.3.

12. Form 2106, Employee Business expenses, Part II, sections A, B, C.

13. Form 2688, Application for Extension to File, Lines 1-4.

14. Form 2210, Underpayment of Taxes. Include (a) Line 1, only. (b) part II, (c) part III, (d) Part IV section A, (e) Part IV section B. Assume that you can use the short method (part III) if you did not check box 1b, 1c, or 1d. In all cases, outputs (if any) go to the appropriate Form 1040 line. That is, don't worry about forms 1040A, 1040NR, 1041, and so on.

15. Do Form 3903, Part I, Employee moving expenses.

4
Loop Testing

4.1 SYNOPSIS

Loop testing is a heuristic technique that should be used in conjunction with many other testing methods because experience shows that bugs often accompany loops. The techniques discussed in this chapter apply when there are loops in a graph, such as: control-flow graph, **transaction-flow graph**, or **syntax graph**s.

4.2 VOCABULARY

External Prerequisite Terms: application, array, assembly, batch, **BREAK** statement, C, capture/playback, COBOL, code, compiler, copy, corrupt, crash, debug, decrement, end of file, enter (a loop), evaluate, execute, field, file, file length, **FOR**, **GOTO**, hardware, heuristic, implementation, increment, initialize, inner loop, integer, iteration, memory boundary bug, merge, model, nested loop, operating system, outer loop, pointer, pointer error, precondition, process within a loop, processing, program, programmer, programming, programming language, random, record, repetitive process, requirement, runtime, searching, software, sorting, specification, structured programming language, structured software, terminate, transmit, truth value, value, variable, **WHILE**.

Internal Prerequisite Terms: behavior, behavioral testing, black-box testing, bug, control-flow graph, control-flow testing, graph, graph model, loop, link, logical predicate, node, node name, object, outlink, path, predicate, relation, revealing test, selector predicate, specification, structure, symptom, system testing, test case, unit testing.

Loop: A repetitive or iterative process. That part of a graph model which has a loop; that is, a repeated node name on at least one path.

Loop count, loop iteration count: The number of times a loop is repeated. Don't confuse this value with the final value of the **loop control variable** (see below), if any, at the time the loop is exited. Confusion between the loop count and the final value of the loop control variable is a common source of bugs.

Deterministic loop: A loop whose iteration count is known before loop execution begins.

Nondeterministic loop: A loop whose iteration count is unknown before loop execution begins, or a loop whose iteration count is determined or modified by processing within the loop.

Loop control node: A node with at least two outlinks: for one link, the loop will be executed, and for the other, it will not. The node marked "20" in the graph is the loop control node.

Loop exit node: A node that represents a predicate with at least one value that will cause the loop not to be executed. A loop may, unfortunately, have more than one loop exit node. Node 20 in the model just illustrated is a loop exit node.

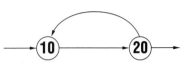

Loop entry node: A node through which a loop is entered. A loop could have more than one loop entry node. Node 10 in the last graph is a loop entry node.

Loop control predicate: The predicate at the loop control node whose value determines if the loop will or will not be executed.

Loop control variable: Any variable within a loop control predicate whose value will affect the (truth) value of the loop control predicate—that is, whether the loop will be executed or not.

Pretest loop: A loop in which the loop control predicate is evaluated before any processing within the loop is executed. In the loop on the right, the loop control node is 20 and no processing takes place between 10 and 20. All processing takes place on link 20–10, so this is a pretest loop.

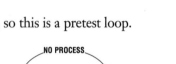

Posttest loop: A loop in which the loop control predicate is evaluated after processing. In posttest loops, processing is executed at least once.

Mixed–test loop: A loop with processing both before and after the loop control predicate is evaluated. *

Nested loops: Two or more loops are **nested** if one is contained wholly within the other. In the model on the right, the 10–20–10 loop is nested within the 5–25–5 loop.

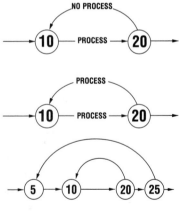

---

* Don't be misled by programming languages and the semantics of constructs such as FOR and WHILE statements. Almost any combination of deterministic/nondeterministic with pretest/postest/ mixed-test loops can be created using almost any construct. See the excercises at the end of the chapter.

4.3 THE RELATIONS AND THE MODEL

4.3.1 General

We use the language of programming in this section and it may seem that we're talking about programs. However, we are not necessarily talking about programs or loops that may or may not exist within them. Black-box testing concerns behavior, not structure. Ours are models of behavior, and there may or may not be corresponding loops in the software we're testing. If you look too closely at the software to find out what kind of loop you have, you might make exactly the same mistake in your model that the programmer made in the code.

You'll notice in the following loop models that I don't use structured programming constructs such as **FOR** and **WHILE** but instead use explicit predicates and **GOTO**s for these *model* loops. We're dealing with models, not with code. I'm *not* advocating dropping **FOR** and **WHILE** constructs in favor of rampaging **GOTO**s. I don't use structured loop constructs in models because they carry baggage that depends on the language in which they're implemented and, in some cases, even the specific compiler for that language. This is especially true for pretest–posttest-mixed loop issues. Precisely this kind of baggage leads to loop bugs in code and in test design.

The relation for these models is *is directly followed by*. However, I will be deliberately vague with respect to the rest of the model. Things will be illustrated here for control-flow models, but loop testing applies to many other models (e.g., syntax testing) where although the objects and relations are different, the testing principles are the same.

4.3.2 Deterministic Loops

In **deterministic loops**, the number of times the loop will be executed is known before the first statement within the loop is executed *and* there is no processing within the loop that will cause that number to change.

```
20    30    loop_control = 0, nmax = 10
30    40    loop_process
40    30    loop_control =< nmax, loop_control = loop_control + 1
      50    loop_control > nmax
50          continue with the rest of the model
```

This example is a posttest loop. The variable **loop_control** is presumed not to be modified by the **loop_process** on link 30–40: It could be *used* in the process but is not itself modified by the process. Node 20 is the loop entry node. Node 40 is the loop exit node and also the loop control node. Although I've used a simple increment (**loop_control** = **loop_control** + 1), almost any function is possible: decrement, increment by value m, some function of **loop_control**.

The loop control variable here is **loop_control** whose maximum value is 10; however, the processing will be executed 11 times. The following is a deterministic loop with pretesting.

20	30	loop_control = 1, nmax =10
30	50	loop_control > nmax
	40	loop_control < = nmax
40	30	loop process, loop_control = loop_control +1
50		continue with the rest of the model

The next example is a mixed-test loop because loop processing occurs both before and after the loop exit node.

20	25	loop_control = 1, nmax =10
25	30	A_processing
30	50	loop_control > nmax
	40	loop_control <= nmax
40	25	B_processing, loop_control = loop_control +1
50		continue with rest of the model

In this model, all iterations are guaranteed **A_processing**. The last time through, however, the processed object will not receive **B_processing**. Note that the loop control variable's value, **loop_control**, is different for the A and B processes. Mixed-test loops should be avoided in specifications, models, and software because they are bug-prone. Mixed loops can't be created accidentally in structured programming languages; the programmer must be deliberate about it. One reason for structured loop constructs is the avoidance of mixed-test loop bugs. In building models, strive to use clear pre- or posttest loops and use mixed-test loops only if accurate modeling of the requirements demands them. If a mixed-test loop *is* required, it should be tested thoroughly because of its bug potential.

Looping processes should be constructed using deterministic loops in each of the following cases because in each one, the number of times the loop will be executed is known before the loop is entered: copying a file with a known number of records, processing n payroll checks, adding a column of numbers, filling an array with numbers, transmitting a file of known length.

4.3.3 Nondeterministic Loops

Nondeterministic loops differ from deterministic loops because the number of times the loop will be executed is not known before the loop is entered. This can come about in three main ways: (1) the value is unknown (2) processing within the loop changes the loop control variable (if any), (3) a condition detected within the loop causes the loop to terminate prematurely .

20	30	Read next record
30	40	process record
40	20	Not End of File (EOF)
	50	EOF
50		continue with rest of model

We don't know, in the above graph, how many records the file has, therefore, the process will continue until the EOF record is reached. This example is vulnerable for several reasons. If the file contains only an EOF record, then that record will receive processing, with possibly disastrous results. Another vulnerability is the problem of a file that has no records, not even an EOF record. If the program implements the given model exactly, the program will loop forever on such files.

20	30	loop_control = 1, nmax =10
30	50	loop_control > nmax
	40	loop_control < = nmax
40	45	loop process
45	46	loop_control = loop_control + INT(3*RAND)
46	30	loop_control = loop_control +1
50		continue with the rest of the model

Processing on link 45–46 of the above model subtracts a random integer between 0 and 2 from **loop_control** each time through. I've picked this example because it's obvious, but it can be achieved without using random numbers. The point is that we can't determine when, if ever, this loop will terminate. Even though it seems to use a deterministic construct, it is nevertheless nondeterministic.

20	30	loop_control = 1, nmax =10
30	50	loop_control > nmax
	40	loop_control < = nmax
40	45	loop process
45	47	Field Value = 17
	46	Field Value ≠17
46	30	loop_control = loop_control +1
47	30	loop_control = nmax +1
50		continue with the rest of the model

Although the above graph appears to be a deterministic loop, it is not. The predicate at node 45 checks the value of a certain field. If this value equals 17, **loop_control** is forced to a value that will cause the loop to terminate. If the field value doesn't equal 17, the loop is iterated up to the value of **nmax**. In either case, the loop is deterministic. I didn't have to modify the loop control variable to do this. For example, the following graph does the same without modifying the loop control variable.

20	30	loop_control = 1, nmax =10
30	50	loop_control > nmax
	40	loop_control < = nmax
40	45	loop process
45	50	Field Value = 17
	46	Field Value ≠17
46	30	loop_control = loop_control +1
50		continue with the rest of the model

Processes with nondeterministic loops include: sorting n records, searching a file, receiving a file on a communication link, solving simultaneous equations, merging two files.

The distinction between deterministic and nondeterministic loops is crucial. Nondeterministic loops are buggier than deterministic loops and should therefore be tested more thoroughly. In structured programming languages the **FOR** construct (e.g., **FOR I = 1 to loopmax DO** ...) is intended for deterministic loops. Conversely, the **WHILE ... DO** construct is intended for nondeterministic loops. The **FOR** loop has an explicit loop control variable, the **WHILE** loop does not. Because **FOR** loops can be nondeterministic and **WHILE** loops can be deterministic, most programmers believe that the choice between them is stylistic. This leads to bugs in which nondeterministic processes are implemented with deterministic constructs and deterministic processes are implemented with nondeterministic constructs. Either one is confusing, an opportunity for bugs, and therefore a good place to go looking for them.

4.3.4 Nested Loops

Nested loops are problematic (i.e., buggy). They include, of course, the usual bugs we would expect with single loops (e.g., missing the first case, terminating too early, terminating too late, never ending) but also bugs that arise from simultaneously hitting the loop termination conditions on both loops. For example, in the following graph:

20	30	outer_loop_control = 1, outermax = 10
30	40	inner_loop_control = 1, innermax = 100
40	45	inner_loop process
45	30	inner_loop_control < innermax, inner_loop_control = inner_loop_control + 1
	50	inner_loop_control >= innermax
50	55	outer_loop process
55	20	outer_loop count < outermax, outer_loop_control = outer_loop_control + 1
	60	outer_loop count >= outermax
60		continue with rest of model

what happens at **outermax** = **10** and **innermax** = **100** and values nearby?

4.3.5 Unstructured (Horrible) Loops

Horrible loops come about when jumping out of the middle of a loop or jumping into the middle of the loop.

The adjacent figure is infamous because in it both types of jump are done. The 30–10 link jumps out of the 20–30–40–20 loop while the 40–20 link jumps into the 10–20–30–10 loop. The mixed-test loops are mildly horrible because they jump out of the middle of the loop. Another problem with mixed-test loops is

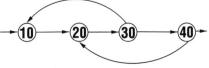

that the loop entry node for the first iteration is not the same as the loop entry node for subsequent iterations.

Programmers must go out of their way to build horrible loops in structured programming languages, but such loops are common in older assembly language software and older programming languages.

There are no good tests for horrible loops. How you handle them depends on where they came from. If they result from the way you modeled things, then remodel with structured loops. Horrible loops could be a correct model of an application's behavior, especially if, as in **transaction flow testing**, you are creating a model of human behavior. For example, if you model a person dialing a long-distance telephone number, it's natural to use a loop to accept the digit. A long-distance call requires 11 digits. So you set up a model loop such as:

10	20	digit_count = 0, digit_max = 11
20	30	digit_count <= digit_max, digit_count = digit_count + 1
	50	digit_count > digit_max, exit loop
30	20	get digit
50		go on with model

Human beings don't and can't be made to behave in a structured manner. They might, for example, exit the loop as soon as they realize that they have made a dialing error.

```
10   20   digit_count = 0, digit_max = 11
20   30   digit_count <= digit_max, digit_count = digit_count + 1
     50   digit_count > digit_max, exit loop
30   40   get digit
40   20   digit okay
     10   digit not okay, hang up and redial
50        go on with model
```

If the loop's poor structure properly models the situation, then you have no choice but to model it that way. However, you must take special care and test such loops more thoroughly than you might otherwise because such situations are especially prone to improper implementation, especially for the special situations that cause the loop to be horrible.

4.4 THE TECHNIQUES

4.4.1 The Critical Test Values

Consider a generic deterministic loop model:

```
10   20   loop_control = startval, itermax = upperval
20   30   loop_control > itermax
     40   loop_control <= itermax
30   20   loop process, loop_control = loop_control + increrval
40        continue with the rest of the model
```

This loop is entered with three numbers:

startval   The starting value of the loop control variable, **loop_control**

upperval   The ending value of the loop control variable

increval   The amount by which the loop control variable will be incremented each time through.

The **critical test values** are the combination of values of these three numbers that experience shows to be especially bug-prone, plus the normal or typical case. The generic test cases follow. Specifics for different kinds of loops will be discussed in subsequent sections.

Bypass: Any value that will cause the loop to be exited immediately.

Once: Values that will cause the loop to be executed exactly once.

Twice: Values that will cause the loop to be executed exactly twice.

Typical: A typical number of iterations.

Maximum:	The maximum number of allowed iterations.
Max + 1	One more than the maximum allowed.
Max − 1	One less than the maximum allowed.
Min	The minimum required.
Min −1	One less than the minimum required.
Null	Discussed below.
Negative:	Discussed below.

Note that we are talking about the number of times the loop will be executed and not the values of the loop control variable (if any). For example, if the loops is: **FOR I = 0 to 8 STEP 2**, the initial value of the loop control variable **I** is **0**, but the loop will not be executed nine times but only five times because the loop control variable is incremented by two each time through.

Many of the preceding cases can overlap. For example, if the minimum value is 0, then the following identities apply:

Min − 1	=	**Negative**
Min	=	**Bypass**
Min + 1	=	**Once**

Similarly, if the minimum value is 1

Min − 1	=	**Bypass**
Min	=	**Once**
Min + 1	=	**Twice**

The null case may turn out to be equivalent to bypass. Typically, instead of the 11 tests just shown, there are only seven tests to design. Some of these cases, such as bypass, may overlap the test you created based on link cover.

In addition to testing the 11 generic situations, in older software (e.g., assembly language software) it may pay to test special iteration values, such as powers of 2: 255, 256, 257, 65,535, 65,536, and 65,537. But don't waste your time with special values related to hardware parameters such as byte or word length in a contemporary programming language such as C– except, of course, if you examine the implementation and see that the programming is very physical.

4.4.2 Deterministic Loops

We're processing paychecks. The software is to handle at least one employee and at most 20,000 employees. Using the prescriptions just given, we obtain, directly, the following test cases:

Bypass:	No employees.
Once:	One employee.
Twice:	Two employees
Typical:	700 employees
Maximum:	20,000 employees
Max + 1	20,001 employees
Max − 1	19,999 employees
Min	One employee: redundant case
Min −1	No employees: redundant case
Null	No employees: redundant case
Negative:	Negative number of employees??

Some of these cases deserve more discussion.

Bypass: no employees. The requirements say that the software isn't supposed to handle this case. But what will it do? Can this case, even though it doesn't make sense, be set up? Say the package is used to do payrolls for many different organizations. It does them in a batch (a nested loop with employees on the inner loop and organizations on the outer loop). A new client is added to the batch for weekly payroll processing, but we haven't been given the employee data yet. We don't expect the software to "process" paychecks for phantom employees. Conversely, we don't expect the program to start printing an infinite number of paychecks for $0.00 for **first_name, last_name**.

We're testing. We're not paid to be nice, or reasonable, or even sensible. If it is at all possible to set up the situation, we should do so and we should expect the software to behave in a reasonable manner, such as telling us that "**organization_name** won't be processed." In doing this test we expect (hope) that some other organization's payroll will be off by one, or bypassed altogether.

Once: one employee. Look for an extra blank paycheck, a duplicated paycheck, or for the next organization to be off by one paycheck.

Twice: two employees. Often revealing, especially for mixed-test loops. Look for duplicated initialization of loops, missing second employee, two paychecks for employee #2, something screwed up for the next organization.

Typical. Unlikely to reveal bugs; but if you don't do it, your testing is sure to be criticized. While it rarely is effective at catching bugs it is politically wise.

Maximum. All the test cases that involve maxima are potentially expensive, especially if there are nested loops. For example, 20,000 employees and 1,000 organizations means 20,000,000 paychecks. Even with computers that's too expensive. It isn't the specific numbers 20,000 and 1,000 that go wrong, but the fact that the maximum values, whatever the numbers, have been reached. If programmers foresee the testing issue, they'll build in the ability to change these maxima for testing—most of which could be done with 20 employees and 10 organizations. If testability has not been a design goal, then you'll have no choice but to test these extreme values at least once. But do it with, say 20,000 employees for only one organization and 1,000 organizations with a few employees each.

Maximum plus 1. The issues are the same as bypass. We don't expect the program to process more than the declared maximum, but because such things could occur by accident, we want to be sure that things don't crash and that files aren't corrupted. Look for this situation: Company X has 20,001 employees; company Y follows company X in the batch, and the first employee in company Y is given a paycheck drawn on company X's account.

Negative. If the number of employees was entered at a keyboard, say, to start the processing, then this would certainly be a potentially productive case. If you can, by fair means or foul, set up this case, try it and look for the program to reject the input. Don't be fooled into thinking that just because you've been told that the case *will be* rejected that it is in fact rejected. For example, company X is declared as having –10 employees through an input error. The case is rejected, as expected, but the first 10 paychecks for the next company in the batch, Y, are not processed. We're dealing with bugs that result in arbitrary and insensible behavior. It makes sense that we use arbitrary and insensible test cases wherever possible.

4.4.3 Nondeterministic Loops

We're searching a file of unknown length for a specific record that could be anyplace in the file or, for that matter, might not be in the file at all. There are two issues: the size of the file and where in the file the record might be found. Two predicates control the behavior of this loop: the predicate that controls getting and examining the next record and the predicate that causes the loop to terminate because the wanted record has been found. We'll deal with file size first and then with where the record is found within the file.

Bypass: A file with no records. This is also the null case. Since there are no records, the wanted record can't be found.

Once: A one–record file.

    a. found: the wanted record is the first record.

    b. not found: the wanted record isn't in the file.

Twice: A two-record file.

    a. found on the first record.

    b. found on the second record

    c. not found.

Typical: A 10-record file.*

      a. found on the first record

      b. found on record 6

      c. found on record 9

      d. found on record 10

      e. not found.

Maximum − 1: Say that we can arrange things so that the maximum file length can be tested for files of, say, 50 records.

      a. found at record 48

      b. found at record 49

      c. not found.

Maximum: a 50-record file

      a. found at record 49

      b. found at record 50

      c. not found.

Maximum + 1: a 51-record file.

      a. found at record 49

      b. found at record 50

      c. found at record 51

      d. not found

Here's my reasoning for the MAX + 1 cases. The software's not supposed to handle files with more than 51 records. If this is really a nondeterministic loop, that fact is unknown until the process (the search) actually takes place. That is, the file length is known only after the EOF record is detected. If it's really done that way, then there's no apparent way to prohibit a 51-record file. Conversely, if the excessively long file is rejected before processing starts, then the file length must have been known and the search loop isn't really deterministic. Only the point at which the process will exit the loop is unknown. How many of these cases you attempt depends on what it is that makes the loop nondeterministic.

1. **Max value unknown and unknowable.** Then there's nothing to bar the maximum value and you should certainly try MAX +1.

2. **Early termination.** We have an essentially deterministic loop that can be terminated early (e.g., by a C BREAK statement) but where that will occur is unknown. MAX + 1 doesn't make sense, but surely try finding wanted data on the last record.

---

* I picked 10 records because we know from experience and theory that the values 1, 2, 3, 4, and 5 can exhibit behavioral differences. Because 5 − 1 = 4 is not a general case, 5 is left out. Because 6 − 1 = 5 is the first general case, 5 is not a good value. The first good general value is probably 7. But powers of two and numbers near them (7, 8, 9) can be problematic, so 10 is the first really good typical value.

3. **Control variable processing.** This could occur with deterministic and nondeterministic loops. Say that the number of records was known and that we wanted to do a spot-check of one out of 10 records rather than check every record in the file. This could be implemented by incrementing the loop control variable by 10, but that leads to a pointer value beyond the end of file. Then we would certainly try the MAX + cases.

4.4.4 Nested Loops

Nested loops should be tested first individually as separate loops. Set the inner loop to a typical value and run through the critical cases for the outer loop. Then reverse the procedure and set the outer loop to a typical value and run the inner loop through the critical test cases. These tests should catch most of the bugs that typically occur for single, unnested loops.

The issue in nested loops is that two or more nested loops hit critical values simultaneously—for example, null–null, MAX–MAX, and so on. You design the test cases by hitting combinations of critical values. That would lead to 64 or more test cases if you followed that prescription religiously. Back off from that a bit and at least test all the combinations of bypass/zero/null, one, two, and MAX for the inner loop with bypass/zero/null, one, two and MAX for the outer loop. That's 16 cases over and above the single–loop tests for a total of 32 tests.

4.5 APPLICATION CONSIDERATIONS

4.5.1 Application Indicators

Every repetitive process deserves loop testing. Any graph with loops should be loop tested, with the possible exception of **finite-state machine** graphs* (Chapter 9) because there are too many loops, and **domain testing** (Chapter 7), where the presence of loops makes the technique effectively impractical.

4.5.2 Bug Assumptions

No deep assumptions here; just the empirical observation that repetitive processes are difficult to start correctly and even more difficult to stop. We do one too many or one too few. Also, many bugs come about because someone assumes that certain preconditions are met when in fact they need not be: for example, assuming that all files have at least one record.

---

* Actually, any strongly connected graph.

4.5.3 Limitations and Caveats

Loop bugs show up mostly in low-level software and tend to have limited impacts. Symptoms tend to show up in time and place close to where the bug is. Many of these bugs will be caught by the operating system or the runtime resident portion of the compiler because they will cause memory boundary violations, detectable pointer errors, reading beyond end of file, and stuff like that. The bugs caught by loop testing are not very subtle, and we would hope that programmers find and correct them in low-level unit testing, where they often can be found by loop testing. Don't expect too much from loop testing on mature software.

4.5.4 Automation and Tools

No special tools really are needed. If you use loop testing as part of system-level behavioral testing, you can exploit a **capture/playback** system to advantage. Individual loop tests, especially if they involve files and nested loops, can be difficult to set up. Once you set up and debug a typical loop test case, you edit that case to modify the input values to create the other loop test cases, especially the combination cases needed for nested loops.

4.6. SUMMARY

Loop testing is a heuristic technique based on the experience that programmers have with bugs in starting and ending loops. Although control-flow examples were used to illustrate this chapter, the technique is effective for most graph models that have loops (excluding strongly connected graphs). The values to test based on the number of times the loop will be executed are: 0, 1, 2, MIN – 1, MIN, MIN + 1, typical, MAX–1, MAX, and MAX + 1, and combinations of these values for nested loops.

4.7 SELF–EVALUATION QUIZ

1. **Define:** critical loop test values, deterministic loop, horrible loop, iteration count, loop, loop bypass, loop control node, loop control predicate, loop control variable, loop count, loop entry node, loop exit node, mixed-test loop, nested loops, nondeterministic loop, posttest loop, pretest loop.

2. Consider the six combinations of (deterministic, nondeterministic) and (pretest, posttest, mixed) for loops in C. Show examples of each combination using the following constructs for creating loops: **WHILE**, **FOR**, **DO–WHILE**, **IF/GOTO**. If a combination is not possible, prove it.

3. Same as problem 2, but for Pascal, using **FOR–TO–DOWNTO, FOR–DO, REPEAT–UNTIL, WHILE**, and all other ways of constructing loops.

4. There's a command in most tax preparation packages to print the tax preparer's forms and worksheets. If each form is considered an item to be printed, is this a deterministic or nondeterministic loop process? Support your position. If you say "deterministic," why might a rational person choose to program this as a nondeterministic loop? Design a set of tests for printing the active tax forms in your tax package.

5. Classify the following processes as to deterministic and nondeterministic (with respect to loop iteration value): (a) spell checking, (b) solve simultaneous equations, (c) sort, (d) merge, (e) add two numbers, (f) square root, (g) long division, (h) do the US census, (i) copy a file, (j) copy a directory, (k) copy the entire disk, (l) check the disk for errors, (m) download a file, (n) count the number of items in a box, (o) recount the number of items in a box, (p) balance your checkbook assuming that you and the bank don't make mistakes, (q) multiply two arrays (element by element), (r) multiply two matrices (element by element), (s) take the square root of a 16-bit number and provide a 16-bit result, (u) evaluate $x^2 h \sin^{-1}$ ABS $((J_2 (ABS (17 \int_0^x e^{-x} dx))))$ where x is a 16-bit number and a 16-bit result is desired, (v) delete n characters from the end of a document starting with the last character and deleting in reverse, (w) add n characters to the end of a document, (x) delete n characters from the middle of a document where the document is known to have at least n characters in it.

6. For each of the deterministic processes of problem 5, what are the operational consequences (e.g., vulnerabilities, RAM and disk) that might exist as a result of implementing the process as a nondeterministic loop?

7. For each of the nondeterministic processes of problem 5, what are the operational consequences (e.g., vulnerabilities, RAM and disk) that might exist as a result of implementing the process as a deterministic loop?

8. Which of the processes in problem 5 have nested loops and how deeply are those loops nested?

9. For each of the processes you analyzed in problems 5, 6, 7, and 8, design a set of loop tests.

10. Model Part IV of Form 2210 as a control-flow graph with a deterministic loop and test accordingly.

5
Data-Flow Testing

5.1 SYNOPSIS

The data-flow graph, a feature of many software design methodologies, is put to profitable use in test design [HERA88, ROPE93].

5.2 VOCABULARY

External Prerequisite Terms: add record, alias, application, array, assign, bug, C, calculation, call tree, **CASE**, close, code, comment, compare, compiler, computation, concurrent processes, constant, constraint, control, copy, count, crash, create, data, debugger program, delete, denote, disk, dummy variable, dynamic call, expression, extract, fetch, field, file, formula, function, global data, halt, hardware, heuristic, hierarchical, **IF-THEN**, **IF-THEN-ELSE**, information hiding, initialize, insert, instantiate, iterate, iteration count, jump, linker, location, logic, loop, maintenance, memory, memory location, merge, message, move, multitasking, network, numerical, object name, object oriented programming, open, output, own data, parallel computer, partition, PASCAL, pointer, processing, program, programmer, programming, programming language, pseudo code, RAM, record, rename, reusable, runtime, search, sequencing, shared data, side effect, software, sort, source code, spreadsheet, statement, store, structured, symbolic, synchronization, table, testability, tester, transmit, truth value, value, variable.

Internal Prerequisite Terms: behavioral testing, blind, branch testing, coincidental correctness, component, compound predicate, control flow, control-flow graph, dangling link, deterministic loop, dirty test, entry node, exit node, finite-state model, graph, initial state, inlink, integration, input, input node, link cover, link list representation of graph, link weight, loop, loop testing, model, negative test, nested loop, node, node cover, node weight, nondeterministic loop, object, oracle, outcome, outlink, output node, path, positive test, predicate, predicate interpretation, relation, requirement, sensitize, simple predicate, specification, state, transaction-flow graph.

Define (an object): An object is **defined** when it is assigned a new value, initialized, created, or instantiated. Don't confuse an object's name or the memory location used to hold its value with the different possible **definitions** of that object. For example, memory location XYZ is used to hold a variable named SAM. SAM may take on several different values in the course of computation. Each value is a *different* **definition** of SAM.

Overload: A variable's name is **overloaded** when it is used to denote different definitions of a variable along a path. In programming the claimed benefit of overloading is that it saves memory,* but in testing models there is no virtue in overloading because its confusing and saves nothing.

Assertion statement: A programming language statement consisting of a predicate that is evaluated at runtime. If the predicate is satisfied, processing continues uninterrupted. If the predicate is unsatisfied, one or more of the following occurs: control is passed to an assertion handler, the assertion is tagged as not satisfied, the program halts, control passes to a debugger program. Assertions usually check relations between values of variables such as: $x > 17$ or $x + y = z$. Assertions are powerful test aids. The main use of assertions in this chapter is as a means of verifying the outputs of calculations.

Computational use: An object has a **computational use** [RAPP82] when it is used to calculate a value of another object. For example, in $Y := X + Z$, there is a computational use of X and Z, and Y is defined. Similarly, in $X := X + Y$, there are computational uses of X and Y, and X is (re)defined. (X is overloaded here.)

Predicate use: An object has a **predicate use** [RAPP82] when it is used in a predicate. In **IF** $X = Y + Z$ . . . X, Y, and Z are predicate uses. In some languages (e.g., C) an object can have predicate and computational uses simultaneously because computation can be embedded in predicates. There is no virtue in creating models with simultaneous predicate and computational uses in behavioral testing—unless confusion is a virtue. Predicates within assertions are not predicate uses because assertions normally don't affect processing flow or output values.

Use: An object is **used** if it is used in predicates and/or in computations.

Input node: An entry node of a data-flow graph at which data are input. The name of the object input at that node is usually written in the node itself or just preceding the node, but by convention it may be written on the outlinks of the node. The examples on the right are equivalent notations for input nodes.

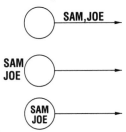

Constants: Constants should be treated as inputs and be modeled as input nodes. Many bugs consist of using the wrong constant, incorrect value of a constant, or modifying the value of a constant during calculations. Constants are as error-prone as other variables and should be treated as such.

Actually, overloading doesn't save memory with optimizing compilers. It probably increases both memory and execution time because it restricts the optimizer's options and forces variables to stay live longer than they might otherwise, thereby reducing the possibility of register-based execution. Because holding time for live variables increases, not only does execution time go up, but so does RAM usage.

Output node: An exit node of a data-flow graph is a node at which data are output. The name of the object whose value is output is annotated to the node, as on the right.

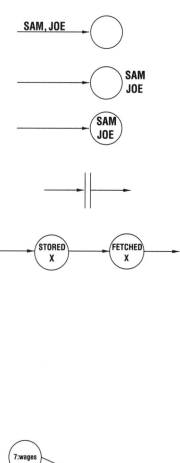

Storage node: A pair of nodes for the same data object. The **STORE** node defines the value of the stored variable (on disk, say). The **FETCH** node defines the value of the variable in memory. The top notation on the right is the way this is usually shown in data-flow graphs, but the bottom notation is clearer. Storage nodes are confusing because in subsequent processing it's not obvious which value of a variable is used. Is it the stored value on disk or the value in RAM prior to storage? In an application on a network with shared files, say, they could differ (and thus be a source of bugs). Use of different names for the two, say **ram_value** and **disk_value**, may help clarify things.

Processing node: A node with one or more inlinks and at least one outlink. The inlinks denote data objects. The outlink denotes a calculated function of those data objects. In the example on the right, **total_income** is a function of the three inlinks, **wages**, **taxable_interest**, and **tax_exempt**. For clarity, you might want to annotate the processing node with the function calculated.

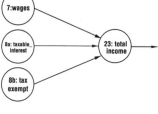

Link value: In data-flow graphs the values of objects are associated with the nodes at which those values are calculated (e.g., processing nodes). In the simplified data-flow graphs used in this book, every outlink of a node has the same data object value. In common usage of data-flow graphs, a node may be used to represent several different computations and therefore may have several different objects associated with outlinks. The typical practice is to place the names of the objects on the outlinks of such nodes. With such usage, we informally call those names **outlink values.** Similarly, because the outlinks of one node are inlinks of a subsequent node, they are called **inlink values.**

Data selector predicate: A predicate whose value (e.g., truth value) is used to select one of several data objects. For example, a pointer to an array selects the data object in the array location to which the pointer points. There is always a data selector predicate for a **data selector node.** (See below.)

Data selector node: A node whose inlinks are controlled by a data selector predicate. The value (truth or pointer) selects a data object associated with an inlink. In the example on the right, the data selector predicate associated with this data selector node has selected the data object **VIV.** A data selector node calculates the special function of selecting the inlink value to use at the outlink. The inlinks of a data selector node can be annotated with the predicate condition that selects that inlink.

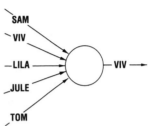

Control inlink: A data selector node may have an inlink whose use is exclusively in the data selector predicate. A common convention denotes control inlinks by dashed lines. In the preceding example, the selection of **VIV** could be based on the values at all the inlinks:

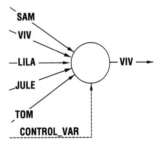

outlink_value:=MAX(inlink_values).

in which case there is no control inlink. Alternatively, the selection could be based on the value at a control inlink that, say, specifies which inlink value is to be used, as in:

outlink_value := SELECT (CONTROL_VAR, inlink_values).

In the last example, the control inlink control variable **CONTROL_VAR** selects one of the inlink values, as in a pointer to an array, say.

Data-flow graph: A graph consisting of **input nodes, output nodes, storage nodes, data selector nodes,** and associated links and properties.

5.3 THE RELATIONS AND THE MODEL

5.3.1 General

Objects (nodes): A calculated function of the inlinks:

7:     **wages**
8a   **taxable_interest_income**
8b   **tax_exempt_interest_income**
9:     **dividend_income**
10:     **taxable_refunds**
11:     **alimony received**
12:     **business_income_or_loss**
. . . . . .
21:     **other_income**
22:     **total_income:=wages+ taxable_interest_income ... + other_income.**

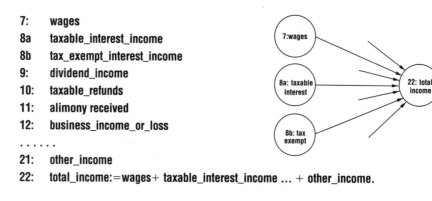

Refer to Form 1040. Nodes 7 through 21 are data sources. Of these, nodes 8a, 9, 10, 12, 13, 14, 15, 18, 19, and 21 probably come from other IRS forms but will be treated here as inputs in order to have a manageable example. Line 22 is a processing node. Node 22 also depends on nodes, 15b and 16b, whose calculation we're ignoring for now (but you should not). Almost every line in Form 1040 corresponds to a data object that is entered without previous calculation, comes from another a form, or is calculated as part of the Form 1040 processing.

Relation (links): *Is directly used to calculate a value of.* In the last example, nodes **7: wages** through **21: other_income**, excluding **15a:IRA** and **16a:pensions** are used directly to calculate the value of node **22: total_income**. These values also are used indirectly to calculate the value of other objects such as node **53:your_total_taxes**, but because the use is not direct there are no arrows from these nodes to node 53. There are, however, data flows from some of these nodes that do reach node 53.

Node Properties (node weights): Annotate nodes with the function of the inlinks that they calculate. This can be as simple as the name of the output of the function (e.g., **total_income**) or the actual function, as in a formula.

Link Properties (link weights): It is not essential to add link weights because that information is specified by the node weights; however, because data-flow graphs can get busy, it is customary to label outlinks with the name of the data object(s) they represent. If the node is a data selector node, label the inlinks with the selector predicate value associated with each inlink.

5.3.2 Control-Flow Graph Equivalences

Constructs in control flow graphs have equivalent constructs in data-flow graphs.

Ordinary Processing: Most ordinary processing is denoted by a single processing node without regard to the order in which the processing is done. Although the previous example for calculating **total_income** appears to have ordering, no such ordering is needed because the IRS doesn't insist that we do our taxes by first entering wages, then taxable interest income, and so on. If we write a program in an ordinary programming language, then we must pick a specific order; but that ordering is of our choosing and not essential to the task. In data-flow diagrams, we don't impose sequencing not implied by requirements.

The link list notation is more convenient than the pictorial representation of the graph. The comment associated with the link applies, by our convention, to the first node of a node pair. This saves us the trouble of writing down a list of nodes and then a list of links. In the following example, the comment **other_income** is associated with the outlinks of node 21.

21:	22:	other_income
11:	22:	alimony received
15a:	15b:	total_IRA_distribution
15b:	22	taxable amount (see your accountant)
16a:	16b:	taxable amount (see your other accountant)
17:	22:	rental_royalties_etc.
18:	22:	farm_income_or_loss
19:	22:	unemployment_compensation
20a:	20b:	social_security_benefit
20b:	22:	taxable_social_security_benefit
8b:		tax_exempt_interest_income
9:	22:	dividend_income
14:	22:	other_gains_and_losses_from_form_4797
10:	22:	taxable_refunds
8a:	22:	taxable_interest_income
12:	22:	business_income_or_loss
7:	22:	wages
13:	22:	capital_gains_or_loss
22:		total_income := wages + taxable_interest_income +
		tax_exempt_interest + . . . + . . . other_income.

It doesn't matter how we rearrange the lines in the above graph. The links are specified, so the order in which we put them on the page doesn't affect the processing or the model. I included node 8b, which doesn't seem to go any place; the IRS wants this information even though it is not used in this calculation. Presumably they use it to calculate something else.

IF-THEN-ELSE: Here's the specification for line 36 of IRS form 1040.

36   If line 32 [Adjusted_Gross_Income] is $83,850 or less, multiply $2,450 by the total number of exemptions claimed on line 6e. If line 32 is over $83,850, see the [IRS 1040] instructions for the amount to enter.

Here's a pseudocode model for this operation.

36.1: 36: IF ((AGI) line_32 <= $83,850) THEN   line_36 := number_exemptions * $2,450 ELSE line_36 : = instructions_calculation.

Here's a classical control-flow graph for this operation.

36.1: 36.2:   predicate node, AGI <= $83,850
36.1: 36.3:   predicate node, AGI > $83,850
36.2: 36:   Line_36 := number_exemptions * $2,450
36.3: 36:   Line_36 := instructions_calculation

The **Line_36** variable is not overloaded. Why? Here's a data-flow graph for this operation.

6e: 36.1:   total_number_of_exemptions
k1:   36.1:   constant_value_of_$2,450
k2:   36:   constant_value_of_$83,850
36.1: 36   total_number_of_exemptions * k1
32:   36:   adjusted_gross_income
P23: 36:   instructions_calculation
36:   ... data selector node   36.1   IF AGI <= k2
                                     P23   IF AGI > k2

I'm not happy with this model because the controls are mixed in with the computation. A really complicated model, could be confusing, so I'd rather add a few links and nodes to make things more explicit, yielding the following flow graph.

6e:	36.1:	total_number_of_exemptions
k1:	36.1:	constant_value_of_$2,450
36.1:	36	total_number_of_exemptions * k1
P23:	36:	instructions_calculation
k2:	36.2:	constant_value_of_$83,850
32:	36.2:	adjusted_gross_income
36.2	36:	selector_value (control inlink)

36: ... data selector node   36.1   IF AGI <= k2 (selector_value = TRUE)
                                      P23   IF AGI > k2 (selector_value = FALSE)

You might want to sketch all of these flow graphs for comparison. The data-flow models seems to be more complicated but are not. They just include more information than is usually put in a control-flow model. The extra detail comes about because every data object must come from someplace. That's why we added the two nodes, k1 and k2, to account for the constants $2,450 and $83,850 respectively. We added the 32:36 link in the first data-flow model (32:36.2 in the second model) because **adjusted_gross_income** had to come from someplace. The 6e:36.1 link for **total_number_of_exemptions** was added for the same reason. If we remove this additional information (thereby reducing the detail of our model), we get an even simpler model (in terms of the number of nodes and links) than the control-flow model.

36.1:	36	total_number_of_exemptions * k1
P23:	36:	instructions_calculation

36: ... data selector node   36.1 IF AGI <= k2
                                      P23 IF AGI > k2

Good software design suggests that constants k1 and k2 be assigned early in the program or stored in a table. That's a lot better than a bunch of $2,450 and $83,850's all over the place. It's good design because it reduces the likelihood of bugs in which the supposedly constant values differ from place to place. It's good maintenance design because there's only one place to change the value when the IRS (inevitably) changes the tax rates.* It's good design, but we can't be sure that the programmer has done it: But why should the tester care? By using symbolic constants in our model, we reduce the likelihood of bugs in our model where we inadvertently use several different values of the supposed constant. Good software design is often also good test design.

---

* I started this book in 1992. I had to revise these numbers in 1993, 1994, and yet again in 1995. However, unlike you, it was not possible to use a symbolic variable for these numbers. It would have been much easier had I been able to do so. If I missed a few of these updates, I'm sure you'll tell me —but I hope you'll forgive me.

IF-THEN: I don't like **IF-THEN** constructs in data-flow graphs because they're ambiguous when the condition isn't met. In control-flow graphs, there's less ambiguity because the next statement is implied. Most **IF-THEN** constructs are better modeled as an **IF-THEN-ELSE** as follows:

IF (predicate is TRUE) then x := function ELSE x := null

Use an explicit specification of what happens to the data object when the predicate is not satisfied. For example:

54   Federal income tax withheld. If any is from Form(s) 1099, check [BOX]

can be represented by the following pseudocode and data-flow model respectively.

54:   If from_Forms(s)_1099 THEN box := check ELSE box := uncheck

54.1:   54: box := check
54.2:   54: box := uncheck
F1099:   54   TRUE/FALSE value from form 1099
54   ...   data selector node: 54.1 IF F1099 = TRUE
54.2 IF F1099 = FALSE

Be careful about values such as zero and **null;** they're not the same. We introduced two input nodes in the last example: **54.1 box:=check** and **54.2 box:=uncheck.** In both cases, **box** has an actual value. Similarly, a value of zero is an actual value, but a **null** is no value. It means undefined.

Consider the specification statement: **IF x>0 THEN sam:=joe.** We know what to do with **sam** if **x > 0,** but supposes **x <= 0?** There are two alternatives: Either **sam** has no value and is created here, or there is another preexisting value of **sam** calculated elsewhere in the data-flow graph. The first case is no problem. We model it as: **IF x > 0 THEN sam := joe ELSE sam := null.** The second case isn't a problem either. It should be modeled as: **IF x>0 sam :=joe ELSE sam:= old_sam_value.** Again we don't need the ambiguous **IF-THEN.**

There's a possible problem if **sam** is calculated in more than one place. Which value should we use in the **FALSE** case? A good question with no simple answer. It depends because there's no obvious answer to an ambiguity. The **IF-THEN** construct is unambiguous in the control-flow graph because control-flow graphs have an implied sequencing. Therefore, there is (usually) an implied (prior) value for this situation. In data-flow graphs that don't have nonessential sequencing, the value is ambiguous. That's why the **IF-THEN** should be avoided in these models. But notice that if there's an ambiguity in the model, then programming bugs are likely.

As an example of the use of **IF-THEN**'s consider how we might model lines 1 to 5 of Form 1040. Here are some pseudocode for these lines.

```
1:    IF filing_status = single THEN check box_1;  GOTO 6a
2:    IF filing_status = married_filing_joint THEN  check box_2; GOTO 6a
3:    IF filing_status = married_filing_separate THEN  check box_3; GOTO 6a
4:    IF filing_status = head_of_household THEN check  box_4; GOTO 6a
5:    IF filing_status = qualifying_widower THEN  check box_5: GOTO 6a
```

This pseudocode is unambiguous if we know that the previous state of all the boxes is "unchecked." Because we can't be sure of that in buggy code, a better model might be:

```
1:    IF fil_stat = single THEN box_1:= check ; GOTO 6a ELSE box_1 := uncheck
2:    IF fil_stat = mar_joint THEN box_2:= check; GOTO 6a ELSE box_2 := uncheck
3:    IF fil_stat = mar_sep; THEN box_3:= check; GOTO 6a ELSE box_3 := uncheck
4:    IF fil_stat = head_house THEN box_4:= check; GOTO 6a ELSE box_4 := uncheck
5:    IF fil_stat = qual_wid THEN box_5:= check; GOTO 6a ELSE box_5 := uncheck
```

Programmers may object that this isn't good code because it has unnecessary complexity that itself makes the code more bug-prone; and besides, that, it isn't structured. That's true, but this isn't code. It's a model—a model in which were trying to make things as unambiguous as we can, even if it takes extra verbiage. Here's a data-flow model for these actions.

```
0.0:    0.1: input fil_stat
0.1:    box_1:          box_1:      6:   selector: IF fil_stat = single
                                         select check ELSE  select uncheck
        box_2:          box_2:      6:   selector: IF fil_stat = mar_joint
        box_3:                           select check ELSE  select uncheck
        box_4:          box_3:      6:   selector: IF fil_stat = mar_sep
        box_5:                           select check ELSE select uncheck
                        box_4:      6:   selector: IF fil_stat= head_house
check:  box_1:                           select check ELSE select uncheck
        box_2:                           select check ELSE select uncheck
        box_3:          box_5:      6:   selector: IF fil_stat = qual_wid
        box_4:                           select check ELSE select uncheck
        box_5:          6:          model continuation
uncheck box_1:
        box_2
        box_3:
        box_4:
        box_5:
```

This may seem like a complicated model, but it isn't because five different outputs (one for each box) are defined. In testing software that purports to implement this process, not only should we confirm that the correct box is checked but also that all other boxes remain unchecked and that at most one box is checked. Note that if the **filing_status** input is not one of the five correct choices, then all boxes will be unchecked.

CASE SELECTOR: The **CASE SELECTOR** construct in data-flow graphs is a generalization of the **IF-THEN-ELSE** construct. A data-flow model for line 34 is:

34.1: 34: input $3,800	(single, deduction := $3,800)
34.2: 34 input $5,600	(head of household, deduction := $5,600)
34.3: 34 input $6,350	(married joint return, deduction := $6,350)
34.4: 34 input $6,350	(qualified widower, deduction := $6,350)
34.5: 34 input $3,175	(married filing separate, deduction := $3,175)
fil_stat: 34 input filing_status	(control inlink for 34 selector)
34: select on filing_status:	single 34.1
	head 34.2
	joint 34.3
	widower 34.4
	separate 34.5

Line 34 illustrates the **CASE SELECTOR** node. I chose to use the variable **filing_status** to model the selector predicate because that's the way the IRS instructions for this line are written. Had the instructions referred to which *box* had been checked in lines 1 to 5, I would have created a variable **box_number** in the model of lines 1 to 5, whose value would be set to the number corresponding to which box had been checked, and then used the value of **box_number** to control the selector predicate in line 34.

As with the **IF-THEN** construct, ambiguity is possible. What happens if none of the boxes (lines 1–5) is checked? What happens if more than one of the boxes on lines 1 to 5 are checked?

5.3.3 Shorthands and Shortcuts

Don't forget that we're dealing with models and not (neither directly nor always) with software. Consequently, you put only as much detail into the model as you need and not all the detail you know. Just as data-flow diagrams used in design are created with various levels of detail, so should your data-flow models used in test design. For example, in dealing with a file, you might profit by having several different levels of detail (and several different data-flow models).

File Level: Treat the whole file as one data object manipulated as a single entity. Concentrate on operations that apply to the whole file and operations between files, for example: open, close, copy, compare, rename, delete, move, transmit, merge, extract, create.

Record Level: The tests you did at the file level (if passed) give you confidence that you have the right file. Concentrate on getting the right record at the record level model. The operations of interest parallel the file level: add record, delete record, copy record, find record, extract, compare, move.

Field Level: Consider individual fields in the record. There could be several levels here. For example, one of the fields could be an array. Consider: insert field, remove field, change field value, copy value, count fields.

Processing Level: Usually you'll integrate processing with the field level, but not necessarily if either the field operations or the processing is complicated. The processing model itself might be created at several different levels of detail.

Data Groups: Whether the application calls for it, or whether it's programmed that way, you might want to group data objects that are processed in a similar way, even if they are not so related in application terms. Doing this will help you to make reusable models. That is, the same model could be used for several different, possibly unrelated, parts of the application. Reuse is good programming and it's also good test design.

Good software designs make the modeling task easy because the designers created a hierarchical set of data flows that are reflected in the way they partitioned the processing. When you partition the model into levels as above, you will probably have to "create" new data objects that aren't in the specifications. Define these as precisely as you would if you were programming: their attributes, definitions, and so on. Once defined, that **pseudovariable** now becomes a variable to use in a higher-level data-flow model.

In creating and using such shorthand methods, you are neither programming nor changing requirements—you're doing groundwork needed for sensible test organization. If the application is complicated, expect the tests to be likewise. If the software benefits from a hierarchical structure, partitioning, and reusable components, so will the test suite. Most methods that make good sense in program design have comparable payoff in test design.

You might criticize this approach to test organization by saying: "Neither the software nor the application is structured. By assuming nice structure in the test design, you're missing the possibility of catching bugs that come about as a result of bad structure—for example, bugs that come about because the file, field, and record levels are mixed up with processing ."

There's merit to such criticism but it doesn't follow that because the programs structure is sloppy, sloppy-structured testing will be more effective. It doesn't take a thief to catch a thief. It takes systematic work.

How should you allocate your scarce test design time effectively? There are many more ways to do bad software design than there are good ways. If you adopt unstructured test design to try to catch some bugs, you've made assumptions about the code as arbitrary as assuming a well-structured design.

You're deceiving yourself. The only way you can make valid assumptions about the code on which to base your test design is to look at the code and to have its structure dictate your test design: which isn't black-box testing.

By adopting a structured model, you're increasing the likelihood that your positive tests will cover requirements. It's also a less biased set of tests from which to create negative tests. For example, by separating the file and field-level tests, you can clearly see that there's an opportunity for dirty tests in which those levels are mixed up. Design of dirty tests will be more straightforward, and make fewer bug assumptions, and the labor will be easier to estimate.

5.3.4 Sequencing, Mixing Control Flow and Data Flow, Loops [RUGG79]

5.3.4.1 SEQUENCING

The data-flow graph doesn't contain much of the unessential sequencing imposed by our programming languages and computer hardware. But some sequencing is still essential and some sequencing information is convenient. Here are four common kinds of sequencing that can occur in a data-flow graph: convenient but not essential, essential, synchronization, iteration.

1. **Convenient, but not essential.** We have a sequence of operations that calculates values with intermediate values. You need **adjusted_gross_income** (line 31) to calculate your tax. The **adjusted_gross_income** depends on **total_income** (line 22), which in turn depends on other fields. Ultimately, these fields depend on data inputs. It might seem that such sequencing is essential, but it isn't. Every line in the tax return could (theoretically) be expressed directly in terms of input data. It could, but it would be silly to do so because each line of the tax form then would be the sum of dozens of input fields. This sequencing is convenient but not essential. If you removed all the convenient sequencing from a typical data-flow graph, you would have only input nodes and (and very complicated) output nodes.

   When you see a data-flow graph that has other nodes between the input and output nodes, examine those **intermediate nodes** to determine if they are essential or just convenient. Can you simplify your graph or make it more regular by removing some of those convenient sequences and expressing outputs more directly in terms of input values? This is the opposite of what you did when you introduced pseudovariables and hierarchical partitions in section 5.3.3.

2. **Essential.** Some sequencing is essential. You can't read a file before it's created (although that's a good test) or close a file that isn't open. You must understand the application to know if the sequencing in a data-flow graph

is or is not essential. Don't remove essential sequencing, because if you do, you'll miss important tests in addition to designing useless tests.

3. **Synchronization.** If there are concurrent processes (such as in shared data systems or networked applications), there is essential sequencing and a synchronization problem. For example, **c:=a+b**, but **a** and **b** come from different places. Synchronization issues lead to five additional test cases depending on which arrives first (why?), which we'll take up in Chapter 6. If there's a lot of this going on, the data-flow model may not be best and you might consider a control-flow or transaction-flow model instead.

4. **Iteration.** If you have selector nodes, you can feed the output of a computation back to some earlier point in the data flow graph and create a loop. The process is repeated until (it is hoped) termination conditions are met. Loops and how to handle them within the context of a data-flow model are discussed in section 5.3.4.3. .

5.3.4.2 MIXED CONTROL FLOW AND DATA FLOW

Control-flow and data-flow models don't mix well [KAVI87]. Every model is a different slice through reality that focuses on some aspects of the problem and ignores others. A model is a way to structure our thinking in order to lead us to useful tests. If the model is too complicated, it will confuse us. Okay, but how *should* we handle essential sequencing within a data-flow model? Here are some ideas.

1. **More than one model.** Do a separate control-flow and data-flow model. Each will lead you to different tests and, it is hoped, there won't be much overlap in the tests created. You may find that the finite-state model of Chapter 9 is the alternate model you want.

2. **Put the control-flow model inside the data-flow model.** You have an iterative procedure within a model dominated by data flows. For example, you have to search a file to get data that are then used in a computation. Treat the file search as a single operation within the data flow model. Use a control-flow model for the file search.

3. **Put the data-flow model inside the control-flow model.** You do repetitive processing on every record of a file, say. The processing is modeled by a data-flow graph. Put the data-flow portion inside the file model (either a control-flow model or a transaction-flow model). Treat the file part as a control-flow model and the processing as a data-flow model.

Once you've designed a test case, no one knows how you got it. The test case consists of initial conditions, inputs, and expected outcomes, and there's no mention (or there shouldn't be) of the fact that you got to those inputs and outcomes via a control-flow model, a data-flow model, or what not.

5.3.4.3 LOOPS

However you model the problem and whatever the loops are, essential or not, you should use the loop testing techniques of Chapter 4. Luckily, we don't often have to deal with loops in data-flow models. We must distinguish between **essential** and **nonessential loops.**

Nonessential loops come about because of the nature of our programming languages. If you wanted to add two arrays in most computers or languages, you would probably do it in a loop. The loop is not essential because you could, in a parallel computer, do this operation in parallel. Most of the loops we find in software are nonessential. Most deterministic loops are not essential.

Essential loops implement iterative or potentially infinite procedures. Solving an equation by an iterative process, such as Newton-Raphson iteration, is a good example. Searching and sorting files whose lengths are unbounded are other examples. Most nondeterministic loops are essential.*

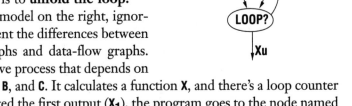

If you have some essential (or convenient) loops that aren't very complicated (meaning not nested, no jumping into or out of them, and not much control logic in them), then an easy and revealing way to incorporate the key loop issues within a data-flow model is to **unfold the loop.**

Consider the model on the right, ignoring for the moment the differences between control-flow graphs and data-flow graphs. There's an iterative process that depends on input variables **A**, **B**, and **C**. It calculates a function **X**, and there's a loop counter **I**. Having calculated the first output (X_1), the program goes to the node named **LOOP**, where a decision is made as to whether to exit or to continue. The controlling predicate might be either a function of **X**, of **I**, or both.

We need an initial value for **X** because the computation done at node **X** depends on the previous value of **X**. I've named that initial value X_0. We also need an initial value for the iteration count I_0. We don't know whether the code actually contains these initial values as explicit constants, but logic dictates that they exist. Experience tells us that initial values bugs are relatively frequent, so it's a good thing to go after.

The first model bothers me. It isn't as dataflowish as I'd like it to be. There's complexity hidden in that **LOOP** node, of which the most important is

---

* We both know that preparing our income tax return is an iterative procedure that seems to never terminate (until April 15, that is). Knowing the bureaucratic mind, I had great hopes of finding many essential loops in the tax laws. I went through all the forms and instructions (some 950 pages of IRS gobbledegook) provided by my tax package. I found many loopholes but not one essential loop. I'm sure that they're there, but I'm no tax expert, so I couldn't find one. Any reader who points me to essential loops to use as examples in a subsequent edition of this book will receive a free copy of that edition.

how those initial values are chosen. The model on the right is more explicit. I added two data selector nodes (marked with "?") to select between the initial values of **X** and **I**. I also put a control link from the **I** selector to the **X** selector to show how the program might pick between the initial value X_0 and a subsequent value X_i. For example, there might be a predicate of the form **IF I = 0 THEN PICK X_i ELSE PICK X_0**. In a real problem, you would have more information

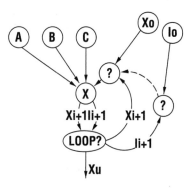

about the specifics of the loop termination conditions, and you would break out as much of that as you could into pure data-flow nodes. For example, the loop terminating condition might be based on the difference between the previous and present value of **X** and compared to some small constant **epsilon**.

I've **unfolded** the loop twice in the following model. The X_1 node does the initial calculation based on the initial values X_0 and I_0. Node X_2 calculates the function based on the constants **A**, **B**, and **C**, using the new values of **X** and **I**. The function for X_2 probably is not the same as the function for X_1, because of initialization. The loop is unfolded yet again for node X_3, which probably has the same function as X_2.

We can continue unfolding and create models with high iteration counts (and therefore many nodes and links). But that's not a good idea. How many times should we unfold? Twice!* That gives you three models: one that stops at X_1, one that stops at X_2, and one that stops at X_3. It is three separate models because you have to consider the three cases: exit without looping, exit after looping once, and exit after looping twice. If you have to test the upper limit of the iteration parameter, use a control-flow model.

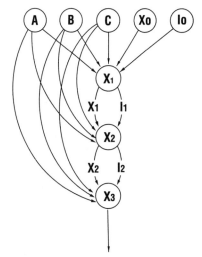

In testing loops with a data-flow model, we are most concerned with possible initialization bugs or with using the wrong values from a prior iteration. For example, at node X_3, instead of using the X_2 value, the programmer uses the X_1 or the X_0 value. Both theory and practice shows us that not looping and iterating once and twice probably will catch most such bugs.

We must unfold once to satisfy the all-uses structural test strategy because we want to cover simple paths. The second unfolding is justified by experience and Huang's theorem. See BEIZ90.

5.4 THE TECHNIQUE

5.4.1 General [SNEE86, ZWEB92]

Test design and execution is the same as for control-flow models, with some minor differences that result from having data-flow graphs rather than control-flow graphs. In the following I'll assume that we don't have loops.

1. Verify the specification—always.
2. Identify input variables, especially constants. Give each input variable a name and assign it an input node.
3. Rewrite the specification as one sentence per function to be calculated.
4. List the functions, starting with those that depend only on input variables.
5. Then list the functions that depend only on the input variables and outputs from the functions listed in step 4.
6. Continue listing the functions this way until you account for all of them. You should have a list of functions such that the ones at the top of the list depend only on input variables and, as you progress down the list, the functions depend more and more on intermediate calculations. Note that in general, a strict ordering is impossible, but it also isn't necessary.
7. Examine intermediate functions (i.e., functions that depend on both input variables and the outputs of other functions) and see if the sequencing is essential or merely convenient. If essential, mark that node and the nodes on which it depends as essential. If not essential, could the model be simplified by removing the intermediate nodes and expressing the function directly in terms of input variables? If you can remove nodes and links without making the calculated function too complicated, do so.
8. Conversely, you may be able to simplify the model by adding an intermediate node for a complicated calculation. If you do this, however, you need a means to verify that your intermediate calculation is correct: possibly by modifying the source code and adding an assertion statement.
9. You now have a set of nodes (each of which has a name) that expresses the processing in a manner that is conceptually simplest for you.*
10. There is a computation or function associated with each node. The variables in that function name the nodes to which this node is connected—that is to say, the links. You now have a model.
11. Verify the model. Check your work.

---

* For you, but not necessarily for me and vice versa. Never forget that models are mental tools and that there's no fundamental right or wrong with them. They can only be useful or useless. You might chooses to keep a nonessential intermediate calculation in the model because you know that it will have utility in another context, or simply because you know that people are used to thinking that way.

Continue as with control-flow models. There will some differences in the details, which we'll see in the following sections. But first, we need definitions.

Subgraph: A part of a graph that conforms to the rules of graphs— that is, entry and exit nodes, no dangling links, no unconnected nodes, and so on.

Slice: A **subgraph** of a graph selected according to a specified criterion, such that for that criterion, the subgraph has all the properties of the entire graph for the selected nodes and links [WEIS81, WEIS84]. There are many criteria and, therefore, many different kinds of slices. If, for example, the graph is a control-flow graph and the criterion of interest is behavior along a path, the subgraph (slice) contains the model of all the code on the selected path. Here we are mostly interested in **data-flow slices.**

Data-flow slice: Data-flow slices are taken with respect to data objects; in our case, usually with respect to an output node. In general, however, a data-flow slice with respect to a given object (node) is a subgraph of the data-flow graph that consists of all the data flows that can reach the specified node directly or indirectly and all data flows that can be reached from that node. If the slice (as usual) is with respect to an output node, then it includes all the nodes that can influence the value of that output.

Practically speaking, you just trace back from the node of interest and mark any inlinks into that node, then inlinks into the nodes that those links come from, and so on, and similarly for outlinks, down to output nodes.*

12. Select test "paths." They're not actually paths; they're slices.
13. Sensitize the slices.
14. Predict and record the expected outcomes.
15. Define the verification criteria for each test.
16. Run the tests.
17. Confirm the outcomes (e.g., output node values).
18. Confirm the values at intermediate nodes.

5.4.2 A Coverage Hierarchy ** [CLAR89, RAPP82, RAPP85, SCHL70, WEIS91, WEYU90, WEYU94A]

Data-flow test techniques are more powerful than control-flow test techniques—more powerful in the sense that they can catch more bugs. They

---

* Obviously obtained by the transitive closure of "is directly connected to."

** For purists, the data-flow testing models discussed in this book are interpretations of the formally defined structural data-flow test criteria but reinterpreted in terms of behavioral testing. The justification for this interpretation is not based on any deep theoretical considerations but on common sense and experience. Be that as it may, although most of behavioral testing is heuristic and justified by experience, such testing should to the maximum extent possible be consistent with, and be based on, the more fundamental underlying structural methods.

also are more powerful in a theoretical sense that the model helps us to create all the tests that we would create with control-flow testing and then some. But power is not without cost. To get more powerful testing you have to do more work—more work in test design, of course, but also more work to verify the results of the test. Here are progressively more powerful test methods to use on data-flow graphs.

1. **Input/Output Cover.** Consider each output node separately (remember that a data-flow graph has one output node for every output.) For each output node, use a set of input values that calculates some output value. There's an obvious weakness to this technique. We'll cover the input and output nodes and probably some intermediate nodes, but if there's a single selector predicate in there, we'll assure that only one value of that selector is used. The others will not be tested. This is too weak to be useful. It only assures us that the software works for one set of inputs and doesn't do anything obviously bad such as crashing. Forget it.

2. **Input/Output + All Predicates.** Let's use something stronger. Beef up input/output cover by insisting that all predicates (including control-flow predicates for loops and other essential sequencing) have been tried with both truth values and analogously for **CASE**-statement predicates.

    Better, but not enough. What if there are intermediate calculations whose values aren't used? We wouldn't catch those, would we? As another possibility, consider this: We calculate a value of X but don't use it because someplace later on that path we recalculate the value of X without having used the first value. There are no selectors involved in this case. Calculating something and then not using the result is probably a bug, which, while merely wasteful in many contexts, can be damaging in others. Some perspective is in order here. Our model is based on what we hope is a correct implementation of the requirements; but we test a buggy implementation. Therefore, an intermediate calculation whose output isn't used is probably a bug, and one that we should try to catch.

    To quote Rapps and Weyuker [RAPP82]: "...one should not feel confident about a program without having seen the effect of using the value produced by ... every computation."

    If all we did was check all predicate nodes (both control-flow and data selector), we would get something a better than control-flow branch testing because of the compound predicate problem. But we wouldn't get much of the benefits we can get from data flow testing.

3. **Partial Node Cover (All Definitions).** The preceding methods covered some nodes and some links, but neither ensured that all nodes and/or all links would be covered. So, knowing that in general, our strategy is to at least cover the computational nodes of our model, let's ensure that we do

so. This is called the **All Definitions** strategy because every computational node in our data-flow model corresponds to the definition of some variable. Note that this doesn't guarantee link cover. So this strategy is not strictly comparable to the input/output + predicate strategy given earlier.

What does this strategy imply? We'll design and execute enough tests to ensure that every computational node in our model has been exercised under test. That means that each function has been executed at least once and produced (we hope) a correct value for that case. Note that we are now responsible for verifying the intermediate calculations because testing every computation node implies verifying the computation done at those nodes.

AD (all definitions) is interesting because the early literature that dealt with heuristic data-flow testing usually suggested this method [BEND70, BEND85, HERM76]. Here our strategies are based on formal, verified theory [FRAN88, RAPP82]. AD also misses too much. For example, it could miss every selector node and every loop in the model. Too much to give up. We need something stronger.

4. **All Nodes.** The next obvious step is to ensure that we cover all nodes, not just computational nodes. This is clearly a stronger prescription because we'll ensure that all data selector nodes and control-flow nodes are covered in addition to the computational nodes. But it isn't strong enough because it doesn't ensure, for example, that we've checked every possibility for selector and control-flow predicates. Something stronger yet is needed.

5. **Link Cover (All Uses).** The next logical step is to cover every link in the data-flow graph. That corresponds to the **All Uses** strategy. Whenever a calculation is done, we will verify every use of the result of that calculation in subsequent processing—this, of course, includes all intermediate calculations and not just the final outputs. This is not testing every possible path through the software. It isn't even testing every way that a definition can get to a subsequent use.

6. **All Uses + Loops.** There are many other data-flow testing strategies not covered here. For an overview, see WEYU94A in MARC94. We should try to keep loops out of our data-flow models, but that's not always possible. If you have such loops, then unfold the model and augment your test cases by covering the unfolded model's links.*

---

* We want something between All Uses but not quite as strong as all-DU paths, which is almost impossible to do in a behavioral testing context. The idea is to bring in the notion of a simple path, without taking all possible simple paths between definitions and uses. Unfolding does that for us. The second unfolding is overkill, but it does reveal enough bugs in practice that I recommend it.

5.4.3 Building the Model

Time to stop gabbing and start building. Let's do a simplified version of lines 54 to 60 of Form 1040. Here's the source material, copied from the IRS, with minor changes to clarify the wording.

54:	Federal Tax Withheld
55:	1994 Estimated Tax Payment and Amount Applied from 1993 Return
56:	Earned Income Credit
57:	Amount Paid with Form 4868 (Extension Request)
58a:	Excess Social Security and RRTA Tax Withheld
59:	Other Payments from Form 2439 or from Form 4136
60:	Total Payments: Sum of lines 54 through 59.

Our first cut at this model is almost the same as the tax form lines, but slightly more formal. In the back of my mind, I'm hoping to use a tool that will help me check the completeness and consistency of this specification, so it's a good idea to formalize early.

54:	60:	Federal_Tax_Withheld
55:	60:	1994_Estimated_Tax Payment and Amount_ Applied_ from_ 1993_ Return
56:	60:	Earned_ Income_ Credit
57:	60:	Amount_ Paid_ with_ Form_ 4868 (Extension Request)
58a:	60:	Excess_ Social_ Security and RRTA_ Tax_ Withheld
59:	60:	Other_ Payments (from Form 2439 or from Form 4136)
60:		Total Payments:= Sum of lines 54 through 59.

That's really not right is it? Line 55 is really the sum of two other items, Line 58a is the sum of two items, and line 59 is the sum of two items (Form 2439 and Form 4136—1994 Estimated Tax and the amount carried over from the 1993 tax return, respectively). We'll redo the model in more detail.

54:	60:	Federal_Tax_Withheld
55a:	55:	1994_Estimated_Tax Payment
55b:	55:	Amount_ Applied_ from_ 1993_ Return
55:	60:	55a + 55b
56:	60:	Earned_ Income_ Credit
57:	60:	Amount_ Paid_ with_ Form_ 4868 (Extension Request)
58a1:	58a:	Excess_ Social_Security_Tax Withheld
58a2:	58a:	Excess_RRTA_Tax_Withheld
58a:	60:	58a1 + 58a2
59a:	59:	Other_ Payments_ from Form 2439
59b:	59	Other_ Payments_ from Form 4136

```
59:          60:     59a +59b
60:                  Total Payments:= 54 + 55 + 56 + 57 + 58a + 59
```

The last line troubles me because of its ambiguous notation. Am I talking about nodes 54, 55, and so on, or about their values? It would be better to make things clear and replace the line with:

```
60:          Total Payments:= L54 + L55 +L 56 + L57 + L58a + L59
```

I've made some assumptions in this model, that might or might not be correct. Wherever I detailed a node (55, 58a, and 59), I assumed that entries could come from none, one, or all of these sources. These nodes are not selector nodes. Selector nodes must deal with mutually exclusive cases. For example, line 38 is a selector node because the cases are (it appears) mutually exclusive. How do you know? You have to understand the application and the intent. Let's now model just line 38 and see what it entails.

```
38    Tax.Check if from a [ ] Tax Table, b [ ] Tax Rate Schedule, c [ ] Capital Gain Tax
      Worksheet, or d [ ] Form 8615. e. Amount from form(s) 8814.
```

I'm not a tax expert, so I had to read the IRS instructions and a tax guide to see what to do about item e. Item e has to be added in to the tax, although the form doesn't say so. Items a, b, c, and d are mutually exclusive and form a proper selector. So here's the model:

```
38a:  38x:     part_of_tax (Use tax table)
38b:  38x:     part_of_tax (Use Tax Rate Schedule)
38c:  38x:     part_of_tax (Use Capital Gain Tax Worksheet)
38d:  38x:     part_of_tax (From Form 8615)
38x:  SELECT (on IRS rules)      38a
                                 38b
                                 38c
                                 38d
38e:  38: Amount_from_Form(s)_8814
38:             L38x + L38e
```

5.4.4 Basic Slice ("Path") Selection

We have several different situations to consider for **slice** selection—the equivalent to control-flow paths in data-flow diagrams. What we do depends on what's in the data-flow graph.

1. No selectors, no control-flow nodes (and no loops)
2. Data flows and selectors only.

3. Control-flow predicate nodes only, no selectors.

4. Control-flow predicates and selectors.

5. Loops.

CASE 1: PURE DATA FLOWS.

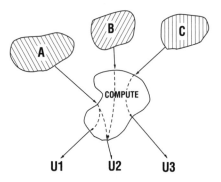

You do this for every output node. Pick an output node. Trace backward from the output node to all the nodes that connect to it. Trace back from those nodes to all the nodes that connect to them, and so on until you have reached input nodes (for that model). You now have a **data-flow slice**. Symbolically, the situation is illustrated by the following:

U1, U2, and U3 are output variables. A, B, and C are sets of input variables. The middle blob contains computation nodes. U1 depends only on the input variables in A. U2 depends on both the A and B variables, and U3 depends on only the C variables. We have three sets of tests corresponding to U1, U2, and U3. If there are no selector nodes and no control-flow nodes, you'll need exactly one test case per output variable. Note that each slice will enclose (possibly) different computation nodes in the COMPUTE blob. For example, we would expect that U3's computation nodes would not overlap with U1 and U2's. U1 would probably have some, but not all, computation nodes in common with U2.

CASE 2. DATA FLOWS AND SELECTORS ONLY.

Start, as before, with a slice for every output variable. However, when you reach a selector node, you must include *every* potentially selected case into the slice. The result is a sort of superslice because there are many alternatives within it. Each superslice will yield a *set* of test cases. Consider each superslice, one at a time.

Assume that there's only one selector in the slice. Select a value for each value of the selector predicate and then exclude from the (super) slice all data flows that do not go into determining that value. If, for example, on line 38 we selected **38a (Use tax table)**, we would exclude from the slice those data flows leading to **Use Tax Rate Schedule**, **Use Capital Gains Tax**, and **Use Form 8615**.

The slice based on U included the three computational blobs, the data sets A, B, C, and D, and the selector node. If we pick the X value, which depends only on data sets A and B, we exclude data sets C and D and the Y computation blob from the slice. Alternatively, if we pick the Y value, then we exclude the A set and the X computation blob because input sets B, C, and D are all used to compute Y and therefore U along that slice.

Suppose that there are two or more selector predicates in a given slice. Here again, we have two cases: Do they branch or do they come back together? We'll take the simpler case first in which the two selector predicates branch. This is depicted symbolically in the next figure.

We start by slicing for all the output variables. Pick one (at a time) as before, and determine the slice for that variable. As before, the first selector predicate we meet divides the graph into more slices, each of which will yield a set of test cases. In the figure, there is a slice for W that yields only one test case and another for V. Following V upward toward the input nodes, we meet the second selector node, which again breaks up into two cases, yielding a slice for X that includes input variable sets A, B, and C and another set for Y that includes input variable sets B, C, and D. Remember that a selector could be for a multiway branch, and you develop a new set of tests for each such branch.

Now for the last case, in which the data flow merges back so that the data flows come back together. If we take the V slice at the bottom selector node and follow the slice upward, we'll come across the next selector node, leading to two new slices and two test cases corresponding the X or Y selection. The W slice, however, goes back to the same selector node (X, Y) where again there are two choices. Does this lead to two more test cases or only one?

That depends on how thoroughly you want to test. If you pick only one choice for W—that is, only one slice (either X or Y)—you have one additional test. More thorough (and more

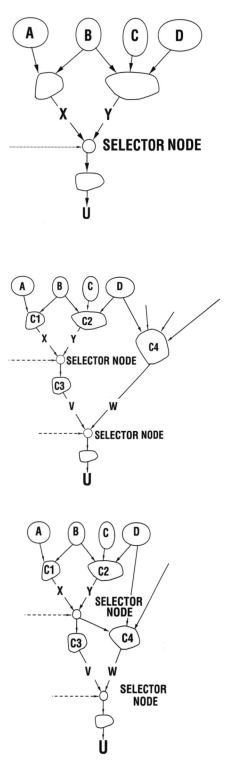

expensive) testing would have you take both slices. In this example it adds only one test, but if we had many selectors stacked up in each slice, the difference in the approaches could be dramatic. The two techniques correspond to applying what is technically known as the **All-Uses criterion (AU)** (take *any* slice that results in a value for W) and the **All-Define-Use-Paths criterion (ADUP)** (take *every* slice that results in a value for W. ADUP is more thorough than AU but takes more work. Such empirical evidence as there is [WEYU90] suggests that you can get most of the benefits by opting for AU. That is, be sure to include at least one slice for every output, but not all possible slices that result from all combinations of selector choices (and as we'll see, all combinations of control flow predicate and loop choices).

CASE 3. CONTROL-FLOW PREDICATES WITHOUT SELECTORS.

You handle this case the same way as you do selectors. Start at the bottom with output variables and create a slice. There is a difference though. In a data selector node, only one of the *inlinks* goes into the slice. That is, each inlink creates a new slice. In a control-flow node (e.g., IF-THEN-ELSE or CASE) each *outlink* creates a new slice. For that reason, it's probably easier to slice control flows from the inputs rather than from the outputs. However, we're dealing with data-flow models here and the control flows are only (we hope) occasional. Symbolically, the situation looks like the following figure.

Start the slice as before, at the output U (for each output). That brings in computational blobs C1 and C2 and their associated data sources, I1 and I2 (which could overlap). Continuing with the slice, you reach the control-flow node, which by definition means that only one of the two alternatives will be followed. That is, you must choose either the C1 or the C2 blobs (and their associated data flows). Each choice yields a test. Both tests need the outputs from blob B and data set I4. Suggestion:

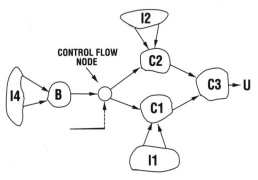

> Data-flow selectors: Slice on the inlinks of the node.
>
> Control-flow nodes: Slice on the outlinks of the node.

Path selection in control-flow testing consists of taking a slice starting at the BEGIN node*. Slicing control flows within a data-flow diagram is more compli-

---

* Technically, it's a slice defined by the selected path, from BEGIN to the EXIT node. That is, select the path and then create a slice that is the union of the slices obtained by slicing on every live variable along that path.

cated because overall, we want to slice from the output, but the presence of control-flow nodes forces us to backtrack and eliminate things from the slice that we may have included before we realized that there was a control-flow node.

Before you do that, however, check if the control-flow part of the model is essential. In the last example, it was not. We could have, for example, replaced the control-flow node by a data selector that selected between the outputs of blobs C1 and C2 and then on to C3. Whether you can do this depends on the application and what things mean. Remember that it doesn't matter how the application may (or may not) have been programmed. What matters is the extent to which the model properly captures the intent of the requirements. You can't do much about the essential control flows and those that denote synchronization and stuff like that. You can play with the convenient ones. If a judicious control-flow node in your model eliminates duplicated data flows, then it's a good idea. If it adds complexity and makes it hard to keep track of slicing, it's a bad idea.

CASE 4. MIXED CONTROL FLOW PREDICATES AND DATA-FLOW SELECTORS.

This case is a combination of the two previous situations, so be careful in building your slices. You should avoid mixed models because it's easy to get confused. Unlike programming, such confusion won't create a bug, but it will waste time and possibly create useless or inexecutable tests.

If you have a mixed model, with both control-flow nodes and selectors, you had better clearly tag each type of node because you'll be doing a lot of backing and filling as you build your slices.

CASE 5. LOOPS.

Data-flow models are just not a good context for loops. The right approach is to do one complete unfolding for each time around the loop and then put in a data selector for each value. If you elect to do three cases, for example, you have: not looping, looping once, and looping twice, and a selector for the three cases.

5.4.5 Putting It Together—An Example

Now let's do a model that we can use for sensitization and the rest of this chapter. It's based on the IRA Worksheet number 1 (for Form 1040, Line 23a/b). With slight rewrite of this worksheet to make it more formal, we have:

		Yours	Spouse
L1:	Min ($2,000, IRA_Contrib_1994)	____	____
L2:	Income	____	____
L3:	Min (L1, L2) (output)	1040 23a	1040 23b
Nonworking Spouse			
L4:	Min (L2a, $2,250)	____	

L5:	Output_from_L3	————
L6:	Line_5 - Line_4	————
L7:	Min ($2,000, 94_Spouse_contrib)	————
L8:	Min(Line_6, Line_7) (output)	————

I'll do this graph for the case that your spouse (if any) doesn't work and that you may (or may not) make an IRA contribution for him. The full model (working spouse included) is left as an exercise. You may think that some of the nodes and links in this model are not really needed, such as: **L1a**, **L3a, L4, L5**, and **L7**. I kept all the nodes following a selector as a precaution and to make sure that the selector in the model was explicit rather than implicit, as in the form. Node 5 (line 5) was kept because there is such a line on the IRS form, and we might be able to confirm its value.

k1:	SL1a	constant = $2000
	SL7	
IL1a:	SL1a	INPUT your_94_IRA_contribution
L2a:	SL3a	INPUT your_94 wages
	SL4a	
IL7	SL7	INPUT spouse_94_IRA_contribution
k2:	SL4a	constant =$2,250
SL1a:	L1a	SELECT min (k1, IL1a)
L1a:	SL3a	
SL3a:	L3a	SELECT min (L1a, L2a)
L3a:	OUTa	OUTPUT to 1040 Line 23a
	L5	
L5:	L6	(note: IRS specification is wrong, should have said "line3a" rather than "line 3" it's of such trivia that bugs are born.)
SL4a:	L4	SELECT min (L2a, k2) (Note another IRS bug here.)
L4:	L6	
L6:	SL8	L4-L5
SL7	L7	SELECT min(IL7, k1)
L7:	SL8	SELECT min(L6, L7)
SL8:	L8	OUTPUT to 1040 Line 23b

We'll do the easy slicing first. That's the case for your IRS contribution, which is entered on line 23a of IRS Form 1040. Slicing upward from the output node, **OUTa**, incorporates nodes **K1, IL1a, SL1a, L1a, SL3a, L2a, L3a**, and **OUTa** and their associated links. There are two selector nodes (and predicates) but only three possibilities, depending on which is the smaller of the three cases: $2,000, 1994 IRA contribution, and 1994 wages. Our superslice then yields three test cases, to be sensitized later.

The line 8 output for spousal IRA contribution is more complicated because selecting this output incorporates the entire graph except for node **OUTa** into the superslice. I'll build my slices in a methodical manner, from the bottom, and always trying to cover links and nodes not covered by a previous test case. Here they are.

Test 1: L8, SL8, L6, L5, L3a, SL3a, L1a, SL1a, IL1a, L4, SL4a, K2
Test 2: L8, SL8, L6, L5, L3a, SL3a, L1a, SL1a, k1, L4, SL4a, L2a
Test 3: L8, SL8, L6, L5, L3a, SL3a, L2a, L4, SL4a
Test 4: L8, SL8, L6, L5, L3a, SL3a, L1a, SL1a, k1, L4, SL4a, k2
Test 5: L8, SL8, L7, SL7, IL7
Test 6: L8, SL8, L7, SL7, K1

Use of cut-and-paste with the word processor helps. Notice that I've put down node names only rather than link names. In general, you have to put down all the links or make it clear that you're defining a set of path segments through the data-flow graph, which together define the slice. For example, a more precise notation would be:

Test 1: L8, SL8, L6, L5, L3a, SL3a, L1a, SL1a, IL1a / L6, L4, SL4a, K2

I used a shorthand because in this case, it's unambiguous. With a more complicated flow graph, it might be ambiguous and just naming the nodes wouldn't be enough.

Note that unlike control-flow testing where we follow only one set of arrows, here, because **L6** has a calculation that involves both **L4** and **L5**, we must include both links in the slice. For the selector nodes, however, you include only the branch for the inlink selected. It may be possible to do this in fewer tests, but frankly, I didn't look too hard. The point is to ensure link cover and not to minimize test cases. The selector nodes are tricky here because they are based on a comparison of two items: that is, **MIN(A, B)**. If both values are the same, you don't know which link you took, so that's not a good basis for test cases (at least in trying to achieve link cover).

5.4.6 Sensitization

Each test corresponds to a slice. If the slices have been defined correctly, then (ultimately) only the inputs of a slice need to be considered in order to sensitize that slice. Sensitization is done much the same way it was done for control flows, except you may find it easier to start at the output and work upward to the inputs. If there are no selectors or control-flow nodes in the slice, there is no sensitization to speak of. Any acceptable input values will work.

If there are selector or control-flow nodes:

1. Note the minimum and maximum values for each input. If the values are members of a set, put down all the set members.

2. Continue upward along all branches of the slice, marking the paths that reach inputs without going through a selector (data or control flow). You can ignore those parts of the slice for now because those inputs are unlikely to be constrained.

3. Move upward along other paths until you reach a selector (for which you've already made a choice). That selector, whether it is a control-flow or a data selector, contains a predicate for which (by the choice of this slice) you have already specified a value. That predicate is now a constraint on all input values that can be reached by slicing upward from that point. Specify the broadest set of input values that satisfy the predicate.

4. Continue to handle every predicate you meet as you slice upward. If there are more than two predicates in a path on the slice, then you'll have simultaneous conditions to consider, and each subsequent predicate you meet further constrains the possible input values.

Sensitization usually is easier for data flows because there are relatively few intermediate nodes and you don't usually have to interpret the predicates in order to express things in terms of input variables. If that is the case, however, you do it much the same way as you would for control flows, except that you deal with data flow slices rather than single paths.

Sensitizing the previous IRA worksheet example is straightforward. Your IRA contributions are compared with $2,000, so that's two possibilities. Your 1994 wages are compared with $2,250 for another two possibilities. Spousal IRA contributions are compared with $2,000 also. There can be at most eight cases, of which only six should be feasible. Taking each of the input variables greater than and less than the things they compare with in all possible ways yielded the following:

Test	Your 1994 contribution	Your 1994 wage	Your 1994 contribution
Test 1:	$1,900	$2,251	$2,060
Test 2:	$2,050	$2,100	$2,060
Test 3:	$2,100	$1,950	$3,500
Test 4:	$2,100	$2,251	$1,500
Test 5:	$ 200	$1,800	$1,500
Test 6:	$ 200	$1,800	$2,500

These are not the only values that achieve link cover, but they were easy to get. Notice that I kept away from the constant values of $2,000 and $2,250. I did it to protect myself against coincidental correctness. If I had picked values of $2,000 for contributions or values of $2,250 for wages, then there is a possibility that both links into the selector nodes based on **MIN(A, B)** would have the same value. If so, it wouldn't matter if that predicate was messed up because we'd get the same value ($2,000) no matter what.

5.4.7 Outcome Prediction

There's nothing special about outcome prediction that wasn't discussed in Chapter 3, pages 62–63. However, you're unlikely to build a model program based on a data-flow model because most programming languages aren't data-flowish. Because there shouldn't be much control flow in your model, a spreadsheet is a good choice for building an oracle. Each cell is an obvious node and provides direct data-flow relations through the formulas in the cell. Spreadsheets, by nature, are very data-flowish, and like data-flow graphs, the presence of control-flow elements makes things more difficult.

5.4.8 Path Verification

It's not path verification as such; it's node verification. You're not getting the full benefit of data-flow testing and you're exposing yourself to possible coincidental correctness if you don't verify intermediate calculations—which is to say, values at nodes. More powerful test techniques mean more work, and verifying those intermediate calculations can be a lot of work. So you need an oracle for those too.

"Testability" here means the ability to examine intermediate calculations. I don't know how to do that except by assertions, more explicit outputs, and symbolic debuggers.

One of the benefits of object-oriented programming is that with proper information hiding, the possibilities of side effects are minimized and the result should be a more robust system. But information hiding doesn't mean that testers should be denied access to that data. The electrical harness on your car has connectors that don't seem to serve any useful purpose—not for you, and you shouldn't play with them; but ask your mechanic how important those test connectors are. Similarly, your PC motherboard has connectors and jumpers that serve only testing—you'd be brave to the point of foolishness if you played with those, but they are useful for testing.

Testing is a legitimate reason for looking at so-called own data and taking the covers off information hiding. If it's your own software you're testing, then use copious assertions as test points. If you're testing someone else's software, exert what pressure you can to get her or him to embed suitable test points or assertions that you can use.

5.5 APPLICATION CONSIDERATIONS

5.5.1 Application Indicators

The applications encompass almost all software, but I wouldn't use data-flow testing for low-level testing of software that had a lot of essential control flows. Some natural applications include:

1. **Object-Oriented Software.** OOP is a data-flow paradigm, which is why data-flow graphs are so often part of the OOP development methodology. If you use data-flow testing for this purpose, you must assume that the objects themselves have been properly tested at a lower level, so that you can trust them and replace each one with a node. You then concentrate on whether the right objects are invoked, the right messages passed, and so on.

2. **Integration Testing.** The main issue in integration is (should be) not if the components being integrated work (that should have been probed during unit testing), but if they are connected correctly and communicate with one another correctly. Each component is modeled by a node, and the data-flow graph can be the program's call tree. That's nice because we have tools to display call trees. The bad news is that the usual call tree isn't enough. If there are global variables, you must include the data flows through them. And because some calls and intercomponent communications may be dynamic, the static call tree determined by the compiler/linker won't tell you the whole story—but it's a start.

3. **Spreadsheets?** Spreadsheets are about as close to a popular pure data-flow language as we have. Don't disdain spreadsheets as not being real programming. They are very real programming to people who create complicated business applications using spreadsheets but have few tools and techniques to use to verify them. Also, if you buy ready-made spreadsheets and plan to entrust a hunk of your business to them, some kind of testing might be in order.

5.5.2 Bug Assumptions

All the bugs that will succumb to control-flow testing will succumb to data-flow testing because it includes control-flow testing as a subset. Because we are avoiding unessential control flows within data-flow models, we are assuming that the programmers have learned to rid themselves of simple control-flow bugs. This biases our bug assumption toward data bugs. Those are the 42xx bugs in my bug taxonomy [BEIZ90] such as: initial and default values, duplication and aliases, overloading, wrong item, wrong type, bad pointers, data-flow anomalies (e.g., closing before opening a file) .

5.5.3 Limitations and Caveats

Data-flow testing won't be any better than your model. And it isn't going to work if *you* don't do the work.

1. You still won't find missing requirements.

2. You're likelier to find gratuitous features, but only if you make sure to verify every output.

3. Data-flow testing is likelier to reveal bugs at the higher levels of integration.

4. Data-flow testing might lose effectiveness when software and test design are done by the same person, but less so than for control-flow testing, because data-flow testing and control-flow testing are such different paradigms that the paradigm shift alone is likely to bring new outlooks even when done by the same person.

5. You still might be blind to coincidental correctness, but the possibilities thereof are easier to spot.

6. Your tests are no better than your oracle.

7. Data-flow testing won't buy you much if you don't find ways to verify those intermediate nodes.

5.5.4 Automation and Tools

As of late 1994 there were no commercial tools to support behavioral data-flow testing. There are many private test tools to support structural data-flow testing in C and Pascal [FRAN85, HARR89, HORG92, KORE85, KORE88, LASK90, OSTR91, WILS82]. If you have a design tool that supports data-flow diagrams, ask the tool's vendor why it doesn't support test design.

5.6 SUMMARY

Data-flow testing is a more powerful technique than control-flow testing. It is based on defining a data-flow model and using that model as a basis for test designs. Tests are created by selecting slices from the output nodes to all the input nodes of the slice. Several coverage metrics were defined, but all-uses supplemented by unfolding loops (twice) is recommended as the minimum.

5.7 SELF-EVALUATION QUIZ

1. Define: all definitions cover, all du-path cover, all nodes cover, all predicate cover, all uses cover, assertion statement, control inlink, convenient sequencing, computational use, data-flow graph, data-flow slice, data selector node, data selector predicate, define, essential loop, essential sequencing, inlink value, input node, input/output cover, link value, loop unfolding, nonessential loop, outlink value, output node, null, overload, predicate node, predicate use, processing node, pseudovariable, slice, storage node, subgraph, use.

2. Show that line 6 of the IRA worksheet (page 260) can never be negative so that it's not necessary to put in a comparison with zero. Hint: MIN is transitive.

3. Redo the IRA worksheet (page 260), including the logic and data flows for both a working and nonworking spouse. Slice, sensitize, and design the test cases.

4. Do data-flow graph models for Form 1040. Treat data that come from other forms as inputs. For each case, do the model, select slices, and design tests using the following criteria: (i) input/output cover, (ii) node cover, (iii) all-uses. Check your work with a tax package or spreadsheet model as an oracle. You may have to override the tax package and insert values from other forms as inputs. (a) lines 1–6, (b) lines 7–22, (c) lines 32–40, (d) lines 41–46, (e)lines 47–53, (f) lines 54–60, (g) lines 61–65.

5. As for problem 4. Form 1040, Schedule SE, short form, lines 1–6, but include the logic to determine if the short form can or can't be used. (a) use a pure data-flow graph, (b) redo using a control-flow graph model with predicate condition cover, (c) redo problem 5a using a hybrid control-flow, data-flow model.

6. Form 1040, Line 10 Worksheet. Entire form.

7. Form 1040, Line 22 Worksheet, social security income. Entire form.

8. Form 1040, Line 34 Worksheet, dependent deductions. Entire form.

9. Form 2106, Vehicle expenses only. Assume one vehicle. Include sections A, B, and C, but not D, and not lines 1–10.

10. Form 2688, Application for Extension to File. Entire form.

11. Form 2210, Underpayment of Taxes. (a) Line 1, only. (b) Part II, (c) Part III, (d) Part IV section A, (e) Part IV section B. Assume that you

can use the short method (part III) if you did not check box 1b, 1c, or 1d. In all cases, outputs (if any) go to the appropriate Form 1040 line. That is, don't worry about forms 1040A, 1040NR, 1041, and so on.

12. Model Part IV of Form 2210 as a control-flow graph with a deterministic loop and test accordingly.

13. Do all of Form 2210 as a data-flow graph with one node for each of parts II, III, IVA, and IVB. Model part I as you wish as long as the high-level model correctly specifies when to use part III.

14. Do the entire Form 3903, Employee moving expenses, as per problem 4.

6
Transaction-Flow Testing

6.1 SYNOPSIS

The transaction-flow graph is used in system testing of on-line applications and batch-processing software. It has both control-flow and data-flow attributes.

6.2 VOCABULARY

External Prerequisite Terms: absorb, acknowledge, application, archival data, auditing, batch, call, capacity, checkout, code, communications, concatenation, concurrent, crash, data, data base, data block, data error, data logging, debug, design, device driver, diagnostic, discrete, dynamic, error, global data, hierarchy, incoming, initialize, input, input error, integer, installation, interface, logic, model, multientry, multiexit, multitasking, network, operating system, outgoing, partition, performance, priority, probability distribution, processing, processor, program, programmer, programming language, protocol, query, queue, random, receipt, record, recovery, reset, resource, routing, scenario, security, sequence, server, simulator, simultaneous, snapshot, software, sort, sort key, stack, subroutine, system, task, test environment, time stamp, trace, value.

Internal Prerequisite Terms: branch, bug-free, component, component test, compound predicate, control flow, data flow, entry node, exit node, finite-state model, graph, inlink, input, integration, intermediate node, link, link cover, link weight, loop, loop testing, model program, node, node cover, outcome, outlink, path, predicate, relation, sensitize, slice, specification, state, submodel, superslice, system test, test design, test path, testing, validation criteria.

Transaction: A unit of processing work.

Transaction token: A mark (such as dot) that depicts the presence of a transaction on a model link.

Transaction control record: A hypothetical or actual record that contains data about the transaction. There need not be an actual record, but in many systems, there is. The term "transaction record" will be used for "transaction-control record" when the context is clear.

Transaction state: Potentially the values of all data in the transaction-control record or its implicit equivalent. Usually, however, the state is expressed by only part of the record's data; often an integer.

Transaction type: A designation, such as an integer, used to identify different transaction types.

Origin node: A node in a transaction-flow graph model at which the transaction begins to interest us. An entry node of a transaction-flow graph model.

Death node: A node in a transaction-flow graph model at which the transaction ceases to interest us. An exit node of a transaction-flow graph model.

Task: Each task in a transaction-flow graph is represented by a node.

Branch node: A node at which an incoming transaction takes one of several alternative outlinks: on the right, the incoming transaction has exited on the uppermost link.

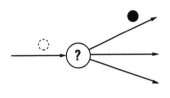

Branch predicate: A predicate that controls which outlink of a branch node is taken. It may be based on transaction data values (i.e., in the transaction control record) or, often, on a combination of the transaction type and state.

Control inlink: An inlink that controls which outlink of a branch node a transaction will take, possibly independent of values in the record. A branch node with a control inlink is like a railroad switch (i.e., "points"). There must a predicate associated with the control inlink. Control inlinks are denoted by dashed lines.

Junction node: A transaction entering at any inlink of a junction node will emerge at the junction node's outlink. This is the same as junction nodes in control-flow graphs.

Birth node: A node at which an incoming transaction produces more than one outgoing transaction. In the figure on the right, the incoming transaction (the **mother**) has given birth to a **daughter** transaction. Daughters have individual properties that may (in part) be inherited from parents.

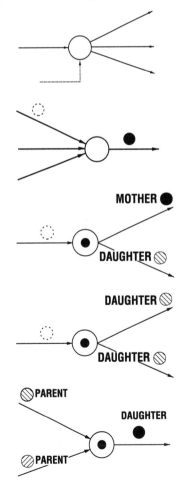

Split node: A node at which an incoming transaction (mother) gives birth to daughters but itself ceases to exist. Daughter transactions need not be identical. Each daughters is presumed to have its own properties: for example, type and state.

Merger node: A node at which two or more incoming transactions (**parents**) merge to create a new, outgoing daughter. The parents do not exist after the merger.

Absorption node: A node with incoming transactions, one of which (the **predator**) absorbs the others (the **prey**).

Markovian node: A node whose action (processing, branch, birth, split, etc.) depends only on the type and state of incoming transactions and not on the path by which the transactions reached the node.

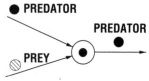

Markovian transaction-flow graph: A transaction-flow graph all of whose nodes are markovian.

6.3 THE RELATIONS AND THE MODEL

6.3.1 General [MURA89, PETE81]

Objects (nodes): Steps in transaction processing such as program steps, but they need not involve computers at all. Nodes represent actions of interest that transform incoming transactions and produce outgoing transactions and/or change the state of incoming transactions. Nodes may model programs, but also human actions, network operations, or anything that makes sense. Nodes are presumed to have a model of their own, whether the control-flow model, data-flow model, or whatever model is useful. The action taken by a processing node depends only on the data contained in transaction records of the incoming transactions. The transaction processing models are assumed to be markovian.

Objects (transactions): A transaction is represented by a transaction-control record (real or hypothetical). This record contains at least a transaction type and state. All other data of interest are assumed to be contained in the transaction record. The interpretation of the data in a transaction record does not depend on the values in any other transaction record.

Relation (links): *Directly follows.* Connect nodes A and B by a link from A to B if an outgoing transaction from A is next handled by B.

Link weights: Zero or more transaction tokens can be associated with any link. Each token represents one transaction.

We'll model part of the processing of Form 1040 as if it were done by a compulsive taxpayer who insists on doing each operation in the order in which it appears on the form. The IRS has no such requirement, and you can fill in the forms in any order that make sense, but that behavior doesn't lend itself nicely to transaction-flow modeling. (Data-flow models are better for that.) Note that we're not modeling a computer or program here (but we *could* be): We're modeling how Wylenia Wysteria (our subject) fills out an income tax return.

11:	12	Previous step in model
12:	13	NO branch node (any business income?)
	12.1	YES
12.1:	12.2	birth node,1040 goes on
	C:	daughter transaction, to Schedule C processing
C:	12.2:	filled-out Schedule C (split node)
	C-out	filled-out Schedule C to IRS
12.2:	13:	absorption node, Schedule C data are absorbed into 1040
13	...	node 13 is a junction node

Node 12 is a branch: The transaction must either go on to fill out a Schedule C or bypass that if there's no business income. Node 12.1 is a birth node that gives birth to a daughter transaction for Schedule C. At this level, we'll assume that a blank Schedule C enters node C and a filled-out Schedule C exits node C. Node 12.2 is an absorption node because the Schedule C data are entered on Form 1040. Node C is a split node because we need a copy of Schedule C for the IRS and also must enter the data on Form 1040. Node 13 is a junction node because Form 1040 could appear on either, but not both, inlinks.

6.3.2 Markings

Marking: The set of all tokens (and their associated states) on all links at any instant of time is called a **marking** of the transaction-flow graph. A marking is to the entire transaction-flow graph what a state is to an individual transaction.

Queues: A link that can be marked with more than one token represents a queue. This could, of course, be a processing queue, but it also could represent people waiting on a human queue.

We follow one transaction through the transaction-flow graph at a time. If there were no splits or births, this would be equivalent to marking a path in a control-flow graph. But two things make this simple interpretation unlikely: (1) the presence of queues, and (2) merger and absorption nodes.

We can show different markings by designating which tokens appear on which links at each step. There are two kinds of tokens in this model: Form 1040 and Schedule C, abbreviated as "T1040" and "SC-C" respectively. If there is only one transaction in the model, there are two possible markings, depending on whether we do a Schedule C.

Without Schedule C:
Step 1:   11/12   T1040
Step 2.   12/13   T1040

With Schedule C:
Step 1.   11/12 T1040
Step 2.   12/12.1 T1040
Step 3.   12.1/12.2 T1040, 12.1/C SC–C
Step 4.   12.1/12.2 T1040, C/12.2 SC–C, C/C–OUT SC–C
Step 5.   12.2/13 T1040, C/C–OUT SC–C

Suppose Wylenia's children have their own businesses and that Wylenia does their tax returns. Her children fill out their individual Schedule Cs if needed, but she'll do the 1040 forms for all of them. Form 1040s are initiated (for this **submodel** only) at node 11. The 1040s arrive at node 12, which is processed by Wylenia. She decides if a Schedule C is needed. She has many other things to do, so she may not process that decision immediately. Consequently, a queue of 1040s accumulates at the inlink of node 12. When she gets time she puts the 1040s that didn't need Schedule Cs on the queue to node 13. For those that do need one, she takes a blank Schedule C, fills in the child's name, and puts it on the Schedule C queue (12.1/C)—Schedule C processing is done by Wylenia's children. Finished Schedule Cs emerge on the C/12.2 queue where Wylenia absorbs them by transferring the data to the appropriate 1040. A queue also builds up on the 12.1/12.2 link.

The number of tokens on any link is potentially infinite, and, therefore, the number of potentially different markings for the entire graph is potentially infinite. Although Wylenia seems to have an almost infinite number of children, she has near infinite patience, so this is not a problem for her—but it is for us. Ideally, we should test transaction-flow graphs for all possible markings. Practically, this is impossible so we'll compromise.

6.3.3 QUEUES [COOP81]

All real queues are **bounded,** that is, they have maximum capacity. Systems that are not well tested often can be crashed by exceeding those capacities; queue capacity is worth testing. If there is a queue, there must be a **queue discipline**—a rule that determines the order in which transactions will be taken off a queue for processing. Here are some popular disciplines.

FIFO: first-in, first-out (also called First-Come-First-Served): The oldest transaction to enter the queue is processed first. This is the simplest discipline and very common. But imagine if Wylenia insisted that all filled-out Schedule C's were returned to her in the order in which she gave them out for processing.

LIFO: last-in, first-out (also called LCFS, Last-Come-First-Served): The youngest transaction on the queue is processed first; a processing stack in which incoming transactions are placed on the stack's top and removed from the top.

Batch: When specific conditions are met, such as the number of transactions on queue or a specific time, all transactions on the queue are processed. New transactions build up on a new queue during the processing.

Random service: Service is provided at random, possibly based on a probability distribution over some value in the transaction-control record.

Priority queues: There is a priority for each transaction. The priority might be fixed or depend on a transaction property such as age. Each priority is treated as a separate queue with the highest-priority queue processed first. Within a priority, service could be FIFO, LIFO, and so on.

Multiple servers: Queues may have one server (**single-server**) or several (**multiserver**). There can be a **server selection discipline** beyond the individual queue discipline. Examples: go to the server of your choice—the supermarket; stay on a master queue to be served by the server who says "next!"—airline ticket counters, post office, banks.

I'll use the term **"simple queue"** to mean a single-server, no-priority, FIFO queue. The simple queue is the likeliest queue if no discipline is specified. The next likeliest is FIFO within priorities: Each priority is treated as a FIFO queue, but the highest-priority queue is cleared first, then the next priority, and so on. If it's not a simple queue, test to make sure that the priority discipline and server selection discipline (if any) are properly implemented.

6.3.4 Mergers and Absorptions

The possibility of merging and absorbing nodes brings a new set of testing problems. We now need **synchronization tests**. The new problems are:

1. Have the right types of transactions been merged?

2. Is the right kind of transaction output? For absorption, the predator and for mergers, the daughter.

3. For two transactions A and B that are to merge (or for A absorbing B) there are five additional situations to test:

a. A arrives, but B never does.　　　　(A)

b. B arrives, but A never does.　　　　(B)

c. A arrives before B.　　　　　　　(A, B)

d. B arrives before A.　　　　　　　(B, A)

e. Arrive simultaneously (i.e., within a specified time). (AB)

Each of these cases must be considered during testing. A three-way merger requires 25 test cases. We'll use concatenation to denote simultaneous arrivals and commas to denote separate arrivals. For example, (AB, C) means that A and B arrive simultaneously, followed by C. There are 25 test cases to consider. Here are the test cases for a three-transaction absorption or merger:

Each alone:　　　(A) , (B) , (C)

Two at a time:　(A, B), (A, C), (B, C), (B, A), (C, A), (C, B), (AB), (AC), (BC)

Three at a time: (A, B, C), (B, A, C), (C, A, B), (A, C, B), (B, C, A), (C, B, A), (A, BC), (B, AC), (C, AB), (BC, A), (AC, B), (AB, C), (ABC)

The number of tests needed grows rapidly for mergers with several merging transactions. Test design is easy to automate, but getting transactions to arrive at the specified nodes in the specified order usually is difficult. Because mergers and absorptions usually are of transactions that have already undergone some processing rather than transactions that arrive from the outside, doing these tests is almost impossible unless consideration of them and appropriate facilities are built in to the system under test.

6.3.5 Loops

The bad news about loops within transaction flows is that, in general, they're problematic. The good news is that they are rare and when they do occur, they are simple and localized. The most common loop you'll find in transaction flows are retry loops after detecting a data input error. For example, your ATM machine allows you three tries to enter your personal identification number. Similar retry loops can be expected at most interfaces, such as communication links with other systems, device drivers, and so on. Batch service queues obviously have a loop to clear the batches. Similarly, each processor served by a queue is in a loop to service the next item on queue and to continue doing so each time it is activated until the queue is depleted. Such loops should be tested in the context of the individual processor, at a lower level of integration and testing. That is, do loop testing of the various transaction processors within the context of component testing for those processors.

6.3.6 Focus and Hierarchical Models

The transaction-flow model can be used at various levels of detail, right down to code, but it's not a good idea to build code-level transaction-flow models. Nodes in a transaction-flow graph may not represent the operation of software. I've used the term "processing" in a general sense to include any manipulation of data, whether by computers, people, or other systems. The transaction-flow model typically is used as a high- rather than low-level model. Its most common use is in system testing. Correct operation of the components should be verified by component testing, typically in a prior stage of integration. How you partition a complicated operation into the components you'll represent in a transaction-flow model is arbitrary. But here are some things to consider.

1. The model components have interfaces through which data transfers occur. Note that global data can satisfy this requirement.

2. Components don't interact except through their interfaces. If you have such components, group them and model the group as a single entity.

3. Component behavior is determined by the transaction type and state.

4. The behavior of the processor does not depend on the prior history of the transaction except insofar as that history is reflected in the transaction type and state, the individual process is markovian.

5. You can verify correct behavior of a processor by examining output transactions (or associated records) from each process in the model.

6. It is possible to do meaningful tests on the component by itself, in a suitable test environment.

The focus in transaction-flow testing should not be on the correct workings of the individual processes but on the entire system, especially on correctness of the interfaces between components, correct transaction routing between components, queue management and discipline (if not FIFO), mergers, absorptions, splits, births, synchronization, simultaneity, transaction creation and destruction, and transaction duplication and loss.

6.4 THE TECHNIQUE

6.4.1 General

I'll assume that we don't have looping transactions. If you do, hope that it is reasonable and possible to test them within a submodel that includes the loop. You'll have to use the loop testing techniques of Chapter 4 on any loops that you can't handle at a lower level.

1. Verify the specification.

2. Identify and name all the transactions that the system is required to process. You should have no trouble with "normal" transactions because these should all be in the specification. The difficulty is usually with transactions implied by the specification but not made explicit. Here's a sample of transactions often missing in specifications but that must be in your model.

   a. Acknowledgments, receipts, negative acknowledgments.

   b. Special transactions for installation and checkout.

   c. Special transactions for operational diagnostics.

   d. Transaction auditing transactions.

   e. Transactions used in human operator training modes.

   f. Initialization or reset transactions for all external interfaces.

   g. Transactions used in system recovery.

   h. Transactions used to measure system performance.

   i. Transactions used to test system security.

   j. Transactions used in protocols not otherwise considered above.

   k. Transactions used to ask about the status of other transactions.

   l. Responses to transaction status requests.

   m. Transactions generated by your system used in transaction recovery.

   n. Recovery transactions from an outside systems.

3. Define a hierarchy of transaction types that includes all of the transactions discovered in step 2 above. Usually you'll be able to use the same hierarchy used by the developers; doing so will make communications easier.

4. Define the transaction state for each transaction type. The states should correspond to the processing sequence appropriate to the transaction type. If the states are a simple progression of numbers, such as "Step 1, Step 2, Step 3, ... Exit", a list will suffice. If more complex behavior is indicated, you may have to use a **finite-state model** (Chapter 9).

5. Identify how every transaction is: born (or enters the system), dies (or leaves the system), merges (with whom), absorptions, splits, births, and so on.

6. Define a hypothetical transaction-control record for every transaction type. The record must include at least the transaction type and state. Again, in most decent transaction-processing systems, you should be able to adopt an actual transaction-control record implemented in the software. For external transactions, such as those processed by other

systems or by humans, say, you will have to define an appropriate hypothetical record.

7. Identify all queues. For each queue, define: the origin(s)—where the transactions come from, queue discipline, priorities within discipline, batch versus continuous. Check limits for all queues that have capacity limits.

   a. How are items placed on the queue by all entities that can do so?

   b. How are items removed from the queue by all entities that can do so?

   c. Single or multiserver. If multiserver, what is the server selection discipline?

8. Identify processing components (not necessarily software). Group the components according to the principles of section 6.3.6 above. You may have to redefine transaction types, merge transaction types, remove queues, and so on, if this modeling stage results in your grouping several components in order to satisfy the criteria of section 6.3.6 .

9. For each component defined in step 8, decide how you will test that component by itself. It could in itself be yet another, lower-level transaction-flow model or a different kind of model.

10. Even though the real components don't necessarily operate that way, separate split/births and mergers/absorptions from their associated processing nodes by putting an explicit split/birth node after the processing node and an explicit merger/absorption node before the processing node.

11. You should, after doing the above, have a set of nodes and links that define the full set of transaction flows to be tested.

12. Confirm the model by using a model program in a convenient programming language. This can be effective in transaction-flow models because they tend to be big. The typical transaction-processing system has many simple transactions. By "many" I mean thousands. By "simple" I mean that branches, junctions, splits, births, mergers, and absorptions are sparse.

13. Select your test "paths"—they have aspects of both paths and slices.

   Continue as with other techniques:

14. Sensitize the slices.

15. Predict outcomes.

16. Define validation criteria.

17. Run the tests.

18. Confirm outcome.

19. Confirm values at all intermediate nodes.

6.4.2 A Coverage Hierarchy

As always, there's a range of coverage criteria to use, from the simplest (but least effective and cheapest) to the strongest (thorough but expensive).

1. **Origin/Exit, Birth/Death Cover.** Run enough tests to ensure that *every* transaction origin and birth has been exercised and that all outgoing transactions (including those born in the system) have been produced. This may seem very weak, but it is more than many systems get. Include *all* the transaction types mentioned in section 6.4.1 above (and any I didn't mention that are specific to your application). This is the least that a rational person can do. The commonsense notion is equivalent to ensuring that every line of code has been tested at the component level. If someone proposes not testing a transaction type, then he or she is either asserting that the transaction is bug-free or not needed. If not needed, take it out because that's one less source of bugs. The buggiest transactions are those that occur most infrequently. Recovery-related transactions are notorious in this respect.

2. **Node Cover.** Node cover alone also doesn't make sense because it only reaffirms what should have been tested in a lower-level model, in component testing, say. Node cover is better than nothing because we'll confirm that all births, splits, mergers, absorptions, and queue disciplines work correctly. That's also more than many systems get.

3. **Link Cover.** With link cover we confirm not only the correctness of the individual nodes, but how they work with one another. Without link cover we're not really doing system testing. With link cover, we ensure that every transaction is not only correctly processed (node cover does that for us) but also that the *right* transactions are processed at every step.

4. **Slices.** The notion of slice here is almost identical to that of data-flow slice discussed in Chapter 5. If there are only branch and junction nodes, a **slice** corresponds to an entry-exit path of the model. If there are births or splits, a **slice** is constructed by following all outlinks of the birth or split node and following those transactions to their death nodes. If there are merger or absorption nodes, a **slice** is constructed by following the inlinks back to the points at which the merged (predictor/prey) transactions were born or came into the system. We'll have more on slicing below in section 6.4.4.

6.4.3 Building the Model

I'd like to create a transaction-flow model for tax returns, but because there is no order implicit in doing tax returns, this model is really not appropriate. A data-flow model is probably the best choice. However, in order to base as many exercises as possible on the tax forms and to show you that almost any model can be used with any application, we'll model the Employee Business Expense Form 2106. I'll treat each input or group of inputs as if they were transactions.

Ex1:	L6a	General employee expense data treated as a single transaction containing: Line 2 (parking, tolls, etc.), Line 3 (travel excluding meals and entertainment, Line 4 (other business expenses excluding meals and entertainment), Line 5 (meals and entertainment). This is an incoming transaction—i.e., from an origin node.
Gv1:	L11	General vehicle data, including the data entered on Lines 11, 12, 13, 15, 18, 19, 20, and 21. There could be more than one vehicle, so there can be zero to n tokens on this origin node. One of these is needed for each vehicle claimed.
Ae1:	L23	Actual expenses, including the data entered on Lines 23, 24a, 24b, and 25. You do not need this data if you elect to use the standard mileage rate. However, you can elect to use the actual expenses. You could have zero to n for this origin node. The number can be less than the number for the Gv1 tokens, but not greater.
De1:	L30	Depreciation. This includes the data on lines 30, 31, 33, and 36. This origin node cannot have more tokens than Ae1 because you do not have to depreciate all the vehicles you own.
F1:	F1a	An origin node with a blank form 2106 (except for name, social security number, and occupation). This form will be processed and eventually pass back to Schedule A, Line 20, which is where it originated.
F1a:	L1	F1a is a branch node that decides if there is or is not to be vehicle processing. This (L1) is the NO branch. The 2106 transaction either goes along this branch or the F1y branch, but not both.
	F1y	The YES branch assuming that there is at least one vehicle.
L1:	L6a	L1 is a junction node that will accept a 2106 transaction either from F1a (no vehicle expenses) or V1 (vehicle expenses completed).
L6a:	L10	An absorption node that absorbs the general employee expense data (Ex1). Form 2106 is the predator. Ex1 is the prey and ceases to exist.
L10:		Exit (pass this transaction back to Schedule A).
F1y:	L11a	L11a is a birth node where you give birth to the appropriate number of transactions: one for each vehicle.
	V1	This is where you pass the blank 2106 waiting for the vehicle deduction.
V1	L1	V1 is an absorption node where the vehicle deduction is entered on the Form 2106.
Vsum	V1	Vsum is the node at which the data for all the vehicles are merged.
L11a:	Vsum	The details are left to you as an exercise (2).

Some explanatory notes are in order. **L11**, **L11a**, **L23**, and **L30** are in a processing submodel where most of the actual processing required by the form is done. At this level of the model, we assume that processing is done correctly, with the result presented at node **Vsum**. You are asked to provide a detailed model of this processing in exercise 2. After you've done a transaction-flow model for this processing, I hope you'll agree with me that either a data-flow or a control-flow model is more appropriate. The way I partitioned this model was sensible to me and closely follows the structure of the forms provided by the IRS. You may have a different way of looking at this that will result in a different, but equally effective, partition of the problem.

6.4.4 Select Test Paths and/or Slices

We have several different situations to consider, depending on whether we have births/splits and/or mergers/absorptions. In all cases, we assume that there are no loops or that the loops can be embedded in submodels. Because transaction-flow models usually consist of many small, independent submodels, it is likely that even though you elected to use the transaction-flow model, some of the submodels might have been better done by control-flow or data-flow models. Here are some common cases to consider:

1. Pure control-flow model, only branches and junctions.
2. Mergers and absorption nodes, no branches, no junctions.
3. Mergers and absorption nodes with branches and junctions.
4. Control flows with splits and births, no mergers or absorptions.
5. General case.

CASE 1: PURE CONTROL FLOWS.

This case is just like control-flow testing. If all the transaction flows were like this, a control-flow model would be a better choice. If, as most parts of the model will be, a single transaction enters the model and the same transaction eventually leaves the model, there is not much to add that hasn't been said in Chapter 3. There are three differences, however, for transaction-flow models as compared to control-flow models.

1. There are usually many transaction flows to consider, even though each of them is relatively simple.
2. Multientry/multiexit models are likely. Transactions can come from different sources and therefore be placed on different input processing queues. Transactions can go to different destinations and therefore be placed on different output queues. It is not enough to confirm the correctness of the transaction processing; you must confirm that the transactions went from the right entry to the right exit. In principle, *you*

should not be satisfied with mere link cover, but you should consider redoing link cover for every entry-exit combination that makes sense.

3. You still have queue disciplines to consider and test.

CASE 2: MERGERS AND ABSORPTION NODES, NO BRANCHES, NO JUNCTIONS.

This is effectively a pure data-flow model, as discussed in Chapter 5, section 5.4.4 You must create one slice for each possible output. You create a slice by starting at the output node and working backward toward the origin node(s) for that output. Include all back-branches because all of them contribute to the processing. In our example, slicing back from **L10** we come to **L6a**. We must then include the link from **L1** (and all that feeds into it) and the link from **Ex1**, because both contribute data to the processing at **L6a**.

CASE 3: MERGERS AND ABSORPTION NODES WITH BRANCHES AND JUNCTIONS.

No births or splits. Several transactions enter and fewer will exit, having absorbed incoming transactions. This is similar to Case 3 in Chapter 5, section 5.4.4. If you have read the chapter, you should reread this case and translate the concepts to their equivalent transaction-flow concepts. If you have not read the chapter, read this case and ignore what it has to say about selector nodes. Be sure to provide at least enough paths to guarantee link cover (as always).

Do a slice as in Case 2, but for junction nodes, you must follow both inlinks to that junction to ensure that all data sources have been included. This slice (actually, a **superslice**) defines a *set* of test cases. Consider the branch nodes. Each branch control value defines an alternate path. Select an alternative. Now some of the source transactions will no longer be needed. Eliminate them. Continue until you have picked only one specific path (and associated input transactions). Do it again with another choice for the branch, for another test case. Continue until you have achieved (at least) link cover.

CASE 4: CONTROL FLOWS WITH SPLITS AND BIRTHS, NO MERGERS OR ABSORPTIONS.

This is an easy case. Start at the output and create a slice for each transaction that eventually gets to the exit nodes. Create one slice (from the exit to all affected origin nodes) for each output transaction. Within that slice, further subdivide (more test cases) to provide link cover for branch nodes.

CASE 5: GENERAL CASE.

There are no simple rules. The idea is to slice for each output transaction. Include all incoming transactions that provide data. If there are control flows in any of those slices, be sure to subdivide them into further test cases to ensure at least link cover for each such slice. This may seem to create redundant test cases because the slices overlap and having provided link cover for transaction type A (slice A, say) it seems redundant to do it yet again for transaction type B (on a different slice that incorporates some of the same branches). The justification is provided by asking "For what are we testing?" I said earlier that system testing was not the place to test the workings of the individual nodes but the place to test to see if the transactions are passed around properly from process to process. Because most processing (in a transaction-flow context) contains conditional branches that are in part based on transaction types, it is not redundant to test the same logic with different transaction types. In fact, it is likely that such "redundant" link cover may be the only way to exercise some deeply buried compound predicates.

The preceding prescriptions yields two families of tests:

L10/L6a/ex1, L6a/L1/F1a/F1
L10/L6a/ex1, L6a/L1/V1/F1y/F1a/F1, V1/Vsum/...L11a...Gv1/Ae1/De1

These are *families* of tests because the case with vehicles yields many tests and also because we must check synchronization issues and queue behavior.

6.4.5 Synchronization Tests

Whenever two or more transactions merge or one absorbs another, we must design and run synchronization tests. For our example, we can consider either node **L6a** or node **V1**, both of which are absorption nodes. Node **L6a** is straightforward; we need five tests. Node **V1** is more interesting and likelier to be productive because it involves merging a form (vehicle deduction) that was born within the same model. You might look at this model and wrongly say: "I don't need five cases. The path from **F1y** to **V1** is obviously shorter than the path through the vehicle processing (from **L11a** to **Vsum**). Therefore, I can assume that the 2106 transaction is always at node **V1** before the vehicle data and is waiting for it. So the only cases to consider are: (1) Form 2106 arrives before vehicle data and (2) no vehicle data."

If you do think that way, you've made a bad assumption and possibly fallen into the same trap that the programmers whose software you are testing fell into. Those *are* rational assumptions, but the buggy world isn't rational. Furthermore, the inlinks to **V1** could both be queues (not for this discussion), and queue disciplines could cause all kinds of rearrangements.

Unless you can show that only one specified order is possible (Form 2106 arrives before vehicle data, say), you better test all the cases. The system should behave reasonably for all cases—by which I mean that it doesn't crash or corrupt or lose data, but it can reject incomplete transactions (with notification).

How far should we take synchronization tests? Should we consider the interactions of one merger node with another farther down the slice? Hypothetically yes, but practically no. The number of tests grows exponentially and there's no evidence that higher-order synchronization tests are productive. Furthermore, setting up synchronization tests for one merger will be difficult enough; setting them up for a sequence of mergers may be impossible.

"The same merger node appears in several slices," you say. "Should we repeat the synchronization tests of such nodes in each slice?" Probably not, mainly because trying that will lead to a vast expansion of test cases. But there's a better reason: You'll probably exercise those cases cheaper and faster with automatically generated, suitably crafted random test cases.

6.4.6 Queue Tests

Any queue that isn't a simple one should be given a battery of queue tests. Where should it be done, in system testing or in lower-level component testing? If the node has one inlink representing one queue and I have reason to believe that management of that queue is done by the component that the node represents (because I peeked at the design), then my preference is to do the queue tests in the context of the component tests. If it is a merger or absorption or junction node (several inlinks), then I would do the queue tests at the component level and repeat those tests during system testing. The tests you need depends on the queue discipline and server selector discipline (if any). Here are some good tests.

1. **Queue Length Limit Tests.**

   a. Maximum queue capacity. Attempt to put more items on the queue than allowed by the capacity limit.

   b. Null-queue. Activate the processor with nothing on the queue.

   c. Loop tests. The queue processor has an implied loop to process the items on queue (especially for batch servers). Use loop testing methods on the number of items on queue.

   d. Dynamic changes in queue length. Attempting to add a transaction to a queue (especially batch processing queue) while the queue is being processed is an obvious test case. But if the system's working permits it, remove an item from the queue while the queue processor is active.

2. **Sorting and Selection Tests.** Many queue disciplines include a sort process. For example, say that the discipline is to serve the oldest transaction first. This is not the same as a FIFO queue. A FIFO queue is based on the position of the item on the queue. The oldest-first discipline is based on a time stamp in the transaction control record. Because transactions take different paths to get to any given queue, the FIFO order may not correspond to the time stamp order. Another example is priority queues where there is an implied sort on a priority value.

The processing could have an explicit sort or, if the queues are short, a scan through the entire queue to select the next item to be processed. Both of these are an implied sorting process. Sorting always is done on an actual or implied sort key. There are some elegant ways to test sort processing routines, but they are beyond the scope of this book. We'll stick to some simple but productive heuristics. Here are some good cases to try.

a. Perfect ordering

b. All items have identical sort key values

c. Items in reversed order

d. Only one item on queue; try for all discrete key values (e.g., priority)

e. One item for each discrete key value

f. If there are multiple keys (e.g., age within priority), consider combinations of the above tests in the spirit of nested loop testing

3. **Queue Discipline Tests.** If there is a queue discipline other than FIFO, you should run queue discipline tests to ensure that the correct discipline has been implemented. If the discipline has an implied sort (e.g., priority) then use sort tests, as above. Beyond that, it's hard to generalize because queue disciplines can be so varied.

4. **Priority Tests.** Distinguish between: (a) multiple priorities on a single queue and (b) a separate queue for each priority. The first case is a sort test based on the priority. The second case yields some additional tests:

a. Only one priority present, separately for each priority.

b. All priorities present, one item for each.

c. All priorities present, several items for each.

d. Priority changes while processing (if allowed by the application). Test both priority upgrades and downgrades.

Priority queues deserve special attention, especially if there are other keys used by other processes. For example, say that on one queue, the key is based on a value field, while on another queue, the key is a security field. On the value key, first the highest-value transaction is processed, then the next, and so on. On the security queue, first top-secret transactions are processed, then secret, then confidential, and so on. Both are priority queues because even though one field is called "value" and the other is called "security," the behavior of both is a priority queue. Why the concern? Because when this situation occurs, there's a high likelihood that a programmer confuses the two and uses the wrong key. I've seen "privacy" confused with "security" and both confused with "priority."

5. **Server Selection Discipline Tests.** Test multiple servers on a single queue in lower-level component testing. If you have several queues as

inlinks to a multiple server, then server discipline should be tested (or at least retested) during system testing. The server selection discipline should be thoroughly tested, and the flavor is much like the sorting tests:

a. All items on one queue

b. All queues with one item

c. All queues with the same number of items

6.4.7 Sensitize

The sensitization issue is different for transaction-flow testing than for control-flow or data-flow testing. The problem is not finding the transaction data that will cause the transaction to follow a specific path. The problem actually is creating a transaction that will do that and getting such transactions into the system. While ordinary transactions tend not to be very difficult, the transactions types listed in section 6.4.1, step 2, page 130 are sometimes impossible to get. Here are some generic problems and what you can do about them.

1. **Errors, Negative Acknowledgments and Recovery Transactions from Other Systems.** These have been my bane. You can't get these without getting the other system to misbehave. You want a transaction from the other system that informs you that one of your data blocks has been lost or garbled. You can't not send it the block or send it a garbled block because that error may be detected by intervening systems. You have to get the other system to send you an error message even though there has been no actual error. You try to cooperate, but these guys, as a matter of national pride, insist that "Our system never sends erroneous messages!" You try to push the issue, and you end up talking to an irate flunky in a pin-striped suit from State Department headquarters in Foggy Bottom—you didn't expect to create an international incident.* I don't have a satisfactory technical solution because it's not a technical problem. At least you'll have to build a simulator of each such uncooperative interface and test all the cases with the simulator; then hope for the best when you go live.

2. **Internal Transactions Related to System Recovery and Illogical Conditions.** The system should protect itself from abuse, such as hardware or software failures. You can't test such protective mechanisms without the ability to create the very situation against which the system is intended to protect itself. Are there security measures? You must violate security doctrines. Is there failure recovery? You must simulate every failure mechanism and transactions that result therefrom.

---

* It really happened to me.

3. **Internal Transactions for Data Recovery and Illogical Conditions.**
If the system detects lost or duplicated transactions, then the tester
must be able to lose them or duplicate them. Every data recovery mechanism responds to specific data loss or garble scenarios. You must stim-
ulate each such scenario with appropriate transactions.

The practical issue in sensitization is how to generate and inject the
transactions you need to test a system properly. The only sane way to do that
is have a transaction generator built in at an early stage in the design. At the
very least, the generator should be able to:

1. Create any specified transaction, both correctly and incorrectly.

2. Put that transaction at any point on any specified queue.

3. Remove specified transactions from queues.

6.4.8 Predict Outcomes

It is not your objective to confirm detailed transaction data during system
testing. The issue in system testing (under a transaction-flow model) is to
verify correct routing of transactions, including births, deaths, and the like.
The expected outcome, then, is identifying what transactions should be on
which queues before and after the test—to predict the final marking given
the initial marking.

The practical issue is not predicting the outcome but verifying it. You
must compare all affected queues before and after the test. At least you'll
need the ability to run a test and freeze the system or, alternatively, some
means of taking a snapshot of all the affected queues. Test tools are implied
and are best built in to the design.

6.4.9 Path Verification

It's really slice verification if there are mergers or births. The problem (as it
always seems to be in system testing) is not how to verify a path, but how to
build in the tools by which you do it. There are two primary sources of supporting data, and in both cases you'll probably have to build a fairly elaborate verifier program because it's unlikely that a general-purpose tool can
handle all the possibilities of your transactions.

1. **Existing Records.** Transaction-processing systems usually have transaction activity records required by the application, such as: billing
information, security logs, recovery data, archival data. The points at
which such data are recorded are often also the points that you want to
verify. For example, it is common for a recovery system to record the
contents of all active queues. Before you ask for extensive data logging
to be built in to the system, examine all logs and records required by the

application and see how well that data helps you to verify the path.

2. **Built-in Logging.** Augment the application data just discussed with other records as needed to fill in blank spots. Keep these to a minimum so that the system's behavior is not materially affected by the additional data logging. This is usually possible, and often the total processing resources needed to satisfy even lavish transaction logging amounts only to a few percent of the available processing resources. As usual, such logging facilities must be built in because they are very difficult to retrofit.

3. **Trace Mode Operation.** This is the nicest kind of logging. Transactions can be run in a **trace mode,** during which a running record of all invoked processes and queues on which the transaction passed are recorded. It has to be built in, of course. Whatever a trace mode's value is to the tester, it is completely justified as a system debugging tool.

6.5 APPLICATION CONSIDERATIONS

6.5.1 Application Indicators

How much of the system's behavior can you model this way? The applicability can be judged from positive answers to most of the following questions.

1. Are there discrete units of work?
2. Do work unit pass between processes by queues or similar interfaces?
3. Are there multiple servers?
4. Do processes work quasi-concurrently?
5. Do processes communicate by messages?

6.5.2 Bug Assumptions

The primary bug assumptions should be that individual processes work correctly (having been extensively tested at an earlier stage of integration) and that the bugs to be found result from the incorrect implementation of inter-component communications and the vagaries of multitasking.

1. **Wrong queues.** Queues missing, extra queues, wrong kind of queues.
2. **Incorrect births or splits.** Wrong type born, wrong parent, duplicated.

3. **Incorrect mergers or absorptions.** Wrong merged or absorbed, lost.

4. **Queue routing errors.** Connections of outputs to the wrong input queue.

5. **Queue discipline errors.** Wrong queue discipline invoked.

6.5.3 Limitations and Caveats

We've assumed a decent design: The design is hierarchical, there is clear separation between processing and queue management, with explicit transaction types, explicit transaction control records, and centralized transaction routing. The better the design, the likelier you are to achieve good coverage with transaction-flow testing. That means that you'll be able to make reasonable predictions (with suitable tests) of the software's fitness for use. Suppose that it's a bad design; is transaction-flow testing then not useful? It is still very useful. The tests discussed here will break a bad design easily. What you lose with a bad design is the ability to make statistically reasonable predictions about fitness for use.

The single most important limitation of this model is the insistence on markovian behavior. With nonmarkovian behavior you have no choice but to test every possible path for every possible transaction, because behavior depends not only on the data in the transaction but on its past history. That kind of testing rarely is practical. Reasonable notions of coverage are useless for nonmarkovian behavior. If you have such behavior and you do the tests suggested here, you will only achieve false confidence. Nonmarkovian behavior can be arbitrarily complex, so whatever you do cover can represent an insignificant sample of the possibilities. What should you do if you encounter nonmarkovian behavior?

1. **Remove it by redesign.** Always the best option. The nonmarkovian behavior usually isn't required. It comes about because people didn't consider the issue.

2. **Isolate it.** Put a fence around it. You may have to do this when your model must include things such as human behavior or the behavior of other systems that you cannot control. Putting a fence around it can be done by imposing operational restrictions (change the specification) or by grouping that behavior in a submodel that you will test very thoroughly before you get into the high-level system test.

3. **Accept the risk.** This may be appropriate. What's acceptable for entertainment software is not acceptable for life-critical software.

6.5.4 Automation and Tools

Consider test execution automation and test design automation separately.

1. **Test Execution Automation.** Execution automation needs were dis-

cussed in part in sections 6.4.7 to 6.4.9 above. As for commercially available test tools, capture/playback systems and scripting languages are the most likely tools for test execution automation. In most systems worthy of the name, however, a built-in test tool is mandatory.

2. **Test Design Automation.** This can range from trivial to a system in its own right. Test generator languages and systems (commercial, private) abound. It would not be unreasonable to expend five work years to create a special-purpose automatic test transaction generator for a project whose labor content was 100 work years. While there are rarely insurmountable technical problems, I'll admit that convincing the appropriate people that a test tool of this kind is worth the time and effort can be difficult and frustrating.

6.6 SUMMARY

The transaction-flow model is an effective model for high-level system testing of many systems. Modeling begins by identifying the transactions to be modeled, especially their birth and death places and the circumstances thereof. The markovian assumption is basic to this model. It is also assumed that detailed processing models have been constructed and used in lower-level component testing at a prior stage of integration. The focus in transaction-flow testing is the queues and how transactions are routed within the system. A heuristic coverage hierarchy based on a form of slicing was provided.

6.7 SELF-EVALUATION QUIZ

1. **Define (in the context of transaction flow testing):** absorption node, batch service, birth/death cover, birth node, bounded queue, branch node, branch predicate, control inlink, daughter transaction, death node, FCFS, FIFO, junction node, LCFS, LIFO, link cover, marking, markovian node, markovian flowgraph, merger node, mother transaction, multiserver queue, node cover, origin/exit cover, origin node, parent transaction, predator transaction, prey transaction, priority queue, priority tests, queue discipline, queue discipline tests, queue tests, random service, server selection discipline, single-server queue, slice, sorting tests, split node, synchronization tests, task, trace mode operation, transaction, transaction branch node, transaction branch predicate, transaction control record, transaction junction node, transaction logging, transaction selection tests, transaction state, transaction token, transaction type.

2. Do a detailed model for the vehicle expenses portion of Form 2106. Allow up to n vehicles. You enter with the appropriate data for each vehicle (**Gv1, Ae1, De1, L11a**), taking into account that you can use actual expenses and depreciation only if you own the vehicle; but you do not have to use actual expenses and if you do, you do not have to claim depreciation. Assume that you will pick the method that provides the greatest deduction (standard versus actual). Enter this submodel with the data for all the vehicles and exit with a single number for the total vehicle deduction (**Vsum**). Do the model, pick the paths, sensitize them, define what you will confirm, handle the synchronization for merging transactions, and so on. Do only clean tests.

3. Design dirty test cases for problem 2 above. Assume that vehicle data can be lost, duplicated, or spurious. Note that you can't use detailed expenses from one vehicle and depreciation for another. Each vehicle's data (**Gv1, Ae1, De1**) must be part of a consistent set for that vehicle.

4. It takes five test cases for a two-transaction merger and 25 tests for three transaction mergers. How many does it take for a four transaction merger? How many does it take for n transaction mergers?

5. Do transaction-flow models for Form 1040: (a) lines 7–22, (b) lines 23–30, (c) lines 32–40, (d) lines 41–45, (e) lines 47–53, (f) lines 54–60. In each case, assume that all input values enter as a single transaction, possibly from a previous block of lines. Model these calculations as a single processing element that need not be tested. Model every form and schedule mentioned as transactions that may be born and/or absorbed as appropriate. Include the logic used to determine if such forms are or are not needed. For example, on line 14 if there are "other gains" a Form 4797 will be created and returned properly filled out, to be absorbed back into the 1040 Form: similarly for W2, Schedule B, Schedule C, Form 3903, and so on. Do not attempt to model these forms. Create blank forms as needed by the logic, pass them to an appropriate forms processor then merge the returned forms' data back into the appropriate Form 1040 line. Design the following kinds of tests: node cover, link cover, birth/death cover.

6. Do problem 5 assuming that the subsidiary forms, even though opened, may be abandoned because it turned out they weren't needed after all.

7. Redo problem 5 under the assumption that the various lines can be filled out in any order at all as long as the prerequisite data are present (e.g., you can't add numbers until they are entered). Design the required synchronization tests assuming that incoming forms arrive one at a time, but in any reasonable order.

7
Domain Testing

7.1 SYNOPSIS

Domain testing is used to test software or portions of software dominated by numerical processing. It replaces the common heuristic method of testing extreme values and limit values of inputs.

7.2 VOCABULARY

External Prerequisite Terms: algebra, ambiguous, application, approximate, array, calculate, **CASE** statement, classification, code, coefficient, collinear, constant, contradictory, coordinate axes, coplanar, data validation, dimension, equation, equidistant, expression, **FALSE**, function, hierarchy, **IF-THEN-ELSE**, implementation, inequality, intersect, line, linear, logic, maintenance, mean, model, nonlinear, numerical, overlap, parallel, plane, point, polynomial, precision, processing, program, programmer, radius, region, round-off, set, software, space, subset, surface, symbolic substitution, system, table, table-driven, testability, transformation, tree, **TRUE**, underflow, user, variable, value.

Internal Prerequisite Terms: blind, bug, coincidental correctness, control flow, data flow, graph, input, link, link cover, link weight, object, outcome, node, node cover, node weight, output, predicate, relation, specification, test, test case, transaction flow.

Input variable: A numerical object presented to the system under test for processing by it. In general, the system processes n input variables.

Input vector: A set of values of the n input variables consisting of one value for each variable. For our purposes, the input vector is treated as it if were an array. Alternatively and equivalently, **test vector, test point**.

Input space: The n-dimensional abstract space over which the input vector is defined. With input variables, you have an n-dimensional input space.

Output variable: In domain testing, a numerical variable of the system under test. In general, the system calculates values for m different output variables.

Output vector: A set of m values of the output variables. As with the input vector, the output vector can be treated as if it is an array.

Output space: The m-dimensional space of the output vector.

Domain: A subset of the input space over which processing done by the system under test is defined. We ask that it be possible to determine if a given input vector is or is not within that domain. In domain testing, domains are defined by a set of **boundary inequalities** (see below).

Range: A subset of the output space consisting of the values calculated (output) by the system under test. There is a range corresponding to every domain.

Domain boundary: A means by which a domain is defined. Typically, these take the form of algebraic inequalities. The term "boundary" by itself will be taken to mean "domain boundary" where such usage is unambiguous.

Boundary inequality: An algebraic expression over the input variables that defines (in part) which points in the input space belong to the domain of interest. For example, the inequality $x >= 7$ states that the points in the domain of interest all have a value of 7 or greater in the input variable **x**.

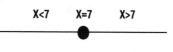

Boundary equation: The equation obtained by converting a boundary inequality into an equation (e.g., by changing a ">=" symbol to "=").

Domain boundary set: A set of inequalities which together define a domain: example, $x >= 7, x < 44$ define a domain as the numbers between 7 and 44, including 7 but not including 44.

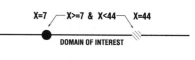

Because a proper set of boundary inequalities define a domain, we will often speak of that set of inequalities as being the domain itself.

Closed boundary: A boundary of a domain is closed if the points on the boundary are included in the domain of interest: For example, in $x >= 7$, the boundary is closed because the value 7 is included in the domain of interest. In one dimension, closed boundaries will be designated by a solid dot.

Open boundary: A boundary is open if it is not closed: the points on the boundary do not belong to the domain of interest, they belong to the **adjacent domain**, if any. In the previous example, the domain of interest is closed at $x = 7$ and open at $x = 44$ because the point $x = 44$ is not in the domain. In one dimension, open boundaries are designated by a hatched dot.

Closed domain: A domain all of whose boundaries are closed.

Open domain: A domain all of whose boundaries are open. Domains need not be either open or closed: as in a domain with at least one open and one closed boundary. In the example on the right, the domain of interest is bounded by five inequalities: $X > 0$, $X <= 12$, $2Y <= X + 4, 2Y >= X - 8$, and $Y > 0$. In two dimensions, the hachure indicate the side on which the

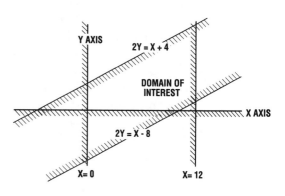

domain is closed. In the previous example, the X (**Y = 0**) and Y axes (**X = 0**) are not included in the domain of interest, but the line **X = 12** and the two diagonal boundaries are included.

Hyperplane: In n-dimensional space, a **hyperplane** is a linear surface of fewer than n dimensions. For example, in the two-dimensional plane, a line or a point is a hyperplane; in one-dimensional space, points are hyperplanes. In three-dimensional space, hyperplanes are planes, lines, and points. Domain boundaries are hyperplanes, usually but not always, of dimension n–1.

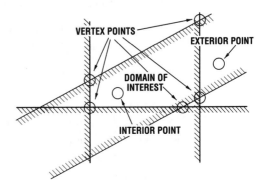

Vertex point: A point where two or more domain boundaries cross: also called "extreme point" in the literature. For n dimensions, a vertex point is a solution to n simultaneous (**linearly independent**) boundary equations.

Interior point: A point within a domain of interest.

Exterior point: A point outside of a domain of interest.

Degenerate domain: In n-dimensions, a domain of less than n dimensions. For example, in two dimensions, a degenerate domain consists of a point or a line. In three dimensions, a degenerate domain consists of a point, line, or plane.

Degenerate boundary: In n-dimensional space, a domain boundary of less than n-1 dimensions. In three dimensions, for example, a degenerate domain boundary is a boundary that consists of a line or a point rather than a plane. In two dimensions, it is a domain boundary that consists of a point rather than a line.

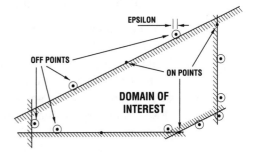

Adjacent domains: Two domains are **adjacent** if they have a boundary inequality in common. If the domain of interest is closed with respect to a boundary, the adjacent domain (for that boundary) must be open, and vice-versa. For example, on the right, the domain of interest is closed with respect to the upper diagonal boundary line so the adjacent domain above that line is open with respect to that boundary.

Epsilon neighborhood (of a point): A small region surrounding a point, at a radius of ϵ (epsilon), where ϵ is an arbitrary but small value. Practically speaking, we pick ϵ to be smaller than the smallest numerical value that interests us in the application. That is, it is the largest value ϵ such that an error of ϵ or less is tolerable for that application.

ON point: A point on a domain boundary or as close to the boundary as possible while still satisfying the conditions associated with the boundary.*

OFF point [COHE78]: If the domain is open with respect to a boundary, then an OFF point of that boundary is an interior point, just inside the boundary (within an ϵ-neighborhood). If the domain is closed, then an OFF point is an exterior point, just outside the boundary. That is, ". . . an OFF point is one that does *not* satisfy the . . . conditions associated with the boundary[JENG94]." Obviously, two adjacent domains can share the same OFF point. You can remember this definition by using the following acronym: **COOOOI**—**C**losed **OFF O**utside, **O**pen **OFF I**nside.

Linear inequality: An inequality of the form: $a_1x_1 + a_2x_2 + a_3x_3 \ldots a_nx_n + k >= 0$, where x_i are elements of the input vector (i.e., input variables), a_i are numerical coefficients, and k is a constant term. In domain testing, domain boundaries are often described by linear inequalities.

Linear domain: A domain all of whose boundary inequalities are linear.

Nonlinear domain: A domain with at least one boundary that is not linear.

Linearly dependent: Two inequalities are **linearly dependent** if you can transform one into the other by dropping the constant term (k) and then multiplying all the coefficients (a_i) of the inequality by a suitable value. For example, $x + 2y >= 7$ and $3x + 6y < 5$ are linearly dependent because dropping the constant terms and multiplying the first inequality by 3, we get $3x + 6y$. Linearly dependent hyperplanes are **parallel** to one another. In the previous sketch, the diagonal boundaries are dependent.

Linearly independent: Inequalities are linearly independent if they are not dependent. A set of inequalities are independent if none of them are linearly dependent on any other; the boundary equations of linearly independent inequalities must intersect.

Linearly independent points: A set of p points (e.g., input vectors) v_1, v_2, $v_3 \ldots v_p$ are **linearly independent** if the only solution to $c_1v_1 + c_2v_2 + c_3v_3 \ldots c_pv_p = 0$ is that all the coefficients ($c_1, c_2, \ldots$) are zero. If a set of points are not **linearly independent**, then they are linearly dependent and it is possible to express some of those points in terms of the others.

---

* This might be necessitated by the limitations of computer's number representation method [JENG94]. For example, a function defined over integers might have no exact solution on the boundary itself.

Complete boundary: A boundary that extends to $+-\infty$ in all of its variables. We will assume that boundaries are complete, unless stated otherwise. The upward slanting boundary on the right is complete because it presumably extends to $+-\infty$ in both variables.

Boundary segment: Part of a boundary inequality between two or more domains: that is, one of the edges of a domain. Generally, a boundary inequality defines boundary segments for many different domains.

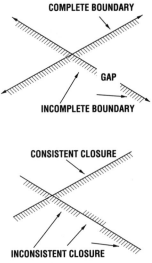

Incomplete boundary: A boundary with one or more gaps. The downward slanting boundary in the sketch is incomplete because it has a gap. Gaps, when they do occur, are between vertex points; that is, they consist of boundary segments.

Consistent closure: A boundary for which the closure direction (open versus closed) is the same along its entire extent. We will assume in the sequel that boundary closures are consistent unless stated otherwise. The boundary marked "consistent" in the previous sketch has the same closure all along its length.

Inconsistent closure: A boundary for which the closure direction changes at least once along its extent. The boundary marked "inconsistent" in the previous sketch changes its closure. Closure changes, when they occur, usually occur at vertex points. That is, the closure change is usually between boundary segments.

7.3 THE RELATIONS AND THE MODEL

7.3.1 Motivation

I'll change the usual order and start with motivation and semantics for domain testing because the previous definitions may be more abstract than many readers prefer; but I will assume that you understand those definitions.

Domain testing is based on a simple processing model illustrated in Figure 7.1. The system under test accepts an input vector, which then goes

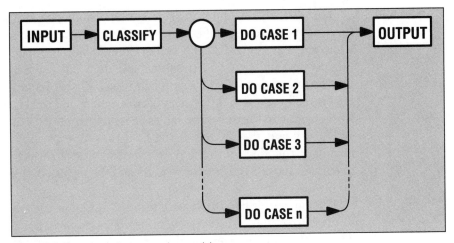

Figure 7.1 Domain testing processing model.

through a classification process. Any input values that are outside of their defined acceptable values are rejected or corrected if possible. The classification process (however it is implemented) continues and classifies the input vector as belonging to one of several cases. The appropriate case is selected and the vector is passed to the appropriate case processor (by a hypothetical CASE statement, say) where the actual processing is done. Our main concern in domain testing is with the correctness of the classification process and the correctness of the hypothetical or real CASE statement used to route the input vector to its corresponding processing as contrasted with the correctness of the processing done for each case; a distinction first noted by Howden [HOWD76].

In domain testing we assume that the classification process is specified by a set of inequalities over the input vector. That is, for each case of interest there is at least one set of inequalities that specifies the domain appropriate to that case. There could be more than one set of inequalities for domains that are defined in, perhaps disconnected, pieces.

As an example, in 1993 the IRS defined the following domains for figuring your taxes if you were single:

Domain	Process
0 < tax_inc =< $22,100	tax = 0.15 × tax_inc
$22,100 < tax_inc =< $53,500	tax = $3,315 + 0.28 × (tax_inc - $22,100)
$53,500 < tax_inc =< $115,000	tax = $12,107 + 0.31 × (tax_inc - $53,500)
$115,000 < tax_inc =< $250,000	tax = $31,172 + 0.36 × (tax_inc - $115,000)
$250,000 < tax_inc	tax = $79,722 + 0.396 × (tax_inc - $250,000)

There is only one input variable in this example, **tax_inc** (taxable income). Five* domains were specified. The first four consist of two inequalities each: a lower and an upper value. The last domain has no upper limit.** The tax instructions said that you shouldn't use these inequalities if your taxable income was under $100,000; you had to use the tax tables. Examination of the tax tables revealed differences between them and the equations. The difference occurred because the tables specified an upper and lower value for each entry and the tax was figured on the value of the upper and lower boundary, rounded off to the nearest dollar. Conversely, the formulas (only to be used above $100,000) were exact and the taxpayer could elect to round off or not.

What does this have to do with testing? Tax tables are what must be used, so that's what you test. If you were testing a tax program and you used the domain definitions given by the equations in your model for testing the *table's* implementation, you would be blind to small errors in the table—typically under $5.00. If you're to test the tables rather than the equations, you must fit equations to the tables that correctly reflect the domains specified by the tables.

7.3.2 General

The description of the graph components and the associated relation isn't as productive for domain testing as it is for most other techniques, but it nevertheless does provide insight as to what should be included in any strategy.

Objects (nodes): Domains defined over the input vector.

Relation (links): The relation is *is adjacent to*. Adjacency is defined as having a common boundary. By convention, we can use the direction of the inequality as the direction of the link. For example, if A and B are adjacent domains and A is closed, draw an arrow from A to B. You might prefer to draw your arrows the other way: it doesn't matter as long as you're consistent.

As with all graph models, you should conduct tests to confirm that the arrows go in the right direction (by whatever convention you chose). This interpretation of the graph modeling paradigm tells us to check the correctness of all closures at all adjacent domains (i.e., link cover). For example, the constants in the domain definition above ($22,100, $53,500, $115,000, and $250,000) appear in two different inequalities and in one processing expression. An error in one instance of these constants could destroy adjacency. You must test the relation in both directions to ensure that nothing has been left out and that nothing overlaps.

---

*But actually there are six domains. The specification is wrong and differs from the requirements. Why?

**Because there is no limit to what the IRS will take from us in taxes.

Link weights: The inequalities that specify boundaries between domains. Because there can be many inequalities at which domains meet, there can be many links between any two domains. You need at least two dimensions to see this. You can model this by one link for each inequality.

An inequality (in two or more dimensions) can be a boundary for many domains. Two lines crossing in the plane defines four regions and therefore, four domains. Three inequalities in the plane can define seven domains.* Our strategies center on testing the inequalities rather than the domains.

Node weights: The calculation associated with the domain. Note that a given calculation does not have to be unique to a domain. The domain as specified could consist of adjacent pieces or even disconnected pieces. For example, we could have a specification such as:

$0 < x = {<}17$	**Process A**
$17 < x = {<}34$	**Process B**
$34 < x = {<}39$	**Process C**
$39 < x = {<}44$	**Process A**
$44 < x$	**Process D**

The domain for process A consists of two disconnected pieces. How should we treat this? I prefer to consider each part of the specified domain as a separate **subdomain** that has processing in common with some other subdomains (its other pieces). I do that because that's what we'll have to do in testing anyhow. In the sequel assume that anything I say about testing a domain applies to each of its subdomains (if any).

Node cover: You must do at least four things for node cover.

1. At least one test point in each domain to confirm that correct processing has been selected by the CASE statement and, if selected, correctly processed. That's at *least* one test per domain. But there's no assurance that one test will confirm processing correctness. A domain's processing could be an entire program for which control flow, data flow, transaction flow, or some other technique is warranted. Use the appropriate model.**

2. For domains that consist of subdomains (whether adjacent or not), confirm that all the required pieces exist and that all get the required processing.

---

*The number of domains that can be defined by k inequalities grows very rapidly with dimensions. (How many are possible is a very difficult mathematical problem called the "pancake problem" in two dimensions and the "orange problem" in three dimensions.)

**Confirmation of the processing itself can be done by domain testing if, say, the processing is defined by an algebraic equation. It can be viewed as confirming the correctness of a degenerate domain defined by an equality predicate [AFIF92].

3. Confirm that no domains overlap. That's done graphically for one and two dimensions. For more than two dimensions, you must use appropriate algebraic tools [WHIT95] (beyond the scope of this book). Usually, however, domain overlaps occur on boundaries.

4. Confirm that the input space is complete. Every input vector must be handled, even if "handling" means rejecting the input. You can do this by inspection in one and two dimensions. For more than two dimensions, it is done by algebra and not within the scope of this book [WHIT95]. As with overlaps, most bugs of this kind occur on domain boundaries.

Link cover: There's a hierarchy to consider here also.

1. Confirm that all the domains that should be adjacent are adjacent—that they have a boundary inequality between them.

2. Confirm that there are not extra boundaries. Domain testing strategies help with that.

3. Confirm the correctness of every boundary inequality. That's what most of domain testing is all about.

As an example of developing a domain testing model, here's a version of lines 32 to 38 of Form1040*. My purpose is to create an example that involves at least two input variables. My modified specification for lines 32 to 38 are:

32:	Adjusted_Gross_Income (AGI)	Used as an input for this example.
33:		Unchecked and treated as 0.
34:	Standard Deduction	Assumed $6,200 for this example
35:	AGI − $6,200	Specified arithmetic
6e:	Exemptions (Exp)	Used as an input for this example
36:	$2,350 × Exp	I'm ignoring an upper limit of $81,350 for this example
37:	tax_inc = Max (0, L35 − L36)	Taxable income. We'll use this tax rate schedule for all values
38:	Tax from tax rate schedule	

0	< tax_inc =< $22,100	$tax = 0.15 \times tax\_inc$
$22,100	< tax_inc =< $53,500	$tax = \$3{,}315 + 0.28 \times (tax\_inc - \$22{,}100)$
$53,500	< tax_inc =< $115,000	$tax = \$12{,}107 + 0.31 \times (tax\_inc - \$53{,}500)$
$115,000	< tax_inc =< $250,000	$tax = \$31{,}172 + 0.36 \times (tax\_inc - \$115{,}000)$
$250,000	< tax_inc	$tax = \$79{,}722 + 0.396 \times (tax\_inc - \$250{,}000)$

Our objective is to develop a domain testing model that we can use to test the correct implementation of the tax table. To do that, we must express the tax tables directly in terms of the input variables (**AGI** and **Exp**). Do this by sub-

---

*These modifications do violence to the tax form, so please don't use them for any tax purposes.

stituting the input variable names into subsequent expressions and continuing with symbolic substitution until you reach the tax table. I did that, and eliminated the lines I didn't need as a result. Here's my rearranged model.

32:   **AGI (Adjusted_Gross_Income)**   **Input**
6e: **Exp (Exemptions)**   **Input**
38:   **Tax from tax rate schedule**

Domain 1:   **tax = 0.0**
           AGI − 6,200 − 2,350 × Exp <= 0

Domain 2:   **tax = 0.15 × (AGI − 6,200 − 2,350 × Exp)**
           AGI − 6,200 − 2,350 × Exp > 0
           AGI − 6,200 − 2,350 × Exp <=22,100

Domain 3:   **tax = 3,315 + 0.28 × ((AGI − 6,200 − 2,350 × Exp) − 22,100))**
           AGI − 6,200 − 2,350 × Exp > 22,100
           AGI − 6,200 − 2,350 × Exp <= 53,500

Domain 4:   **tax = 12,107 + 0.31 × ((AGI − 6,200 − 2,350 × Exp) − 53,500))**
           AGI − 6,200 − 2,350 × Exp) > 53,500
           AGI − 6,200 − 2,350 × Exp <= 115,000

Domain 5:   **tax = 31,172 + 0.36 × ((AGI − 6,200 − 2,350 × Exp) − 115,000))**
           AGI − 6,200 − 2,350 × Exp > 115,000
           AGI − 6,200 − 2,350 × Exp <= 250,000

Domain 6:   **tax = 79,772 + 0.396 × ((AGI − 6,200 − 2,350 × Exp) − 250,000))**
           AGI − 6,200 − 2,350 × Exp > 250,000

I used my word processor's search-and-replace command to do this. First I moved line 6e to the top. Then I removed lines 33 and 34 because their values have been assumed for this example and are included in the source model given first. I then substituted "**AGI−6,200**" for "**L35**", removed line 35, and cleaned up the arithmetic. I put parentheses around expressions before substituting to prevent errors: for example, sign reversals due to double minus signs and multiplication of an expression by a constant as in the **tax** calculation. The next substitution was for line 36. The **Max** on line 37 was removed by adding another domain, as you can see, for negative taxable incomes. I then substituted for **tax_inc**, yielding the inequalities you see (after a little rearrangement to get them all pointing the same way). I then simplified the algebraic expressions for the taxes, resulting in the following model:

32:   **Adjust_Gross_Income (AGI)**   **Input**
6e: **Exemptions (Exp)**   **Input**
38:   **Tax from tax rate schedule**

Domain 1:   **tax = 0.0**
           AGI <= 6,200 + 2,350Exp

Domain 2:	tax = 0.15AGI − 352.5Exp − 930.0
	AGI > 6,200 + 2,350Exp
	AGI <= 28,300 + 2,350Exp
Domain 3:	tax = 0.28AGI − 658.0Exp − 4,609.0
	AGI > 28,300 + 2,350Exp
	AGI <= 59,700 + 2,350 Exp
Domain 4:	tax = 0.31AGI − 728.5Exp − 6,400.0
	AGI > 59,700 + 2,350Exp
	AGI <= 121,200 + 2,350Exp
Domain 5:	tax = 0.36AGI − 846.0Exp − 12,460
	AGI > 121,200 + 2,350Exp
	AGI <= 256,200 + 2,350Exp
Domain 6:	tax = 0.396 AGI − 930.6Exp − 21,683.2
	AGI > 256,200 + 2,350Exp

Figure 7.2 may be a more palatable way to present these domains; and for one and two dimensions, it's a good idea to plot them as I did. The domains consist of several parallel lines. That's typical of domains we see in practice. But it did take algebra slinging to simplify those boundaries and express them in terms of the input variables.

Predicate interpretation: The symbolic substitution I did above to express the domains in terms of input variables is called **predicate interpretation**. Each inequality has the form of a predicate that can be evaluated in terms of TRUE and FALSE; the predicates we interpret in terms of the input variables.

Why bother interpreting the domain boundary predicates? Why not work directly with IRS form lines in the specification? If you do that, you won't have a domain testing model—it'll be a control-flow model. Our objective is to verify that the boundary predicates (or whatever their equivalent might be in the code) have been correctly implemented.

Our final model is redundant. The boundary inequalities appear twice (once for each domain they define). This model isn't elegant, and it's not likely that a programmer would set up calculations this way. A programmer will analyze the calculations, arrange them in a better order (e.g., easier to maintain), and not necessarily implement the specified intermediate calculations but something that appears to be different but that is supposedly equivalent. And that's the point. The analysis we do to design domain tests is driven by different goals from the programmers'; so we're unlikely to make the same mistakes. We testers have our own errors to make.

The main justification for predicate interpretation is to provide an independent check of the rationality of the specification. I suspect specifications

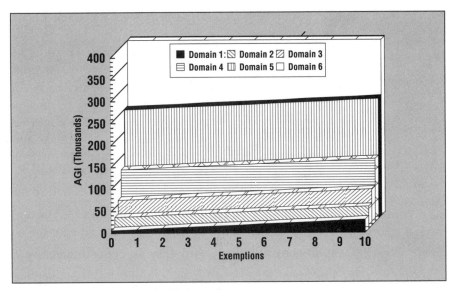

Figure 7.2 Domains for tax schedule inequalities.

that contain many intermediate calculations to get from the input data to the output. I'm suspicious because I smell a frustrated programmer instead of a specification writer. Such intermediate values are often not essential and are just that specifier's concept of how it should be programmed—something our programmers should notice and ignore. We not only provide an independent check of the programmer's work, but if our modeling effort turns up contradictions and ambiguities in the domain specifications (as it often does), then we've earned our pay for that day.

Predicate interpretation isn't usually difficult. Typically, you don't have to do it at all because the domains are given directly in terms of the input variables. If you have to do it, and if the predicates are simple enough, use your word processor as I did (but don't forget to enclose every expression you substitute in parentheses to avoid all kinds of algebraic substitution errors). If the wordprocessor is clumsy, then use an algebraic processor. My HP-28C calculator is adequate. If that's cumbersome, then use an algebraic package.

7.3.3 Ambiguity and Contradiction Analysis

About 30 percent of all bugs concern errors in requirements. These bugs are expensive because often they're not discovered until the software is put to work. Approximately 5 percent of all bugs are caused by wrong domain definitions.* Contrary to popular myths, no one bug type dominates. Most bugs

---

*This is underestimated for contemporary software, because value is based on data now almost 10 years old (as of 1994). As component testing methods have improved, the relative frequency of requirements bugs also has increased. I wouldn't be surprised if domain bugs were 10 percent overall and up to 30 percent in some applications.

appear in numbers under 3 percent, so a 5 percent frequency is high and worth going after.

A program can't be self-contradictory. Whatever it does is self-consistent. A program can't be ambiguous. It will always do *something* to an input. Specifications, however, can be both contradictory and ambiguous. When a programmer implements from a self-contradictory or ambiguous specification, he or she must resolve the ambiguities and contradictions either consciously or unconsciously. Bugs result because the contradictions and ambiguities are usually unrecognized and because their resolution is usually unconscious. The domain testing model and the analysis done to create the model is an effective way to check specifications for ambiguities and contradictions.

Domain ambiguity: The specification of a set of domains is ambiguous if the set of domains do not cover the entire input space.

Domain contradictions: Two domains are contradictory if they overlap.

The first place to look for ambiguities and contradictions is at the boundaries between domains. Here's an example:

Domain 3:	AGI $>$	28,300	+ 2,350Exp
	AGI $<=$	59,700	+ 2,350Exp
Domain 4:	AGI $>=$	59,700	+ 2,350Exp
	AGI $<$	121,200	+ 2,350Exp
Domain 5:	AGI $>$	121,200	+ 2,350Exp
	AGI $<=$	256,200	+ 2,350Exp

The boundary between domains 3 and 4 is contradictory because both domains claim the same closure along the **AGI = 59,700 + 2,350 Exp** line. The boundary between domains 4 and 5 is ambiguous because the input values along **AGI = 121,000 + 2,350 Exp** are not specified.

Once you have a set of interpreted domain boundary specifications you should examine them for ambiguities and contradictions. Most of this is easily done by inspection. For one and two input variables you can do it graphically. For more than two input variables, algebra is essential. See WHIT95.

1. Is every input value from -∞ to +∞ included? If not, are there mechanisms that will prevent values below the minimum and above the maximum from entering the system? Make a special check for zero values. The specification on page 151 is ambiguous—why?

2. Is the closure consistent from -∞ to +∞ for all variables for all domain boundaries? If not, there must be several (at least two) inequalities that specify the same boundary but with different input value ranges for at least one variable and with different closures. Group those sets and check for overlaps and/or gaps in the closure. Here's an example of an inconsistent closure with closure ambiguities and contradictions.

Domain 3: $\text{tax} = 0.28\text{AGI} - 658.0\text{Exp} - 4,609.0$

$\text{AGI} >= 28,300 + 2,350\text{Exp}, \quad 0<\text{Exp}<4$

$\text{AGI} > 28,300 + 2,350\text{Exp}, \quad 4<=\text{Exp}<7$

$\text{AGI} >= 28,300 + 2,350\text{Exp}, \quad 7<\text{Exp}<=10$

$\text{AGI} > 28,300 + 2,350\text{Exp}$

$\text{AGI} <= 59,700 + 2,350\text{Exp}$

3. For one and two dimensions, plot all the specified domains, one at a time, by plotting all the domain boundary equations for each specified domain.

The example on the right shows an ambiguity for input values less than 7, and domains 1 and 2 overlap. Remember that the likeliest ambiguities and contradic-

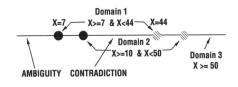

tions will be a closure ambiguity or contradiction at a boundary, so be sure to mark the closures of every boundary.

4. What about three or more dimensions? The analysis is algebraic; see WHIT95. You may be able to analyze three-dimensional models by brute force and heuristics, but beyond that, there's no helping the math. As of 1995, no commercial tools will tell you when a set of domain specifications is consistent and unambiguous. Organizations that regularly need such analyses get expert help and program their own tools.

7.3.4 Nonlinear Domains

There's good news, good news that may look bad to some of you but not to others, and the best news.

1. **Good News.** The good news is that nonlinear domains (meaning domains with at least one nonlinear boundary inequality) are uncommon in practice. Early studies [COHE78] showed about 85 percent linear predicates in COBOL code. It's mostly a linear world.

2. **Good News That Looks Bad (Optional).** The issue of linearity is not the simple issue of linearity in an elementary algebraic sense, but in the more general sense of linear vector spaces. Ordinary polynomials are linear in this expanded sense. Because polynomial approximations can be used to fit any decent functions, it is possible, by choosing suitable approximations, to convert a nonlinear domain testing problem into a linear domain testing problem, albeit at the cost of adding dimensions. Nonlinear boundary equations can also often be linearized by suitable transformations. Among these are

hyperbolas, exponential functions, power functions, and logarithmic functions. Approximations of functions in terms of ordinary polynomials are seldom used because they are usually computationally inefficient. With today's fast computers, this is far less a problem than it used to be. Which do you want, computational efficiency or testability?

3. **The Best News.** The best news [JENG94] is that if you are only concerned with determining that there is a bug and not with the specifics of the bug (e.g., the kind of domain error) and you're willing to take a calculated risk over the possibility of being blind to some bugs [AFIF92], then the issues of nonlinear domain boundaries do not, for the most part, matter.

7.4 THE TECHNIQUES

7.4.1 General

There are many domain testing strategies [AFIF90, AFIF92, CLAR82, COHE78, JENG94, ONOM87, PERE85, WHIT78A, WHIT80A, WHIT85B, WHIT90, ZEIL83, ZEIL89]. We won't discuss all of them. If you've programmed, then you have surely learned the fundamentals of domain testing strategies. If you've been programming for a while, then you've used heuristic domain testing methods. Before getting to the effective strategies, let's see what's wrong with the heuristic strategies.

1. **Heuristics Strategy Number 1. Test the extreme points.** This strategy recommends that any numerical input be tested at and near the minimum and maximum allowable values for that input. This heuristic strategy goes under various names, such as boundary value testing, [MYER79], extreme value testing, and special value testing, [HOWD80]. As pointed out by Richardson [RICH85] and many others, these heuristic strategies are all subsumed under domain testing. The main difference between formal domain testing and heuristic domain testing (which has been in common use for decades) is that with the former we'll do better testing and learn more about the bugs we find with fewer test cases.

2. **Heuristics Strategy Number 2. Test the extreme point combinations.** The typical next heuristic strategy, and a very popular (but misguided) strategy at that, is to test the combinations of extreme points. Although this strategy is supported by commercial automatic test generators, it is a fundamentally foolish strategy—as we'll see later.

7.4.2 What's Wrong With Extreme Point Combinations?

The "strategy" of using extreme point combinations, if it can be called that, assumes that there is an upper and lower acceptable value for every input variable. Below the minimum value and above the maximum value, presumably the software corrects or rejects such inputs. Obviously, the minimum and maximum values (in part) specify domain boundaries, and the strategy asks first that we test the domain boundary and then values just above the maximum and just below the minimum. That's for one dimension. For two dimensions, the strategy recommends that we test the combinations of extreme values. If I call the four interesting cases for each variable, respectively, "under," "min," "max," and "over," for two variables we would, under this strategy test: (underA, underB), (underA, minB), ... (overA, overB), for a total of 16 tests, plus one test for a typical value. For n input variables, the number of test cases needed to follow this prescription is $4^n +1$.

On what kind of bugs are we betting? The processing, whatever it is, must define a functional relation between the input variables. There are two possibilities for functional relations between input variables: (1) They appear in the same output function, or (2) they appear in the same domain boundary.

1. **Same function.** The calculated function is either right or wrong. We are assuming, by testing combinations, that it is not possible to see the bug except at a particular combination of input values (the extreme cases) because the program is correct at other combinations of input values. What we are saying, if reinterpreted, is that the normal processing and the erroneous processing for the combination of extreme values lie in different domains. If that's the case, we'd better check the domain boundaries.

2. **Same domain boundary.** The input variables might appear in the same (interpreted) domain boundary inequality. Either they do or they don't. If they don't, then they are independent. There is no functional relation between them and we are hypothesizing a bug that will create a relation where none existed. That's no bug, that's sabotage. If there is a functional relation, then that's what should be tested, because testing raw combinations of extreme points tells us nothing about such relations.

In the example of Figure 7.3 on the next page, I applied the heuristic combination strategy and got the points marked with hashes. We have three domains whose boundaries are given by the solid lines. Only eight of the test points—those adjacent to the upper boundary's extreme points—tell us anything at all about the correctness of the domains' boundaries. The tests tell us nothing at all about the correctness of the lower boundary. Suppose we had

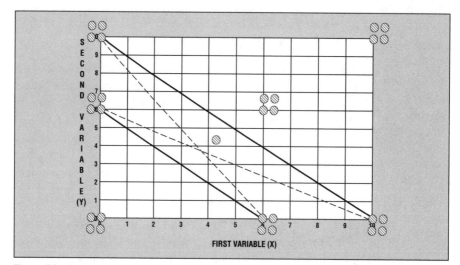

Figure 7.3 Functional relation between input variables.

a bug in which the two domains were implemented with the boundaries shown by the dashed lines. Instead of three domains we have four domains, and who knows what kind of strange processing in them. The extreme point combination tests won't catch this bug.

"But," comes the objection from the sidelines, "we know that there are domains and we should have tested the inputs at and around **X = 6** and **Y = 6** and their combinations!"Better, but not good enough. This supposed refinement adds 12 tests but still doesn't catch the crossed boundary bug. It comes down to: (a) the only way to test a functional relation is to test the functional relation and (b) betting on a bug that creates functional relations where there were none is a bad bet.

Testing combinations of extreme points is a poor-man's n-dimensional domain testing. It generates many tests, most of which are meaningless and/or misleading. In the last example, we did 29 tests but didn't catch the bug. A proper strategy will find the bug with only four tests. The worst part about this "strategy" is that the number of test cases grows exponentially with the number of input variables. Consequently, even if automated, coverage is impossible. Only a small part of that awesome number of combinations (1.2677E30, for 50 inputs, or 4E19 years of testing at one test per millisecond) can be attempted so those that will be executed are effectively arbitrary. Properly designed random testing will find more bugs and tell you more about the software's dependability. Proper domain testing does even more for less work.

7.4.3 Weak 1 x 1, One Dimension

The first strategy (and the one you'll most often use) is the weak 1×1 strategy. It is called "weak" because it only does one set of tests for each boundary inequality instead of one set of tests for every boundary segment, and "1 × 1" because it will require one ON and one OFF point per boundary inequality.

Figure 7.4 shows all the possible bugs for a one-dimensional domain boundary. As specified by the strategy, there are two tests per boundary (a point in one dimension), consisting of a single ON point and an OFF point. I've illustrated this with a closed boundary. I leave it as an exercise for you to demonstrate that the strategy works for any combination of open and closed boundaries. The following cases are all the bugs that there can be for one-dimensional domain boundaries.

1. **Closure Bug.** The boundary is open when it should be closed or closed when it should be open. The ON point test will catch this bug because the input will receive B domain processing instead of A domain processing. This will work if there is no coincidental correctness at the boundary.

2. **Boundary Shifted Left.** The OFF point should have had B domain processing, but instead gets A domain processing.

3. **Boundary Shifted Right.** The ON point should have A domain processing, but gets B domain processing instead. We can't tell from this test if this is a closure or a right-shift bug, but we know there is a bug.

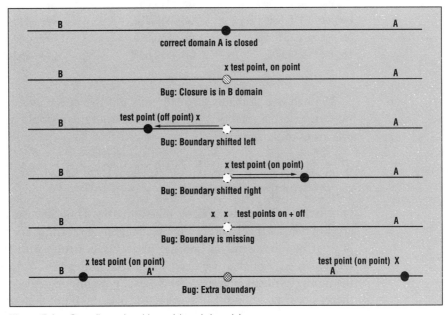

Figure 7.4   One-dimensional bugs (closed domain).

4. **Missing Boundary.** Both the ON and OFF points get the same processing, but they should have had different processing.

5. **Extra Boundary.** The extra boundary divides the original domain into two domains. The presence of the new boundary must result in distinguishable processing difference or else we can't find it. The comparison of the two processing for the original boundary points must show a difference.

Let's compare this strategy now with the heuristic domain testing strategies for one dimension. The heuristic strategies call for an ON point, an OFF point, and a point near the boundary but on the other side (an "anti-OFF point"?)—or three tests per boundary where the 1 ×1 strategy calls for two tests. Not bad. We've cut our test cases by a third and lost nothing—the payoff is more dramatic in higher dimensions.

Let's apply this strategy to a few cases. The domain specification on page 151, after expressing each boundary as a single expression, are:

Domain	Tests	
tax_inc > 0	ON=0	OFF=0.00001
tax_inc =< 22,100	ON=22,100	OFF=22,100.00001
tax_inc > 22,100	~~ON=22,100~~	~~OFF=22,100.00001~~
tax_inc =< 53,500	ON=53,500	OFF=53,500.00001
tax _inc > 53,500	~~ON=53,500~~	~~OFF=53,500.00001~~
tax_inc =< 115,000	ON=115,000	OFF=115,000.00001
tax_inc > 115,000	~~ON=115,000~~	~~OFF=115,000.00001~~
tax_inc =< 250,000	ON=250,000	OFF=250,000.00001
tax_inc > 250,000,	~~ON=250,000~~	~~OFF=250,000.00001~~

We had five domains (actually, six) and five specified boundaries, which we tested with a total of 10 tests; the naive strategy would have used 15 and told us nothing more.

7.4.4 Weak 1 x 1, Two Dimensions and Higher [JENG94].

Our first task should be to determine if there is a bug associated with a boundary. Boundaries that have no bugs need no further testing. For boundaries with bugs, it may be useful to find out just what is wrong with the boundary as implemented. For that, we need a stronger strategy (N × 1, see below). For the more restricted (and more immediately useful) objective of determining if there is or is not a bug, 1 × 1 works for two and more dimensions.

I call this a "weak" 1 × 1 strategy because it assumes that: every boundary extends to ±∞, there are no gaps in the boundary, and that the closure is consistent all along the boundary's length. The strategy is *not* restricted to linear domain boundaries, or for that matter to functions defined over real numbers—it applies across the board to almost any domain that might be specified in the context of software.

The strategy calls for one ON and one OFF point for every boundary inequality, the two points being chosen as close as possible to each other while satisfying the definitions of ON and OFF points. Note that the "ON" point does not actually have to be on the boundary if that is not possible in the computer's or language's number representation system. The "ON" point merely needs to satisfy the conditions of the boundary. The situation is shown in the figure on the right.

The correct boundary is shown by the solid line with the closure, as usual, indicated by the hachure. A possibly buggy implementation is shown by the dashed curve. Note that we are not restricted to linear domain boundaries. Play with the two curves and (with the exception noted below) you can see that one way or another, either the ON point will fall into the B domain or the OFF point will fall into the A domain.

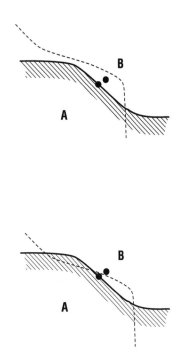

The exception is illustrated by the next figure: Our buggy boundary just passes between the selected ON and OFF points. Before considering what to do about this possibility, we should explore the likelihood of its occurrence. It's not likely because we're dealing with natural bugs and not sabotage. Domain bugs tend to be fairly gross with obvious symptoms (if you test them with the right strategy, that is). For example, a decimal point is left out of a coefficient or put in the wrong place, a constant term is left out or changed, or an entire term is missing. Such bugs cause fairly big distortions of the buggy boundary compared to the correct boundary. How can you protect yourself? By choosing the ON and OFF points as close to one another as you can. It's no guarantee that a buggy boundary won't sneak in between your selected test points, but it's a good bet.

"How good a bet?" you ask. Here the theory gives us qualitative guidance [AFIF92, JENG94]. Jeng and Weyuker [JENG94] provide a cogent argument on theoretical grounds that the bet is a very good one. All testing is a bet about the likelihood of missing significant bugs. Jeng and Weyuker's argument is probably good enough for testing ordinary software, but for life-critical software or for software that creates considerable financial exposure, one might want to play it safe and user stronger (and far more expensive) methods that guarantee that sneaky bugs won't get by unnoticed. Let's apply 1 × 1 to an example.

Domain 4:   tax = 0.31AGI − 728.5Exp − 6,400.0
AGI > 59,700 + 2,350Exp
AGI <= 121,200 + 2,350Exp

We weren't told this, but it's obvious that the number of exemptions (**Exp**) is an integer greater than zero. We start by picking the ON point, because that's easiest to do. Pick any value that satisfies the domain boundary. We have two boundaries. For the second boundary, we have **AGI**= **121,200 + 2,350Exp**, so picking **Exp = 5**, say, yields **AGI = 132,950**. We want the OFF point to be very close. In this application, the smallest sensible value is a penny, so going two orders of magnitude smaller should be adequate. That yields **AGI = 132,950.0001** at **Exp = 5**.

Note that there's nothing wrong with picking the OFF point as close as you can within the limits of your number representation system as long as calculated values won't get destroyed by round-off or a Pentium bug. For example, you could pick **AGI = 132,950.00000000001** if your computer and/or language carried floating point calculations to that many significant digits. The advantage of doing this is that it minimizes the possibility of not catching a bug that sneaks in between your selected ON and OFF points. Conversely, if in the last example the number representation system only did calculations to 10 significant digits, then your ON and OFF points would in fact be exactly the same and you wouldn't actually be using the strategy. I leave it to you to design tests for the other boundary of this domain and to calculate the expected value for the tests you design.

7.4.5 Degenerate Cases

For n-dimensions, a degenerate situation occurs when a domain is defined as a region of less than n-dimension. A and B are adjacent domains and both are open with respect to the boundary shown. C is the boundary and is a separate domain. By definition, it must be closed. The 1 × 1 strategy works here if you interpret things correctly. A is open, so we need an ON points on the boundary and an OFF point inside A. B also needs an ON points, but it can be the same as is used for A. B also needs an OFF point, which is inside B. How about C? It is

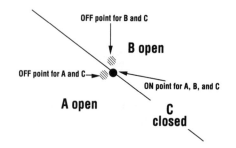

closed so, by definition, the OFF point should be outside. Outside of what? Outside of C and therefore both in A and B. Again, the points can be shared. Thus, degenerate situations don't require additional tests if we interpret what we mean by an "OFF point" for such situations.

7.4.6 Higher-Order Strategies for Two Dimensions and More [AFIF92, COHE78]

7.4.6.1 WHY HIGHER-ORDER STRATEGIES?

There are two reasons to use higher-order strategies: (1) to be assured that various kinds of domain boundary bugs can't sneak by the selected ON and OFF points of the basic 1×1 strategy, and (2) to learn something about the bug we have when the simpler strategy reveals that we have a bug. However, there are three reasons to *discuss* higher order strategies: the above two reasons and (3) for the insights that these strategies provide for testing in general.

7.4.6.2 TESTING SAFETY

The higher-order strategies all take more test points—a lot more test points. Typically, the number of additional tests *per boundary* is proportional to the number of dimensions. If **b** is the number of boundaries, then 1×1 requires **2b** tests. All the surer methods require of the order of **b x n** tests, where **n** is the number of dimensions. That's a lot worse, but not nearly as bad as the naive strategies based on raw extreme point combinations that suggested **4ᵇ** tests.

The bet gets worse with increased number of dimensions—that is, the probability of not catching a bug because the buggy boundary sneaked in between the chosen test points increases with increasing dimensions; but theory aside, we had as of 1995 no hard statistics that we could use to quantify the risk.

Afifi and coauthors have shown [AFIF92] that to *guarantee* that no bug sneaks by in between the chosen ON and OFF point, and to handle many other kinds of possible domain bugs, you need n + 2 properly chosen tests per domain boundary (weak assumptions). At least one point must be an ON point and one must be an OFF point. Further properties (i.e., what does "properly selected" mean) of the selected test points and algorithms for selecting the points are beyond the scope of this book but are clearly described in AFIF92.

7.4.6.3 TYPES OF DOMAIN BUGS

Our second and third objectives for considering higher-order strategies can be met by examining the first of these strategies, $N \times 1$ [COHE78]. $N \times 1$ appears to be reasonable strategy to use to try to diagnose the specifics of the bug once you have determined that a boundary *is* buggy. It also provides valuable insights into domain testing and bugs in general. Last, all of the advanced literature on domain testing presumes an understanding of this strategy.

N × 1 provides diagnostic support because by selecting n ON points we can confirm the correctness of an n - 1 dimensional boundary hyperplane in n dimensions (e.g., a line in two dimensions, a sheet in three).

The possible domain boundary bug situations for two (and more) dimensions can be described simply if the domain boundaries are all linear. In fact, domain testing is one of the few areas in which it has been possible to describe bugs with mathematical precision. The strategy requires n ON points and one OFF point for n dimensions.

1. **Closure Bug.** What should have been an open boundary is implemented as closed or what should have been a closed boundary is implemented as open. We'll 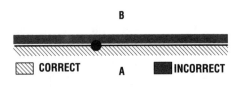 assume that the boundary should have been closed and leave the analysis of open boundaries as an exercise. The single ON point will catch this bug if there is no coincidental correctness at the boundary. Closure bugs are the most common domain bug.

2. **Domain Shift "Up" or "Down."** This is equivalent to the one-dimension left or right shift. A **domain shift bug** is an error in the constant term of the inequality: an increase, decrease, or sign change. That applies for n-dimensions. Before the shift (the correct implementation) the ON points got A domain processing and OFF point got B processing. After the 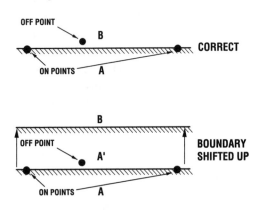 upshift, all three points get A domain processing. I leave it as an exercise to show that the N × 1 strategy in two dimensions works for all kinds of shifts (increase, decrease, or reverse sign of the constant) for both open and closed domains.

Domain shifts tend to be big. The likeliest shift is caused by a gross F 1p2error, such as leaving out the decimal point or putting it in the wrong place. But simple digit transpositions can occur, causing small shifts. That's why it's important to keep the OFF point close to the boundary.

3. **Domain Tilt.** This has no one-dimensional equivalent but applies to two or more dimensions. A **domain tilt bug** is any error in a coefficient in the inequality we're testing. I tilted the domain boundary counter-

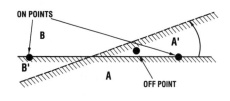

clockwise. Before the tilt, the OFF point got B domain processing. After the tilt, this point is in domain A and so we know we've got a bug.

Domain tilts are caused by errors in coefficients (of linear domain inequalities) and, like shifts, they're likelier to be big tilts rather than small ones. Again, keeping the OFF point very close to the boundary helps to reduce blindness to small tilts.

4. **Extra Boundary.** The N × 1 strategy works for an extra boundary also. Instead of two domains A and B (for this example), there are four. Presumably, some processing differences are associated with the extra bound-

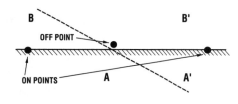

ary so that domain A and A', for example, are distinguishable. A comparison of the two ON points, assuming that the new boundary passes between them, spots the discrepancy. The N × 1 strategy will be blind to extra boundaries for which there is no processing change as a result. But that's not too bad because the users won't see it either.

5. **Missing Boundary.** Compare either of the ON points with the OFF point. The missing boundary will cause the A and B domain processing to be the same (but we can't tell whether it will be A or B processing).

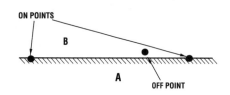

7.4.6.4 N × 1 Illustrated

What test points should we select? For weak N × 1, where we test only the boundary equations rather than domain boundary segments, keep the ON points as far apart as convenient and the OFF points midway between them. Some additional comments for more than two dimensions:

1. ON points must be linearly independent. For example, in three dimensions, they can't be **collinear**—that is, lying on the same line. In four

dimensions, where the boundary is a volume, the points can't be coplanar. Picking ON points near vertices of a domain is profitable because the vertex points of a domain always are independent.

2. OFF points should be chosen at or near the **centroid** of the ON points. For lines, pick midway between the ON points. For planes, pick the point at the center of the triangle formed by the ON point that is as close as possible to being equidistant from the triangle's vertices.

Let's apply the N × 1 strategy to testing the upper boundary of domain 4.

Domain 4:   tax = 0.31AGI − 728.5Exp − 6,400.0
AGI > 59,700 + 2,350Exp
AGI <= 121,200 + 2,350Exp

The number of exemptions, **Exp**, can't be negative; so zero is our lower bound. We weren't given an upper limit, but we might as well pick a very big value so that we can decrease the likelihood of not spotting some small shifts or tilts; 100, say. Exemptions are integers, so the smallest value we can pick that isn't a vertex point is 1. Substituting for 1 and 100, respectively, we get 123,550 and 356,200 respectively. So our ON points are (1, 123,550) and (100, 356,200). Our next step is to pick the OFF point. We start by picking a point on the boundary, midway between the two ON points we picked, or **Exp = 50**. Substituting this back into the boundary equation, we get 238, 700. But our OFF point must be outside this domain, in this case, a little larger, so our OFF point becomes (50, 238,700.01). The last step is to substitute these three sets of values into the equation for taxes to get our predicted outcome. However, be sure to substitute for the domain 5 taxes for the OFF point, because the OFF point is in domain 5, not domain 4. Doing that, we have the following test cases:

Exp	AGI	Tax
1	123,550.00	31,172.0000
50	238,700.01	31,172.0036
100	356,200.00	31,172.0000

This is not an instance of coincidental correctness because the issue is not to distinguish between points in the same domain but to determine if a point is in the wrong (e.g., adjacent) domain. The tax calculation for the OFF point in this domain (4) yields 31,172.0031, not 31,172.0036. The tax is almost the same for all three points, but the domains and the tax rates are not linearly independent. In general, as in the next example, you won't have this situation.

Inequality	ON point #1 (x, y)	ON point #2 (x, y)	Off point
$y >= 0$	0, 0.0001	0, 10	$-0.0001, 5$
$x >= 0$	0.0001, 0	10, 0	$5, -0.0001$
$2y < x + 4$	2, 3	12, 8	6.999, 5.499
$4y >= x-4$	4, 0	20, 4	12.0001, 1.999
$y <= -x + 16$	0, 16	16, 0	8.0001, 8.0001

I'll ignore the value of the function calculated in this domain, but let's assume that we have it and that there is no coincidental correctness with adjacent domains. I'll illustrate the procedure by designing the tests for the last of these boundaries. We want to pick the ON points as far apart as possible, and recall that in weak N × 1 we just verify the entire boundary and not the segment within the domain of interest. Therefore, I can pick any values along the line, and the farthest ones possible are (x = 0, y = 16) and (x = 16, y = 0). The mid-point between these is (8, 8), so a good value to test with might be x = 8.0001, y = 8.0001. The X and Y axes are also included in this domain's boundaries; things rarely go wrong with coordinate axes, but you might still want to do that test. The minimum y value is zero, so (0, 0.0001) and, say, (0, 10) are decent choices for the ON points, resulting in (−0.0001, 5) for the OFF point. The next equation is an open boundary, so I had to subtract a trifle to get the OFF point inside. I suggest that you plot these lines, their closures, and the test points on graph paper to see what I'm doing here.

7.4.7 Strong Domain Testing

The difference between weak and strong domain testing is that in weak testing we do only one set of tests for each boundary inequality, while in strong testing we do a separate set of tests for every boundary segment.* Furthermore, it isn't a question of using either one or the other strategies. You can be weak with respect to one set of boundaries and strong with respect to another. It depends. Use weak testing unless you have reason to use strong, such as:

1. There's a gap in a boundary inequality. That means that there's at least three segments to test. You certainly would want to test the gapped segment by itself, but you might test the two parts of the boundary inequality on both sides of the gap as inequalities rather than as segments.

2. A closure change at one or more segments is a good reason to go strong with respect to that inequality.

---

* Actually my distinction between weak and strong is specious. A proper set of specifications for situations in which "strong" was needed would require at least one inequality for every point at which the boundary closure changed and/or at beginning or ends of boundary gaps—with such additional data, all is weak—you never needed to test the intersection anyhow.

3. The processing is such that some test points fall into a region that will not be processed. Suppose there are several domains and that any input not in one of those domains is rejected. The code proceeds in three steps: data validation, input classification, processing. You use weak testing and pick points that fall into the reject region. They are rejected properly, but you really didn't test the input classification logic. What you actually have here are two sets of overlapping domains. The first set defines the accept/reject boundaries and the second set defines the processing. The implementation is in a sense redundant, but it's a very common way of doing this. If you go weak in this situation, you could be misled. Many inputs will be correctly rejected because they fall outside of the processing domains, but they are rejected for the wrong reason—coincidental correctness. By going weak here, you conclude that processing boundaries are correct based on your examination of accept/reject boundaries; dangerous assumption. Strong testing would be safer. You'll have to look at the code to decide.

4. Look at the coding style. If I saw a neat, explicit, table-driven, processor in which the boundary inequalities were explicitly identified as such and there was, furthermore, a general-purpose processor to do the classification, then strong testing would probably be wasteful. Conversely, if the implementation had ad-hoc code to define each domain, pots full of complicated IF-THEN-ELSE trees, and various boundary defining predicates appearing redundantly, then strong testing would be prudent. If this was old code that previously worked and had been maintained, there would be no choice because weak testing would pass too many domains as being correctly implemented when, in fact, they were not. If it was new code, however, programmed in such a junky way, then I would start with weak testing because it would probably be a great bug catcher. If the design was changed as a result of the bugs we caught with weak testing, then staying weak would be safe. Conversely, if all the programmers did was patch up the ugly logic to the point that it worked, I'd go strong.

7.5 APPLICATION CONSIDERATIONS

7.5.1 Application Indicators

Domain testing can't be used to test all of a system or even all of a program. No single technique can do that. Here are some application characteristics that suggest that domain testing may be appropriate.

1. The parts of specifications given directly in terms of numerical inequalities.

2. Heavy numerical processing with lots of conditional logic: tax forms, payroll processing, financial calculations, most things you do with a spreadsheet

3. Numerical inputs and heavy input data validation and categorization, even if the subsequent processing isn't intensively numerical.

4. *Don't restrict your notion and application of domain testing to software.* This is black-box testing, so we make as few assumptions as we can about what is being tested and how it is implemented. Domain testing can be a powerful paradigm for testing systems that may or may not have software in them (as rare as that is these days). If the system, however it is implemented, is (in part) described by algebraic inequalities, then domain testing is indicated.

7.5.2 Bug Assumptions

The bugs we hope to catch are, in the typical order of importance:

1. **Domain Specification Bugs.** Ambiguous domains—the specification of the input space is incomplete; contradictory domains—domains overlap, especially at boundaries with closure to both sides; overspecified domains—too many inequalities conspire to define a domain out of existence; degenerate domains where not intended.

2. **Domain Boundary Bugs.** These bugs include, in a typical order of likelihood and importance: wrong closure, shift, tilt, missing boundary, extra boundary.

3. **Domain Processing Bugs.** Here domains appear to be correctly specified but the processing function is wrong for the domain. Wrong function chosen is likelier than an error in the implementation of the function.

4. **Domain Vertex Bugs.** These are expressed only at the vertex points of specified domains, especially if there's a lot of ad-hoc logic.

7.5.3 Limitations and Caveats

Every technique has limitations, and domain testing is not an exception. Here is a summary of the limitations discussed in this chapter.

1. **Loops.** It's assumed that there are no loops in the domain selection processing. Loops within the domain processing are okay as long as you can guarantee that once in a given domain, the processing will never cause the program to leave that domain. There are theoretical methods for handling loops that affect boundaries, but they are far beyond the scope of this book.

2. **Coincidental Correctness.** Coincidental correctness is a problem for all test techniques. The likeliest situation is coincidental correctness

with respect to rejected input domains. That is, because of coincidental correctness, bad inputs are rejected for the wrong reason.

3. **Blindness Limits and Epsilon.** Domain testing is blind to errors of less than your chosen ϵ. You may not be able to pick a single value for all your testing. Your processing might push the limits of small numbers in your system (e.g., 10^{-399}) and an appropriate ϵ can cause underflow.

4. **Difficulty with OFF Point Selection for Closed Domains.** For domains that have boundaries with input rejection domains, the OFF point may tell you nothing because the input validation occurs before domain selection.

7.5.4 Automation and Tools [TSAI85]

To date, no commercial tools implement proper domain testing. Some automatic generators use heuristic one-dimensional domain testing and then create raw combinations of extreme point values. The good news is that you don't need any special tools except a calculator and a willingness to do some elementary algebra to apply 1 x 1. You do need algebraic tools to determine if a set of domain boundaries is complete and consistent [WHIT95]. Also, all the tools you need for higher dimensions abound in mathematical libraries [BISW87, KOLM88]. The bad news is that they're not strung together in a sensible way to support domain testing.

7.6 SUMMARY

Domain testing is a formal, automatable technique to replace the common but flawed practice of testing extreme input values and their combinations willy-nilly. Domain testing is based on formally defining processing domains as sets of boundary inequalities defined over the input space. Weak 1 x 1 domain testing is used to test the inequalities when suitable, and strong 1 x1 when not suitable. Higher strategies such as N x 1 and the strategies described in AFIF92 can help diagnose bugs (e.g., shift, tilt), if that's one of your objectives. Full automation of test design and execution is possible without pushing the state of the art, but support by commercial tools is scant.

7.7 SELF-EVALUATION QUIZ

1. **Define:** adjacent domains, boundary equation, boundary inequality, boundary segment, centroid, complete boundary, closed boundary, closed domain, closure bug, collinear, consistent closure, degenerate boundary, degenerate domain, domain, domain ambiguity, domain boundary, domain boundary

set, domain contradiction, domain shift bug, domain tilt bug, epsilon neighborhood, exterior point, hyperplane, incomplete boundary, inconsistent closure, input space, input variable, input vector, interior point, linear domain, linearly dependent inequalities, linearly dependent vectors, linearly independent equations, linearly independent vectors, linear inequality, nonlinear domain, N × 1, OFF point, 1 × 1, ON point, open boundary, open domain, output space, output variable, output vector, parallel, predicate interpretation, range, shift bug, strong domain testing, subdomain, tilt bug, vector, vertex point, weak domain testing.

2. What is the sixth domain for the example on page 151?

3. Identify the ambiguities in the specification on page 153.

4. Identify all the specification problems in the example on page 159.

5. Schedule SE defines the following domains: test them.

Self-Employment Income	Rate
SE_inc < 433.13	0
433.13 <= SE_inc <= 57,600	0.153 X Net_SE_inc
57,600 < SE_inc < 135,000	0.029 X (Net_SE_inc − 57,600) + 8.812.80
135,000 <= Net SE_inc	11,057.40

6. Show that 1 x 1 works for any combination of open and closed boundaries in one dimension.

7. Plot the domain boundaries for the inequalities on page 171 and identify all the domains. Design a set of tests using strong (a) 1 ×1, (b) N × 1.

8. In each of the following, design a set of tests using (1) 1 × 1 and (2) N ×1. By set of tests, we mean input values and predicted outcomes.

a. calculated function: $u = 3x^2 + iny − exp(x^2 − y^3) + 17$.

inequalities: $−37 <= x^2 + y^2 − 10x − 8y <= −25, x >=1, y >=0$.

Tests: (x = 5, y = 8), (5, 6), (5, 2), (5, 0), (6.999, 4), (9.001, 4). I've given you test cases; your job is to justify them.

b. calculated function: $3x + 7y − 908.7345$

inequalities: $1 <= x <= 3, 2 <= y <= 10, x^2 y^{1.135} >= 30$

c. calculated function: $14x + 3.5x^2 + 17$

inequalities, $0 <= 14x + 3.5x^2 + 17 <= 31, 0 <= x <= 4$

8
Syntax Testing

8.1 SYNOPSIS

Syntax testing is a powerful technique for testing command-driven software and similar applications. It is easy to do and is supported by commercial tools.

8.2 VOCABULARY

External Prerequisite Terms: algebra, ANSI, application, ASCII, boolean, character, code, command, communication, content, control, data base, drive, file, file name, identity, input, integer, juxtaposition, language, level, logical OR, macro, model, MS-DOS, name, number, operating system, optional, Pascal, piping, program, redirection, sequence, set, software, tree, UNIX, value, variable.

Internal Prerequisite Terms: bug, clean test, coverage, dirty test, domain testing, link, link cover, link weight, loop, loop test, node, node cover, object, outcome, path, relation, specification, state machine testing, system, test.

Alphabet: A set of distinct characters of interest: for example, ASCII, hieroglyphs, {a, b, c, x, y, %, 7}. The alphabet may vary with application and even differ from test to test. Confirm the alphabet because many bugs (found by syntax testing) arise because the wrong alphabet is used; such as, ASCII instead of ANSI.

dash – : A dash between two items of the alphabet means all the items in the alphabet starting with the first item and ending with the second, assuming that there is an understood, natural order to those characters, such as "a–z." "1–9" means the integer characters 1 through 9 inclusively.

Metasymbols (also **metalinguistic symbols**): Symbols we use to describe languages. The metasymbols used here include: {, }, |, [,], (,), *, +, <, >, ?, β, σ, λ, Φ, ::=, = , – , , (the comma), , (a space), and the characters used in ordinary text. The interpretation and usage of these metasymbols follows. We'll be talking about words and commands formed using characters and how to test them, so it's important to distinguish between the characters we test and *the characters we use to describe the characters we test*. To describe a test that includes the | character, the usual practice is to double it as follows: | |. So, for example, "[[" does not mean two of the metasymbol "[" but a single square bracket that might appear in a test case.

Null (λ): A metalinguistic symbol used to designate no character. Don't confuse λ with a **space character** (σ) or a **blank character** (β).

Space character (σ): A metalinguistic symbol that denotes a space character (e.g., in printed text). The spaces between words in this sentence are for your reading convenience and not part of our descriptive language.

Blank character (β): A metalinguistic symbol that denotes a blank. This may or may not coincide with the space character, if any. The typical difference between a space character and blank character is that the σ creates a visual space in printing or display while the β does not.

String: A sequence of zero or more characters of the alphabet: for example, abd567xββ111, 1776, 666999, {:-{|)> , ~~//\\~~. Strings are denoted by uppercase letters: for example, A.

String set: Sets of string are denoted by curly braces: e.g., {A}. The set consisting of the null string λ—for example, {λ}—also is denoted by λ.

String name: Another way to denote strings is to enclose a string name in a pair of angled brackets, such as <**string_name**>. A string name also can be the name of a set of strings. Example, <**string_set_alpha**>:: = { **x, xx, ab, cde** }.

Command: A string used to control. Commands consist of **fields** and/or **operators,** and/or **operands,** and/or **delimiters** (see definitions below).

Command-driven software: A software system or a part of one in which the primary means of control is through input strings: for example, MS-DOS, UNIX.

Command language: The set of commands used to control command-driven software. Syntax testing is concerned with testing command languages.

Syntax: Rules that define what is and isn't a proper string (e.g., command). There may or may not be rules that apply to all commands, such as the correct form for numbers, but there must be a rule for every command in the command language. Syntax testing is used to determine if the program can recognize properly formed strings and reject ill-formed strings.

String field (or "field" alone when the context is clear): A part of a string to which you choose to give a name.

Operand: An object's name as it appears in commands: for example, in **DEL C:**<**filename**>, the object <**filename**> is an operand. Operands usually take the form of a word in normal language, such as: "filename," "drivename."

Operator: Special characters or strings that indicate what actions are to be taken on the specified operands. In the previous example, **DEL** is an operator.

Keyword: An operator (usually) that takes the form of an ordinary word such as: **DELETE, STORE, OPEN.** Although a keyword can consist of many characters, it is nevertheless a single operator.

Delimiter: Characters in the alphabet used to separate operators, operands, and/or to mark the end of a command. Common delimiters include: β, σ, (,), ↵ (carriage return), ≡ (line feed), [,], \, /, ", ", and , .

Parsing: The process of examining a string to identify its fields, operators, operands, and delimiters. A program that does this is called a **parser.** Every command-driven system *must* have a parser; but often the parser is implicit rather than explicit. A primary objective of syntax testing is to test the parser. We don't have to know how parsing is done to design tests for parsers.

Syntactic analysis: Parsing applied to a single field or portion of a command, for example, identifying a **substring** as a <**number**>. Syntax testing is used to test the correctness of syntactic analysis done by the program.

Semantic analysis: Operands have values: A number in a command, in addition to being a properly formed string, has a value. There may be limits on that value, such as a minimum and maximum. Syntax testing is *not* directly concerned with semantic analysis. That's better done by other techniques, such as domain testing for numerical fields.

Command interpretation: A command has been parsed and its component fields semantically analyzed. The extracted data are then passed to a program for processing—that is, executes the command. The act of executing the command is called **command interpretation.**

Lexical equivalence: If you replace the letters of the English alphabet with, say, their Cyrillic equivalents, you create a new command language that is **lexically equivalent** to the original. **DELETE C:*.***, ΔΕΛΕΤΕ Γ:∗.∗, ДЕЛЕТЕ Γ:∗.∗ , and תילאד ג:∗.∗ are lexical equivalents because we've just changed the alphabet. Lexical equivalence can involve transformations from a string of several characters to a single character, as in **PLUS** transformed to +. Lexical equivalence also may entail changing from left to right to right to left, or to up to down. For example, **DELETE C:*.*** might be transformed to ∗.∗:ג מחק. It's important to understand this concept for internationalized products lest you waste effort redesigning tests because of a trivial alphabet change to a lexically equivalent command set. If the differences between two command sets are lexical, then you can (usually) automatically convert the tests written for one alphabet to those for another alphabet.

Lexical analysis: The act of identifying operators and operands and converting them to an internal language in which a number (typically), called a **token,** replaces each operator and operand: also called **tokenizing** because input strings over the defined alphabet are converted into strings of tokens. Lexical analysis, possibly trivial and implicit, *must* take place in any command-driven system. Lexically equivalent command sets tokenize to the same token representation. Syntax testing is used to test the correctness of lexical analysis.

Null set: The set Φ, which contains no string, not even the null string.

Head (of string) (also, **beginning**): The first character of a string going from left to right (in a left-to-right alphabet, of course).

Tail (of string) (also **end**): The last character of a string going from left to right.

Concatenate: If A and B are strings and C is a string obtained by following the tail of A by the head of B, then A and B are said to be **concatenated** to yield C. Concatenation is represented by juxtaposition, for example, AB. For example, if <**string_a**>::={**xxxyzz**} and <**string_b**>::={**111011**} then <**string_a**><**string_b**> = {**xxxyzz111011**}. If {A} and {B} are sets of strings, then {A}{B} means concatenate every string of {A} with every string of {B}, maintaining the order. If {A}:: ={**111, 4 , x** } and {B}::= {**/, %**} then {A}{B} is {**111/, 111%, 4/, 4%, x/, x%**}. If A is a string then $\lambda A = A\lambda = A$. If {A} is a set of strings then $\lambda\{A\} = \{A\}\lambda = \{A\}$.

Or: If A and B are strings, then A | B (also A + B), read as "A or B," means either the A string or the B string or both. Because this is defined for strings, and single characters are strings one character long, the definition also applies to individual characters. This is the same as logical **OR** and is **commutative** and **associative**; that is, A|B = B|A, A|(B|C) = (A|B)|C. Obviously A|B|C|D|... and A + B + C + D +... are the same as {A, B, C, D...}.

Exponent: If A is a string, A^n means exactly n repetitions of A. For example, if **A**::= **##$x** then A^2 = **##$x##$x** and A^3 = **##$x##$x##$x**. By definition, $A^0 = \lambda$. The shorthand notation A^{n-m} is used to denote n to m repetitions of the string: $A^{3-6} = A^3|A^4|A^5|A^6$. If {A} is a set of strings, then $\{A\}^n$ means {A}{A}{A}....{A} concatenated n–1 times. That is, $\{A\}^2 = \{A\}\{A\}$, $\{A\}^3 = \{A\}\{A\}\{A\}$, and so on.

Plus exponent: If A is a string then A^+ means one or more repetitions of the string A: A, AA, AAA, AAAA, ... A^∞. If A::= xy, then: xy, xyxy, xyxyxy... Similarly for $\{A\}^+$ where {A} is a set of strings: {A}, {A}{A}, {A}{A}{A}...

Star operator: If A is a string then A^* means zero or more repetitions of the string A: λ, A, AA, ... Similarly for $\{A\}^*$ where {A} is a set of strings: λ, {A}, {A}{A}, {A}{A}{A} ... ; or $\{A\}^* = \{A\}^+|\lambda$. Evidently, $AA^* = A^*A = A^+$.

Union: If {A} and {B} are sets of strings, then {A}|{B} is the **union** of {A} and {B}, meaning all the strings of {A} and all the strings of {B}, without repetition. Alternate notations: {A}+{B}, {A}$\cup${B}

Behead: To create a new string by removing zero or more characters from the head of a string: For example, **d567x$\beta\beta\beta$11** is obtained from **abd567x$\beta\beta\beta$11** by beheading the first two characters.

Curtail: To create a new string by removing zero or more characters from the tail of a string: For example, **abd567x$\beta\beta\beta$** is obtained from **abd567x$\beta\beta\beta$11** by curtailment.

Substring: String A is a substring of string B if A can be obtained from B by beheading and/or curtailing B.

BNF (Backus-Naur Form) [BACK59]: A way of defining strings using the above operators and notations with minor changes and notational expansion.

::=: A single metalinguistic symbol meaning "is defined as." For example, **<string_name_alpha>::=xyz<string_beta><string_gamma>|<delta>**. This is interpreted as: "the string named 'string_name_alpha' is defined as the characters x, y, and z in that order followed by the string named 'string_beta' in turn followed by the string named 'string_gamma', or the string named 'delta.'" **<string_beta>**, **<string_gamma>** and **<delta>** have their own definitions.

BNF definition: A definition of a set of strings using the definition operator, null, concatenation, OR, exponents, plus exponents, star operator, null set, and string names or string set names. BNF definitions are usually written top down, but eventually the definitions must get around to specifying actual characters from the alphabet. Example:

<zero_entry>	::= λ|β^{0-127}|σ^{0-127}|$(\beta\sigma|\sigma\beta)^{1-63}$|<zeroes>|<dashes>
<zeroes>	::= **<integer_zeroes>**|**<decimal_zeroes>**
<integer_zeroes>	::= $\mathbf{0}^{1-12}$
<decimal_zeroes>	::= $\mathbf{0}^{1-12}.\mathbf{0}^{0-6}$
<dashes>	::= $-^{1-17}$

In the above specification, note that $(\beta\sigma|\sigma\beta)^{1-63}$ is not the same as $(\beta\sigma)^{1-63}|(\sigma\beta)^{1-63}$. The former yields $\{\beta\sigma, \sigma\beta, \beta\sigma\sigma\beta, \beta\sigma\beta\sigma, \sigma\beta\sigma\beta \ldots \}$ while the latter includes only $\{\beta\sigma, \beta\sigma\beta\sigma, \beta\sigma\beta\sigma\beta\sigma \ldots \sigma\beta, \sigma\beta\sigma\beta, \sigma\beta\sigma\beta\sigma\beta\}$. Do not try to simplify these expressions using ordinary algebra. Ordinary algebraic identities do not hold [BRZO62].

Optional field: An alternate notion for optional fields is to use brackets, as in [**<optional field>**]. Obviously the brackets are a shorthand for the 0–1 exponent. That is, [**<optional_field>**] is the same as **<optional_field>**$^{0-1}$.

Single wild card: Denoted by "?", meaning any single character from the alphabet. For example, **????abce.xxx** means any four characters from the alphabet followed by **abce.xxx**.

Multiple wild card: denoted by "*", meaning any legitimate entry for the field it replaces. Don't confuse this with the star operator. The interpretation of the multiple wild card depends on context and can't be presumed. In the string **DELσC:*.exe**, only our knowledge of the operation of MS-DOS tells us that the scope of the wild card * in this case applies just to the characters between the : and the . and that it must be restricted to legitimate strings that could appear in that place (e.g., 1–8 characters long).

Multiple wild cards such as * that can represent an indeterminate number of characters or wild cards that can represent multiple fields or sets of strings are potentially dangerous and should be avoided in test design. They're dangerous because their interpretation is fluid and can depend on context. For that reason, they're always a good place to go gunning for bugs.

8.3 THE RELATIONS AND THE MODEL

8.3.1 General

Conversion of a BNF specification into a graph is a mechanical and, therefore, automatable process [BRZO62]. Repeated application of the following four transformations does it.

Series (concatenation): The BNF segment consisting of <field_a><field_b> is modeled by a link whose weight is <field_a><field_b>.

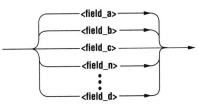

Parallel (or, **disjunction**): The BNF segment consisting of <field_a> | <field_b> | <field_c> ... <field_n> is modeled by a branching node, each of whose links is weighted by one of the or terms (called **disjunct**), which then merges to a single junction node. We don't bother using circles for the nodes in syntax graphs because the nodes have no significant properties in and of themselves: We usually use the second form.

Exponent from nonzero: An exponent such as <field>$^{n-m}$ is interpreted as a loop that is executed at least n and at most m times. I reduced each of the looping counts by one because the field in the loop appears on the bottom link. If I had put the field in the top link (an equivalent model), then the counts are n and m respectively. That's an alternate, acceptable model. The plus exponent operator is a loop from 1 to infinity.

Exponent from zero: The star operator by this definition is a loop from 0 to an infinite number of times. There are several possible, alternative but equivalent models for looping zero or more times. They are shown on the right. Recall that λ is the null string. The star operator is just a loop from 0 to infinity, which is also A+ | λ.

With these preliminaries, we can create some models for data entry on various lines of the 1040 form. The

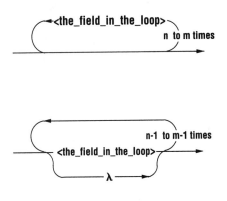

first is the social security number. A social security number consists of three subfields of three, two, and four digits respectively. Between these fields, almost any delimiters are allowed as long as they're not digits. Our first cut at a specification might be:

```
<soc_sec_num>        ::= <digit>³<delim>¹⁻ⁿ<digit>²<delim>¹⁻ⁿ<digit>⁴
   <digit>           ::= 0|1|2|3|4|5|6|7|8|9
   <delim>           ::= β|λ|σ|<other>
   <other>           ::=a|b|c|...A|B|C ...
```

This BNF form isn't unique. You could write this in many different but equivalent ways. I haven't specified how many delimiters are allowed, but I experimentally determined that for my tax package, there did not have to be a delimiter at all between the fields; hence the λ on the third line. I could have written $<delim>^{1-n}$ as $<delim>^{0-n}$ and then not put in the λ on the third line because $<anything>^0 = \lambda$. I intend the <other> specification to mean anything else. However, you'd have to check to see if this included control and alt-shifted characters. Be sure you understand this specification before you go on.

My tax package, but perhaps not yours, is very tolerant with this field. I could find no upper limit to how many entry characters it would allow. There probably is a limit, and anyone testing that software should check it. Let's say that the upper limit is 65,536 for each delimiter. My new model now is:

```
<soc_sec_num>        ::= <delim>⁰⁻⁶⁵⁵³⁶(<digit><delim>⁰⁻⁶⁵⁵³⁶)⁹ (<digit>|<delim>)*
   <digit>           ::= 0|1|2|3|4|5|6|7|8|9
   <delim>           ::= β|σ|λ<other>
   <other>           ::= a|b|c|...A|B|C ...
```

This is not a specification for social security numbers; it is a description of what my tax package accepts. It will accept almost anything and extract the first nine digits to use as the social security number. Once it has a nine-digit number, it ignores everything that follows. The IRS's rule for a proper social security number is less tolerant and more complicated because it includes restrictions on which digits can appear where as well as semantic restrictions on the numerical values of the fields. A simple BNF specification for social security number might be something like:

```
<soc_sec_num>        ::= <digit>³<delim><digit>²<delim><digit>⁴
   <digit>           ::= 0|1|2|3|4|5|6|7|8|9
   <delim>           ::= σ|-|/
```

We can now describe the model in the usual manner.

Nodes: Nodes are just points where inlinks enter and outlinks exit. That is, they are junctions or branches (usually both). A branch node means an OR operator.

Relation (link): The relation is *is concatenated with*. That is, if A *is concatenated with* B, then draw a link from A to B.

Links weights: Link weights are the important part of BNF specifications. A link weight can be the name of another part of the specification with its own graph or that graph itself. For example, the first line in the preceding specification could be as it is, in which case the weights are <**digit**> and <**delim**> with the appropriate exponent. Alternatively, I could have written:

<**soc_sec_num**>   ::= <**digit**>^{3}<σl−l/ ><**digit**>^{2}<σl−l/ ><**digit**>^{4}, or even:

<**soc_sec_num**>   ::= <**0l1l2l3l4l5l6l7l8l9**>^{3}<σl−l/ ><**0l1l2l3l4l5l6l7l8l9**>^{2}

<σl−l/ ><**0l1l2l3l4l5l6l7l8l9**>^{4}

The exponents also are included in the weights for loops.

As is so often the case with these models, while at first you may want to sketch the graph out in graphical form, once you become comfortable with the model you no longer have to do that: You work with the textual form of the graph. Often you'll find in practice that the textual form of the graph can be a page for a single command while the equivalent graphical form takes pages and pages and is more confusing than illuminating.

8.3.2 Comments on Effort

Don't confuse the effort it takes to learn BNF notation with the effort it will take you actually to do the job on real software. Sometimes ideas are easy to explain but they take a lot of effort to actually accomplish. When you think about it, the idea of the Great Wall of China isn't very complicated. Once you get the hang of it, assuming that you start out with reasonably good specifications that are not in BNF but readily available, you should be able to do about one or two typical commands per hour (e.g., an MS–DOS command). If you have to research the command to find out in detail what are all the fields and their limitations, it could easily take a day or more per command. Most examples and exercises in this chapter should take you about an hour or two.

8.4 THE TECHNIQUE

8.4.1 General [HANF70]

Syntax testing has many applications beyond testing typed commands, but that's a good application for which to illustrate this technique. As always, we start with the specifications.

1. Get as formal a specification as you can for all the commands (actually, strings) that you intend to test, in whatever form they are available. This information must exist, or else what did the programmers implement and how do the users know how to run the software? If it's an existing system, look at the help files (such as the MS-DOS command HELP) or, at worst, find the commands' syntax experimentally.

2. Search through the commands to find common parts that apply to many commands. For example, in MS-DOS 6.2, the following fields are used in many commands: **<address>**, **<device>**, **<directory>**, **<drive_name>**, **<filename>**, **<integer>**, **<ONIOFF>**, **<path>**, **<time>**. You do this in order to avoid redundant specifications for common fields. If you specify the same thing twice, there's a possibility that your specification won't be identical each time and, therefore, a possibility for creating a test design bug.

3. Search the commands to find keywords. In MS-DOS, every command has a keyword, but other keywords appear within commands, such as: **AUTO, AUX, COM1, COM2, COM3, COM4, CON, LPT1, LPT2, LPT3, ON, OFF, PATH, PRN.** Again, we do this to avoid repetitious specifications and test design bugs.

4. Start your definitions with the keywords because those are most likely to be modified through lexical changes (e.g., from English to French). This is a simple alphabetical listing, such as:

```
<auto>      ::= AUTOIAUToIAUtOI .... Iauto
<aux>       ::= AUXIAUxIAuXIAuxIaUXIaUxIauXIaux
.........
<lastkeyword> ::=
```

You might be able to save time. Instead of writing out all the possible upper- and lowercase variants, you could have written something like this:

```
<A> ::= Ala, <B> ::= Blb.
```

and so on. Then the specification for the **<aux>** keyword becomes:

```
<aux> ::= <A><U><X>
```

Command abbreviations are allowed in many systems. **DELETE** might have aliases such as: **DEL, DELE, DELET.** There are no general rules; you must research to find what is and isn't allowed.

5. Create BNF specifications for the common fields, such as **<drive>**.

6. List the commands in order of increasing complexity, where complexity is measured by the number of fields in the command and how many lower-level definitions to which you have to refer.

7. Group the commands. We don't order the commands by their operational meaning. That may be good for a sales demonstration, but it is not for testing. Group them by characteristics, such as: uses common keywords, uses common field definitions, follows a similar pattern. For example, we could have commands that followed the same pattern, such as:

<command_keyword> ::= **<drivename>:** **<path>** **<delimiter>[\<sw1>]** **<delimiter>[\<sw2>]<return>**

Well–chosen groups makes designing and testing the tests easier, helps you avoid test design bugs, and can reduce your design labor.

8. For every field that has variable content (e.g., numerical, integer, string, etc.), there is usually an associated semantic specification (e.g., min and max values). Define all such semantic characteristics and decide what test technique you will use, for example, domain testing.

9. Design the tests. Each command creates a separate set of tests—both clean and dirty. Each clean test will correspond to a path through the syntax graph of that command. As usual, you pick the path, sensitize it, predict the outcome, define validation criteria, confirm outcomes, and so on.

You must do the first eight steps whether you use automatic test generators or do it by hand. The first eight items on this list are 50 to 75 percent of the labor of syntax testing. Note how picky I was, such as not taking for granted that upper- and lowercase letters can be used interchangeably. Don't assume that because the operating system is smart about such things, the application you're testing is equally smart.

8.4.2 Coverage Hierarchy
Node cover won't be useful because the nodes have no interesting properties; we need link cover. Because we have loops, we'll also use the loop tests.

8.4.3 Clean Syntax Testing
I like to divide syntax testing into two parts: clean and dirty. Clean testing means (link) covering the graph plus additional tests for loops. It's easier to do than to describe. Figure 8.1 shows a specification for **<real_number>** in Pascal whose BNF is given by:

<real_number> ::= **<digit>+<λ| . <digit>+>< λ|<E|e|D|d >< λ|+|− ><digit>+>**
<digit> ::= **0|1|2|3|4|5|6|7|8|9**

Here's my covering test set, excluding special cases for loops: **01, 2.34, 5.6E78, 9.0e+1, 0.0D−000, 0d0**. These six test cases (and a virtual infinity of

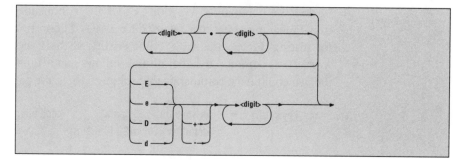

Figure 8.1 Syntax graph for <**real_number**>.

equivalent tests) provide full link cover. The easiest way to see that is to trace the specified paths on a copy of the figure.

Our next set of tests should check the loops. We should try every loop for the following number of iterations: 0, 1, 2, typical, max − 1, max, and max + 1. We can't loop zero times, at least as a clean test, because this would violate the syntax as specified. Has every loop been tested with the 1 case? Yes; so no additional tests are needed. Typical values are specific to the application, so there's no point trying them without supporting statistics. By the way, typical values usually don't pay off in finding bugs—but they're politic because they give people (statistically unwarranted) confidence.

How about the max and near max values? The + and * operators are invitations to a bug hunt. *Nothing* in a computer is infinite, so there must be a maximum value. For example, the actual specification is that no command or statement can exceed a maximum number of characters, such as 255. You must find the rule, whether it is implicit or explicit, and design tests for those cases. Let's say that there's a simple rule, such as:

<**real_number**>::=<**digit**>$^{1-10}$<λl.<**digit**>$^{1-12}$><λl<**ElelDld**><λl+l−><**digit**>$^{1-3}$>

This specification can be tested with the following tests for the max − 1 and max cases: **123456789.12345678901e12, 1234567890. 123456789012e123.** Why did I combine the three max − 1 and max into single tests? Wouldn't three cases, for each loop separately, have been better? Yes, but against what bugs are you betting? You're betting on a bug such that the software will work if any two of the three fields are not at their digit limits but will fail if all three are at that limit. That doesn't seem like a natural bug to me.

What kinds of bugs do we expect when we go hunting against * and + operators? There was a time that the software would break just because that limit had been implemented improperly; that's an unlikely bug in today's software. Programmers know and avoid such problems The likeliest bug is caused by two or more programmers with different notions of the maximum value:

One programmer assumes a limit of 512, another uses 65,536, and the third thinks that 20 is enough. The bug we expect results from inconsistencies among the three notions of computationally infinite loops. For example, the programmer of the software that does the input allows 65,536 digits. A later program to handle this number accepts only 20 digits and assumes incorrectly that the previous program prevented inputs of more than 20 digits.

8.4.4 Dirty Syntax Testing

Our objective in dirty syntax testing is twofold: (1) to exercise a good sample of single syntactic errors in all commands in an attempt to break the software, and (2) to force every diagnostic message appropriate to that command to be executed. If we have done a good job at the first task, the odds are that we will have accomplished second task also; but it's still a good idea to check.

Let's first finish the loop tests. We have to loop zero times on each loop, so here's a few of my tests: **.05, 1. , 1.1e**. For the dirty cases at max + 1 I get: **12345678901.1, 1.1234567890123, 1.1e1234**. Note that my dirty tests have only one error in each and the rest of the fields are as simple as I can make them. The clean tests should be accepted; consequently, the program should read and interpret all the characters if there are no bugs. The situation for the dirty loop tests is different because if there are too many or too few digits in the first field, the number is rejected and the buggy code for the second field is never executed. I want to ensure that all the code, however it is implemented, is tested. If there's more than one error in the test, then whichever error is detected first causes the command to be rejected and the subsequent, possibly buggy code is never tested. Because we don't know, without looking at the code, which field will be processed first, it's safest to have only one error in each field. There are other, more potent reasons for having only one error at a time in dirty syntax testing, which I discuss later.

Dirty syntax testing is straightforward. It consists of applying a few simple rules. Each BNF specification is a tree (actually, a slice). Starting at the top, we work our way down to the tips of the roots, the actual characters.

The tree has levels. At the top of the tree, <**real number**>, we have some syntactic elements directly defined and others that are defined by a specification lower down in the tree. We introduce one error, in one field at a time, or defer the error in that field to a lower level. We plan the errors in each level, one field at a time. For any field, we can make an error in the field directly or defer it to a lower level. If we make an error, it can be either a syntactic or a semantic error.

Here's a BNF specification (simplified in the interest of a reasonable example) for the MS-DOS 6.2 COPY command. The original was almost identical to a BNF specification, with a few notational differences. There are some complexities that I'll ignore—for example, overall limitation on command length, different limits on <**path**> length, where and what kinds of delimiters must or can occur between fields, and the **/A** and **/B** switches. I developed the specification top down, one level at a time, just the way I'm going to design the tests.

Level 1:   <copy> ::= COPY σ [/Y|/−Y](+ <source>)$^{1-n}$ [σ<destination>] [/V]

  L2:   <source>   ::= [<drivename>:] [<path>][<filename>]

  L2:   <destination>   ::= [<drivename>:] [<path>][<filename>]

      L3:   <drivename>   ::= a|b|...z|A|B|...Z

      L3:   <path>   ::= (\<dir_name>)$^{1-m}$\

      L3:   <filename>   ::= <fl_alphas>$^{1-8}$[.<ext>]

         L4:   <dir_name>   ::= <dr_alphas>$^{1-8}$[.<ext>]

         L4:   <ext>   ::= <fl_alphas>$^{1-3}$

           L5: <dr_alphas> ::= <a|b|c − z| A|B|C − Z|0|1|2 − 9| ^ | $ | ~ |!|#|%|&| −− |{| | }| ((|))>

           L5:   <fl_alphas>   ::= <dr_alphas>| < @ | '|' ' >

A word about levels. The field <**ext**> appears at level 4 because that's how many definitions I had to get through to get to that definition. But it also appears in the definition of <**dir_name**>, which would put it at level 5. Which is correct? Both. The point is that this definition tree is **partly ordered** while the notion of "level" is **strictly ordered** and really doesn't apply to **partly ordered graphs** such as our definition tree. But couldn't you argue that the fact that the same field appears in two different places and contexts implies a possibility of a bug caused by different treatments of each case? Correct. If it was good software, that possibility would be unlikely, so don't worry about missing a case or two. If it's real junk, then yes, it may be a good test. Junky software takes more tests to achieve coverage, but it breaks under any systematic test.

The first field is the keyword **COPY**. If this was the first command I was testing, I would start with an attack on that. All MS-DOS commands start with a keyword. If keyword recognition is broken, it's unlikely that any other commands would work. Chances are that we tested this earlier in the game. What can we do to mess up the keyword if we were going to test it?

1. Leave it out.

2. Almost right, but short a character, such as **COP**.

3. Too long, such as **COPYME**.

4. Good keyword, but wrong for this command, such as **COMP**.

Such a bug is unlikely in good software, but numbers 2 and 3 might be worth trying for junk. The rest of the command should be error-free, so we get the following tests: **T1.1.1: COP σ a:*.*** and **T1.1.2: COPYME σ a:*.***

A few comments on these two tests. You'll note that I picked the simplest version possible by eliminating as many subsequent fields as I can. That alone reduces the possibility of having these commands rejected for the wrong reason. I also used the wild card operator (*), because I'm betting that processing the wild card is a common feature to many commands and that it probably takes place along a different program path from the path for processing this command. If I wanted to avoid wild cards at this stage of testing, I would use something like **filename.tst** and have a file like that ready to be copied. Let's continue now with the next field, the delimiter.

Actually, when you do and don't need a delimiter (in this case, σ) is tricky, and my model doesn't show that. You don't need a delimiter if the next character is a backslash for a switch. Also, several delimiters are possible. Let's ignore that nicety and assume that only σ is used and that it is mandatory as shown in the model. That gives us the next two test cases: **T1.2.1: COPY a:*.*** and **T1.2.2: COPY σσ a:*.***

The first test is rejected, as it should be, but the second is accepted. What happened? Either the specification or the model is wrong. It's our model (the BNF version of the specification): It should have had σ^{1-q}, where **q** is the maximum number of delimiters equal to 127 less the number of characters in the command, or 118. So maybe we should do clean and dirty loop tests on that: q = 0, dirty; T1.2.1; q = 1, clean; q = 117, clean; q = 118, clean; q = 119, dirty.

Next we do the switch field. Several options here: wrong switch in this position, too many switches, both wrong switches. That leads me to the following tests, all of which should be rejected.

T1.3.1.	**COPY / σ A:*.***
T1.3.2.	**COPY / /Y σ A:*.***
T1.3.3.	**COPY /V σ A:*.***
T1.3.4.	**COPY /Y/−Yσ A:*.***
T1.3.5.	**COPY /Y/V σ A:*.***
T1.3.6.	**COPY /Y/Y/V σ A:*.***

In examining these tests, I found that I had not followed my own model properly. The correct specification is not as shown. I have forced a + sign on every source, but this is needed only if there is more than one source. So a more nearly correct specification is:

<copy> ::= COPY σ^{1-q} [/Y|/−Y]<source> (+ <source>)$^{0-n}$ [σ<destination>] [/V]

How can we mess up the **<source>** field? First note that the two source file fields are linked. There must be at least one source. Because the destination can be a file name also, the program can't tell if we left out a source file name and had a destination file name instead. So we have to leave both out for a dirty test. Our options then are: no source (and no destination), too many sources, syntactic error in source, semantic error in source, play around with the plus sign.

T1.4.1.   **COPY**
T1.4.2.   **COPYσA:file1.txt file2.txt**
T1.4.3.   **COPYσ A:file1.txt ++ file2.txt**
T1.4.4.   **COPY σA:a+b+c+d+e+f+g+h+i......+aa...** (beyond max source limit, n)
T1.4.5.   =   **T2.1.** Syntactic error in source specification
T1.4.6.   =   **T2.2.** Semantic error in source specification

In T1.4.4, I used very short file names without extensions because I'm trying to force the maximum number of source files into this command, beyond the maximum allowed, I hope. I had to create a lot of files with single-character names, then some with double-character names, and so on. In doing this test, you would have to be sure not to exceed the maximum command length of 127 characters.

Tests 1.4.5 and 1.4.6 are really tests for the next level. My test numbering scheme is systematic. The first digit identifies the level, the second digit identifies the field being messed up, and the third digit identifies the specific way the field is messed up. Leaving out a field or putting in too many fields is a test at the first level. However, syntactic or semantic errors in those fields really are deferred to the next level.

The dirty tests for the destination field and its delimiter have already been done at this level, because there is almost no difference between a source and destination specification. The only thing we can do are syntactic and semantic errors in the destination specifications:

T1.5.1   =   T2.3 Syntactic error in destination specification
T1.5.2   =   T2.4 Semantic error in destination specification

The last productive test we can do at this level is to play with the switch, much in the same way we played with the first switch.

T1.6.1.   **COPY σ A:file.txt /**
T1.6.2.   **COPY σ A:file.txt σ V**
T1.6.3.   **COPY σ A:file.txt //**
T1.6.4.   **COPY σ A:file.txt / V/V**
T1.6.5.   **COPY σ A:file.txt / Y**

The same prescription is followed for the next level of the tree. The semantic error in the source field consists of a syntactically correct file name for a nonexisting file. The source field itself is actually more complicated than our model shows. It must have at least one of the named fields. That is, a drive and/or a path and/or a file must be specified. So the correct specification is really more like:

(<drivename>: [<path>][<filename>]) | ([<drivename>:]<path>[<filename>]) |
([<drivename>:] [<path>]<filename>

If you have one of the two components, the other two are optional. All fields in the destination specification, however, are optional. Level 2 errors, then are syntactic and semantic errors in the source and destination fields. There really aren't many syntactic errors at this level because of the optional fields. That is, if we have any one of the three components for a source, it's okay. About the only test we can do at this level is play with the colon: wrong character (;), too many, leave it out. Except for semantic errors (no such source and no such destination), the rest of the tests are deferred to the next level.

In level 3 we play with <drivename>, <path>, and <filename>. The number of drives permitted by MS-DOS and, therefore, the syntax and semantics of the drivename depends on the MS-DOS version. Because <path> is optional, the only errors we can make at this level are missing the required \ at the end of the path string or having too many of them. An invalid path, semantically, is deferred to the next level. I might try a file name with an (.) but no extension.

The fourth level deals with semantic and syntactic errors in the content or formation of directory names and extensions. The same pattern is applied again: Leave something mandatory out, put too many in, put the wrong thing in its place, make a semantic error. You continue this way until you reach the tips of the rootlets—the place at which you insert actual characters.

I've stuck pretty rigidly to only one error at a time. There are two reasons for this, both of them important.

1. **Too Many Tests.** It probably takes about 75 to 100 tests to do this MS-DOS COPY command and would take many more if we had based our testing on the actual BNF specification with all its switches and complexity. Whatever number of tests you might generate with a single error, you'll generate the square of that number or thereabouts with double errors. Commercial tools [IDEI94, POST94] do all of this once you have a BNF specification or its equivalent. And such tools generate an awesome number of dirty tests. With a typical system that has a few hundred user and operator commands, you can easily create 100,000 tests in a day or so. Even with automated execution, that's a big number. Double errors would probably lead to 10,000,000,000, and triple?

2. **Error Cancellation.** It is theoretically impossible to create a dirty test generator that's guaranteed to generate only dirty tests. Syntactic

peculiarities will lead to supposedly dirty tests that are perfectly fine. The system will "pass" the test and you'll have to investigate. If there are too many false alarms, even with automation, the technique's utility is eroded. With double errors you introduce the possibility of error cancellation. For example, **(x + y + (z − w)** is missing a right parenthesis. If I make two errors to get either **x + y + (z − w)** or **(x + y + z − w)**, we have two syntactically correct strings—the errors have cancelled. Parentheses and other **paired delimiters** (BEGIN-END, DO-ENDO, IF–ENDIF, PARDO–ENDPAR) are simple examples of error cancellation. With multiple errors, not only does the number of tests increase dramatically, but the proportion of false alarms increases even faster.

8.4.5 Outcome Prediction

There are two outcome prediction issues: clean versus dirty tests. Outcome prediction for clean tests is specific to the command tested and the semantics. There are no general rules: You have to do it. For dirty tests, outcome prediction is very easy: **COMMAND REJECTED**.

8.4.6 Nice and Nasty Variations

Several variations of syntax testing can make the job easy and several can make the job much more difficult. The saving grace, however, is that the programs that exhibit the nasty variations are usually the buggiest and therefore syntax testing tends to have a good payoff.

1. **Formal Structure.** Some command languages, such as UNIX, have a formal structure. Instead of hundreds of specialized commands, the language has relatively few command segments that, under the specified rules for composing those segments, create the wanted effect. Conversely, an operating system such as MS-DOS, which does not have this overall formal structure, does have some aspects of it, as in the piping and redirection options. For command languages that have an explicit, formal structure, it is usually enough to test the segments and the rules for composing them without testing the entire universe of possible commands. This is especially important in dirty syntax testing, which tends not to be very productive against formally structured command languages. Because the language has a formal structure, it is usually very easy to find a complete, detailed specification of all commands, often in a metalanguage that's equivalent to BNF. So the tests are easy to design, but they don't reveal much. Clean testing cost, of course, is significantly reduced.

   Command languages that have no formal structure or that appear to have grown by accretion typically are very vulnerable to dirty syntax testing (and also buggy). The most notorious example of this type is the dBASE-II/III/IV data base programming languages for PCs. Macro command languages for PCs also often exhibit such bad traits. Ad-hoc languages, often "designed" without the conscious understanding that a language was being designed, tend to be difficult to research because the commands (and especially their quirky exceptions) are poorly documented. The lack of structure makes test design automation difficult, and automated dirty testing produces many wrong test cases. The saving grace is that systems with ill-structured command languages are pathetically easy to break.

2. **Explicit Lexical Specification.** These are command languages with an explicit lexical specification. Keywords are clearly identified and can never correspond to, say, options within commands or other command strings that might come about naturally. The language specification provides clear rules concerning alphabets and keyword transformations. The cleaner and more obvious the separation between lexical and syntactic aspects, the less testing you have to do. A single set of comprehensive tests for the overall language under one specific lexical transformation provides warranted high confidence in other lexical equivalents. However, if there is an explicit lexical specification, then it is easy to automatically convert a set of clean and dirty tests designed for one lexical specification to another. As is so often the case, good programs are less buggy and a lot easier to test.

   The converse of a clean lexical specification is a language in which lexical and syntactic aspects are hopelessly intertwined. Test design is difficult, research effort is high, but payoff is also high.

3. **Context-Dependent Syntax.** Good command languages have a clear separation between syntax and semantics. In bad languages, these aspects are hopeless muddled. As an example, consider the following specification:

\<command\>	::=	\<keyword\>\<delimiter1\>\<field1\>\<delimiter2\>\<field2\>
\<delimiter1\>	::=	σ|β|−| IF \<keyword\> = \<keyword_list_1\>
	::=	λ IF \<keyword\>= \<keyword_list_2\>
\<delimiter2\>	::=	\\/|,|σ|−| IF \<field1\> = \<field1_syntax_1\>
		λ IF OTHERWISE
\<field2\>	::=	\<field2_syntax_1\> IF \<field1\> = "1"
	::=	\<field2_syntax_2\> IF \<field1\> = "2"
		....
\<field2\>	::=	\<field2_syntax_99\> IF \<field1\> = "99"

Command languages with context-dependent syntax are not usually as clean and regular as the example just given. The problems with this specification is that the syntax of one field depends on the semantics of another. To make matters worse, the syntax of an early string in the command may depend on the specific syntactic form and/or the values (semantics) taken on by a subsequent field. The best thing to do with such languages is to bury them. They're almost impossible to use, impossible to maintain, very difficult to program, but very easy to break. Typically, when we see such languages, the code that implements the parser is totally implicit and as scatterbrained as the language itself. There is a purpose to testing such garbage: to convince the designers that a language change is essential. While research to find the ad-hoc quirks is difficult, there's little point in doing it. This junk is so easy to break that you can do it manually without difficulty. It is one of the few places in testing that makes me feel guilty about the pain I cause—as any adult should when doing violence to little children and small vulnerable beasts.

8.5 APPLICATION CONSIDERATIONS

8.5.1 Application Indicators

Command languages for which syntax testing is effective are a surprisingly common part of most applications.

1. **Command-Driven Software.** This is the most obvious application and probably the most common. If a system is mostly command–driven, then much of its testing can be organized under syntax testing. I have found it useful to use syntax testing with as few as a dozen commands.

2. **Menu-Driven Software.** The popular alternative to command–driven software is **menu-driven software,** in which actions are initiated by selecting from choices presented in a menu. The most appropriate technique for testing menu-driven software is state-machine testing discussed in Chapter 9. However, menu-driven or not, there are still data fields to enter and those fields have a syntax against which syntax testing is effective. It's usually very easy, though, because the syntax tree tends to be shallow.

3. **Macro Languages.** Many commercial software packages for PCs have a **macro language,** also called a **scripting language.** This is a programming language that can be used to automate repetitive operations. Some examples are: operating system (MS-DOS batch command language), operating system shell (Norton Desktop for Windows Scripting Language), Lotus 1–2–3 and WordPerfect (Macro Languages),

CrossTalk (CASL-IV Scripting Language). These languages often are implemented in commercial packages not just for the users' convenience but because they are neat way to implement a lot of complicated features, such as mail-merge in a word processor. In their best form, these are full-blown, albeit specialized, programming languages with formal specifications (often in BNF or the equivalent). Noncommercial software or software that serves a narrow segment of an industry* also may have a macro language, but usually it's not as cleanly defined or implemented as the commercial (horizontal) packages. Such languages, if they are part of an application, warrant syntax testing.

4. **Communications.** All communications systems have an embedded language. It is the language of the format of messages. You might not think that there's such a language in telephony, for example, but you would be wrong. Telephone exchanges use a big language to communicate with each other. But proper telephone numbers, local, long distance, and international, have a very formal syntax called a number plan. Every message used to communicate must have a format (i.e., syntax) that must be parsed.

5. **Data Base Query Languages.** Any data base system has a command language used to specify what is to be searched and what is to be retrieved. The simplest ones allow only one key. The more mature systems allow boolean searches based on user-supplied parameters, which we recognize as being predicates. Such predicates obviously have a formal syntax and semantics, and should therefore be treated to syntax testing.

6. **Compilers and Generated Parsers.** The one place I would *not* use syntax testing, especially dirty syntax testing, is to test a modern compiler. This might seem perverse and strange, but it's consistent with my dictate that a tester should never repeat the tests previously done by another. Modern compilers have a parser, of course. But that parser is generated completely automatically by use of a parser generator given a formal definition in something like BNF. Lexical analyzers are also generated automatically from formal specifications. The best-known tools for this purpose are LEX and YACC [MASO90]. While at first used almost exclusively to generate lexers and parsers for compilers, they and similar tools are being used increasingly to create lexers and parsers for software command languages. That's great, because the generated lexers and parsers are very robust. From a testing viewpoint, there's not much that syntax testing, even when fully automated, can do

---

* General packages that cut across many users, such as word processors, spreadsheets, and data base packages, are called **horizontal packages.** Packages that serve a single industry and provide most of the services needed by that industry (e.g., travel agents, florists, druggists) are called **vertical packages.**

to break such lexers and parsers. Before you spend a lot of effort on syntax testing (even if automated), look at the application and how it has been implemented. If a generated lexer and parser are used or planned, you're unlikely to have great success in using syntax testing; those kinds of bugs have been totally prevented. The only thing left to test is semantics, which, as you've seen, often is done by another technique such as domain testing.

8.5.2 Bug Assumptions

The bug assumptions for syntax testing are best described in terms of a hypothetical parser, whether implicit or explicit. Here's a sample.

1. **Incomplete Syntax.** Operationally meaningful commands are not accepted or, if accepted, are processed improperly because the parser does not handle such strings. As a consequence, the command's interpretation is haphazard, usually wrong, and leads to crashes or data corruption.

2. **Inconsistent Syntax.** Syntax, especially context dependent, results in different, inconsistent parsing and subsequent interpretation errors.

3. **False Rejections, False Acceptance.** Parser bugs lead to rejections of operationally meaningful commands and acceptance of syntactically erroneous commands.

4. **Syntax/Semantics Mismatch.** Errors in the parser lead to rejections or incorrect modifications of the values of fields. For example, integers from 0 to 999 are to be accepted but the implementation insists on having leading zeroes, thereby rejecting good numbers such as 7 and 19.

5. **Alphabet and Lexical Bugs.** Lexical transformation is incorrect leading to interpretation of field contents as delimiters, say. For example, quotation marks are required around strings but there is no ability to handle a string that contains quotes, or a carriage return is interpreted as an end of field but there is no way to insert text with carriage returns.

8.5.3 Limitations and Caveats

The biggest potential problem with syntax testing is psychological and mythological. Because design automation is easy, once the syntax has been expressed in BNF, the number of automatically generated test cases measures in the hundreds of thousands. Yet, as in the case of generated parsers, such tests may be no more cost-effective than trying every possible iteration value for a loop. The mythological aspect is that there is great (undeserved) faith in the effectiveness of what I call **keyboard-scrabbling** or **Rachmaninoff testing,** also called **monkey testing.** This is just pounding away at the keyboard with presumably random input strings until something breaks—the myth is usually completed by the presence of a wily hacker to do the pounding. Early PC software and much amateurish software still can be broken by this kind of testing, but it's rare for professionally created software today. However, the myth of the effectiveness of the wily hacker doing dirty things at the keyboard persists in the public's mind and in the minds of many who are uneducated in testing technology. I have met software development managers who sincerely believed that monkey testing was the only testing a product needed. Now what is syntax testing but highly formalized, scientific monkey testing? The big caveat, then, is that syntax testing leads to false confidence.

8.5.4 Automation and Tools

Perhaps the most attractive thing about syntax testing is the ease with which test design can be fully automated. Perhaps because automation is so easy this technique is supported by commercial tools such as (T) [IDEI94, POST94]. Even without commercial tools, construction of a test language that accepts BNF specifications, an associated test language interpreter, and a clean/dirty test generator is not that big a deal. You define your metalanguage as if it were an ordinary language and then use a lexical analyzer and parser generator such as LEX and YACC to do the hard part of the job. Of course you test your generator using itself to generate the tests. I've had several decent generators built for me: Each one took about one trimester of labor by one good (but not genius-level) senior coop student who had taken a programming language course that included LEX and YACC.

I mention the modest labor required because in many applications, working with a commercial tool such as T proves cumbersome by the time you take into account specialized input interfaces, test execution automation, platform peculiarities, and the like. This is especially true where inputs do not normally come from a keyboard (e.g., telecommunications signaling) but must be integrated deep into the application.

8.6 SUMMARY

Syntax testing is a powerful, easily automated tool for testing the lexical analyzer and parser of the command processor of command-driven software. Syntax testing begins with defining the syntax using a formal metalanguage, of which BNF is the most popular. Once the BNF has been specified, generating a set of tests that covers the syntax graph is a straightforward matter. Beyond mere link cover, we usually supplement the tests with clean and dirty tests to handle exponents, especially the plus and star operator.

8.7 SELF-EVALUATION QUIZ

1. **Define:** alphabet, associative, behead, blank character, BNF, command, command-driven software, command language, commutative, concatenate, context-dependent syntax, curtail, dash, delimiter, disjunction, error cancellation, exponent (metasymbol), generated parser, keyword, LEX, lexical analysis, lexical equivalence, link (in syntax graph), link weight (in syntax graph), macro language, menu-driven software, metalanguage, metasymbol, node (in syntax graph), null character, null set, operand, optional field (notation in BNF), paired delimiters, parallel transformation, parser, parsing, plus (exponent) operator, semantic analysis, series transformation, scripting language, space character, star operator (metasymbol), string, string field, string head, string name, string set, string tail, substring, syntactic analysis, syntax, token, tokenizing, union operator, wild card (multiple), wild card (single), YACC.

2. Play with your tax package to determine experimentally the BNF specifications for the following fields in Form 1040. Having done that, design a set of covering clean tests and dirty tests. (a) tax year ending; (b) first name, middle initial, last name; (c) entire address except zip code; (d) zip code plus carrier route; (e) field 6c(5) number of months dependent lived at home; (f) date field in the signature area.

3. Use your tax package to determine experimentally the BNF specification for the social security field. My tax package is very liberal and allows very wide variations in syntax. However, what it subsequently interprets the inputs to be is a totally different issue. Determine the syntax for valid entries and design tests for them. Then define the total BNF specification that also includes how various strings are to be transformed to extract valid numbers if possible. Design both clean and dirty tests.

4. Create a BNF specification for one- or two-digit integer data entries. Use positive numbers only. Include various means that people might reasonably use for zero or no entries, such as: blank, null, 0, o, –, –0–, etc. Then design a covering set of clean tests and good dirty tests for single errors.

5. Create a BNF specification for dollar amounts including positive and negative entries, blanks, zero entries, with and without cents, with and without commas, and so on, including all the reasonable ways people might enter such data into a tax return. Then design covering clean tests and single-error dirty tests.

6. Define the <**drive**><**path**><**filename**> portion of MS-DOS commands or their equivalent in your operating system. Then design a full set of clean and dirty syntax tests.

7. Research the following MS–DOS (or comparable commands in your operating system) and provide a complete BNF specification for each, excluding the <**drive**>, <**path**>, and <**filename**> fields, which you can assume are tested elsewhere. Then design a covering set of clean and dirty tests. Allow for abbreviations, aliases, and different alphabets. Check ONLY your dirty tests by trying them out. (Note: If you inadvertently design a clean test, it may execute and the consequences to your system are yours to deal with.) The commands are: **APPEND, ATTRIB, BUFFERS, CHDIR, COMMAND, COPY, COUNTRY, DATE, DIR, EXPAND, FC, FORMAT, KEYB, PRINT, SHARE, SORT, TIME, XCOPY.**

8. Design parser tests for Old English currency. You're given an arbitrary number of each item, consisting of a number followed by a coin symbol, such as "3£, 17s, 8p, 7S, 4hc". The parser is for an automatic coin changer. The program will convert the input numbers and express total in terms of f, h, d, s, and £. The coinage: 2 farthings (f) = 1 ha'penny (h); 2 ha'pennies = 1 penny (d); 12d = 1 shilling (s); 1 florin (F) = 2s; 1 half crown (hc) = 2s 6d; 1 crown (c) = 5s; 20s = 1 pound (£); 21s = 1 guinea (G); 1 sovereign (S) = 2£ 18s. No wonder they went decimal.

9. Honorable Pvblivs Jvlivs Lentvlvs,

Tribvnvs Laticlavivs, Legio XXIII *(Confutatore):*

Hail Pvblivs:

There are problems with your tax return for last year to discvss:

1. You did not inclvde XLIV talents of silver that you got from the sack of Rvbidivm last year.

2. Your claim as dependents for all the men of XXIII Legion is allowed, but you cannot claim your men's MMCCCIX slaves nor their MMMXLIV camp followers as these are claimed on the men's own tax retvrns. ....

   Poor Pvblivs; income tax problems probably started back then. Create a BNF specification for positive integers in the Roman numeral system. Note: An underline* under a letter — X, L, C, D, and M,— multiplies it by 1000: for example, X = 10,000, L = 50,000, and so on. Allow both upper- and lowercase letters. Include all integers from 1 to 5,000,000. Then do a covering test set and dirty tests. Hint: Completeness is wanted, not compactness.

---

* The Roman numbering system actually uses an overscore, but frankly, that's too clumsy to do with a word processor. I hope that classical history purists won't take offense.

9
Finite-State Testing

9.1 SYNOPSIS

Originally motivated by hardware logic testing, the finite-state machine model is an excellent model for testing menu-driven applications. It is also important because of its widespread use in object-oriented design.

9.2 VOCABULARY

External Prerequisite Terms: application, behavior, boot, bug, character, close file, control, data, design, hardware, file, function key, integer, load, logic, LSI, menu, menu bar, mapping, memory, message, method, mouse, mouse click, MS-DOS, object-oriented software, open file, operating system, serial port, software, subroutine, symbolic debugger, Windows.

Internal Prerequisite Terms: behavioral testing, coincidental correctness, domain, domain testing, graph, input, link, link cover, link list, link weight, model, node, node cover, node weight, null, output, path, state, strongly connected, syntax testing, system, value.

State: States are depicted by nodes.

Input event: A distinct, repeatable event *or fixed sequence of events* of interest characterized by inputs (or input sequence) to the system. What constitutes an interesting event is specific to the application. In the context of finite-state models, I'll use the term "input" where not ambiguous to denote "input event." Examples: an external stimulus, an input message, a character, a menu selection, a fixed sequence of user commands.

The inputs of finite-state models concern control rather than data: inputs that change the behavior of the system rather than just produce different outputs. Examples: the value of an integer control parameter, inputs whose values cause software to follow different processing paths, a representative input for each input domain. Each of these is considered a distinct input event.

Input encoding: Each event can be given a name or number: that is, the input events can be mapped onto the integers, say, or onto a set of characters. This is called an **input encoding.** The behavior of a finite-state machine is not changed by changing the input encoding.

Input symbols: The set of distinct names or values of the input encoding.

Number of input symbols: The input encoding assigns an integer from 1 to n, say, to every distinct input event. We assume that there are no gaps in these numbers. In most models, the number of input symbols is small—typically under 20. Bigger numbers can be handled, but usually not without tools.

State code: The states can be numbered. This is called a **state encoding.** States have operational meaning. For example, the states of a floppy disk drive might be: (1) start-up, (2) motor-on, (3) seeking track, (4) seeking sector, (5) reading, (6) writing, (7) erasing, (8) motor off. We can call these states by their equivalent numbers—for example, 1 to 8—a state encoding. The behavior of a finite-state machine is not changed by changing the state encoding.

Current state: At any instant, the system is in one state, the **current state.**

Initial state: A special state, called the **initial state,** usually is the state of the system prior to any input. While it is possible to test systems that have no initial state, doing so is beyond the scope of this book.

State counter: A hypothetical or actual memory location that holds the state code of the current state. The state counter often is implicit. The program counter of a computer is an explicit state counter.

Number of states: The state counter has a maximum value. If there are no gaps in the state code, this maximum value is the number of states in the model. As with input symbols, the number of states in a model usually is small (under 30). Bigger models can be handled with appropriate tools.

Finite-state machine: An abstract machine (e.g., program, logic circuit, car's transmission) for which the number of states and input symbols are both finite and fixed. A finite-state machine consists of **states** (nodes), **transitions** (links), inputs (link weights), and outputs (link weights). Finite-state machines in this book are depicted by **state graphs.**

transitions: A system responds to input events; the state may change as a result. This is called a **state**

transition, or transition for short. A system transmits a message to another. While it was transmitting, it was in the "transmitting" state. When it finishes transmitting, it waits for an acknowledgment. It is then in the "awaiting acknowledgment" state. The state change can be thought of as changing the value of the state counter. Transitions are denoted by links. If an input, X, causes a transition from state A to state B, we use a link from A to B, weighted by X, to denote that fact. In the diagram, an input X has caused a transition from state A to state B.

Self transition: Denotes no change of state; it is a link from a state back to that state. There may be an output associated with that transition.

Output encoding: There may be an output associated with a transition: that is, an output action is initiated as a result of a state change. Output actions can also be mapped onto integers. This mapping is an **output encoding.** The behavior of a finite-state model is not affected by the specifics of the output encoding.

Output event: The system may produce an output as a result of a state change. This is equivalent to outputting an integer, such as the output code.

If we were talking about software (and we need not be), then we could say that an output of the integer 7, say, corresponds to activating the seventh subroutine, or sending a message to the seventh method in object-oriented pro-

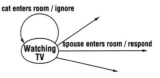

grams. Output events also are denoted by link weights, following a slash mark. In the first example above, output Y is activated by input X. Note in the above model that an input both causes a state change (possibly to the same state as in "watching TV") and an output (possibly null, as in "ignore" for an input of "cat enters room").

Null output: A hypothetical null output event: for example, do nothing.

Reachable state: A state B is **reachable** from a state A if there is a sequence of inputs such that, when starting from state A, the model will end up in state B. That is, the state graph has a path from A to B.

Unreachable state: A state is **unreachable** from other states, especially from the initial state, if it is not reachable. Unreachable states usually mean a bug.

Strongly connected: Most states of practical finite-state machines used in testing are strongly connected if there are no bugs.

Isolated states: A set of states not reachable from the initial state. Within a set of isolated states, the states may or may not be strongly connected. It is their unreachability from the initial state that isolates them. Isolated states in software testing models are suspicious if not buggy.

Reset: A special input that forces a transition to the initial state from any state. If every state is reachable from the initial state and if there is a reset, the state graph is strongly connected. A reset is not essential, but it makes test design and testing much easier. Reset also may be implemented as a reset to a specified state that is not the true initial state of the model.

Initial state set: A set of states with the following properties: It includes the initial state(s). The initial state set may or may not be strongly connected. Once a transition is made out of that set to a state not in that set, it is impossible to return to the initial state set. Consider booting up a system. The software goes through a series of steps, each of which can be modeled by a state. Once the software is loaded, it is impossible to return to the initial state set because you can't "deboot" a program. The system might progress through several initial state sets: for example, the initial sets consist of one state each and denote the stages in booting up. But a good program *does* provide a way to return to the initial state: consider, the **CONTROL–ALT–DELETE** combination in Windows.

Working states: Eventually, the system leaves the initial state set and reaches a strongly connected set of working state; this is where most of testing is done.

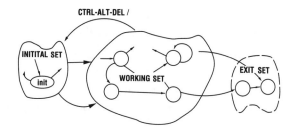

Working set initial state: A state in the working set may be called "the initial state." It is not a true initial state of the model, but operationally, it behaves as such. For example, the menu that appears after Windows has been loaded is not a true initial state—the boot-up sequence is. However, from an operational point of view, in testing, we may call that state "the initial state" insofar as testing the menus is concerned. It's a good idea to identify clearly the various sets of states and which states in those sets serve as initial states for those sets.

Exit state set: A model may have one or more states or a set of states such that, once entered, there is no path back to the working set. The states within the exit set may or may not be strongly connected. A typical example is an exit sequence for a program.

Completely specified: A finite-state machine is completely specified if and only if for *every* combination of input code and state code there is a specified transition (possibly back to the same state) and a specified output (possibly null). Unbuggy state machines are presumed to be completely specified. Buggy versions thereof may or may not be.

Menu-driven software: Software, or a mode of software operation, in which primary control is effected by selecting choices from menus.

Initial state tour (or **tour** alone when unambiguous): A sequence of transitions from a state A (the initial state, say) to a state B and back to A. If the model has an initial state set, then it is a tour from a state in that set designated as the initial state. The term also is used to refer to a tour from the initial state of a working state set.

9.3 THE RELATIONS AND THE MODEL

9.3.1 General [BARN72, BRZO63, CHOW78, CHOW88, MCNA60, MILL75]

I looked for useful examples of state machines in the various IRS forms and instructions but could find none save the perpetual state of anxiety that most of us associate with tax returns. I'll use other familiar examples as illustrations.

Nodes: Nodes denote states. Here's an example based on menu-driven software. The fact that a given menu is active indicates that we are in that state. I've customized my operating system shell to display the following menus: **Exit, File, Disk, Tree, View, Options, Tools, Window, Run Dos, Help.**

BORIS' OWN DESKTOP DESIGN										
Exit File	Disk	Tree	View	Options	Tools	Window	Run DOS=Ctrl+D	Help		
Find	Format	Label	Copy Disk	KeyFinder	DOS	Save Config	Arrange	Editor	Options	Options	Help

There are actually 12 and not 10 states because I didn't include the initial state: the state in which no menu has been selected. I also didn't include the selection of the leftmost dash button, the control menu box.

Links: Links denote transitions. In the current example, it's possible to go from the initial state to any other state by a suitable input action. It's also possible to go from most of the other 10 states back to the initial state (the active menu collapses) by using either the **ESC** or **ALT** key. We can stay in the initial state by doing nothing or by tapping any normal (not **ALT** or **CTRL**) key.

Link weights (input codes): There's a rich input encoding built in to the Windows operating system. Here are some of the ways we can activate menus, thereby causing a state change (new menu displayed).

Exit File		Tree	View	Options	Tools	Window	Run DOS=Ctrl+D	Help		
Find				Copy Disk	KeyFinder	DOS	Save Config	Arrange	Editor	Options
	Format Diskette...					WordPerfect - [CHAPTER 9 – FINITE STATE TESTING]				
A: 5.25 Flopp	Label Disk...			Insert	Layout	Tools	Graphics	Table	Window	Help	Close

Mouse selection: Move the mouse to the appropriate area on the menu bar and click the left button.

Other pointing devices: The mouse isn't the only pointing device; you can use a trackball, joystick, touch-screen, light pen, to name a few.

Alt + Key: If in the initial state, the key combination of **ALT + Letter Key**, where "Letter Key" is the letter underlined on the menu bar, such as **View.**

Function keys: Function keys can be programmed to open menus. For example, **F1** usually opens the Help menu.

Cursor keys: Once any menu on the menu bar has been selected, you can go from menu to adjacent menu by means of the left and right cursor keys.

Each of these methods is a different input encoding. The conversion from what I did (the keys I tapped, the mouse movement, etc.) to an input code often is done by the operating system. If that's your case, you can ignore it unless you're testing the operating system. If, however, your application does the encoding, then you would have to test that. If your application has several different input devices and the software handles those devices directly, each device should be considered to have a separate input encoding that must be validated.

There is an initial state: the state in which no menu on the menu bar is selected. There are several ways to get back to the initial state from most menus, such as the **ALT** key alone or the **ESC** key.

There are self-transitions in most states. Almost any normal key does a self-transition in the initial state. Note, however, that when you're in one of the open menus, some of the normal keys are active. For example, the following underlined keys are active in my **Help** menu: **Quick Help, Contents, Search for Help on, How to Use Help, Readme Files, About.** Other letter keys cause a self-transition, as do various combinations of the **CONTROL**, **SHIFT**, and regular keyboard keys. Most of these signal the fact that they are "dead" with a click. Most keys do click, but some don't: that means that a different output code has been selected. That's something worth checking.

Link weights (output codes): The actions that can take place are complicated in this example: A menu is opened or another window is opened. A selection could lead to a whole string of actions some of which work directly and some which bring up yet more windows.

Let's integrate these concepts into a model of the starship *Enterprise*. It has three impulse drive settings: drive (D), neutral (N), and reverse (R). The ship itself has three possible states: moving forward (F), stopped (S), and moving backward (B). The combinations of which impulse thrusters are firing and how the ship moves creates nine states: DF, DS, DB, NF, NS, NB, RF, RS, and RB.

The impulse drive thruster control requires that you go through neutral to get to drive or reverse. All thrusters are turned off in neutral: **D<>N<>R**. The possible inputs are: **d>d, r>r, n>n, d>n, n>d, n>r,** and **r>n.**

Let's now build a state graph for the *Enterprise.* Our ship obeys Newton's laws of motion. We'll start with **NS**, no thrusters and standing still. If we don't touch the controls (**n>n**), nothing happens and we remain in the same state. There are only two other input choices: forward thrusters (**n>d**) or reverse thrusters (**n>r**). There's a

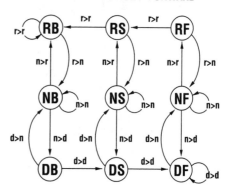

BACKWARD < MOTION > FORWARD

delay between the time we push the thruster lever and the time the thrusters fire. If we elect forward thrust (**n>d**), we move to the **DS** (drive-stopped) state. Similarly, if we elect reverse thrust, we go to the **RS** state. In either case, if we keep the thruster engaged (**d>d**), it eventually fires and we start moving forward. That puts us in the **DF** (drive-forward) state. If we were in **DS** (drive-stopped) and we disengaged the thruster, then we would get back to **NS** (neutral-stopped) state. The **RF>RS>RB** transitions on the top and the **DB>DS>DF** transitions on the bottom state that if we are moving in some direction, it is physically impossible to reverse the direction of motion without stopping at some point.

Here are some observations about the model and its graph.

1. It is strongly connected because there is at least one path from any state to any other state. Notice that these paths are not direct transitions and that the path from one state to the other is not just a simple reversal. For example, to get from **DF** to **RB** you follow the **DF–NF–RF–RS–RB** path, but from **RB** to **DF** you take **RB–NB–DB–DS–DF**.

2. I chose to model two factors: thruster control position and ship motion. Since there were three possibilities for each, the combinations yielded nine states. The number of states is the *product* of the possibilities for each factor. *State graphs grow big fast.*

3. There's a relation between inputs and states. Although there are seven possible input actions, not all of them are possible in every state. A more detailed model (see the state table in section 9.3.3 below) includes every input, including the impossible. Why? Because we're not dealing with a well-behaved system but with a possibly buggy one. For example, suppose the thruster controls were broken and it was possible to get from **REVERSE** to **DRIVE** bypassing **NEUTRAL**? (See problem 2.) In the simplest models, the states and inputs are independent, but that almost never happens in practice. For example, the action of the various keys in the menu model clearly depends on the state (which menu is active).

4. The spaceship model has nice symmetry—also rare in practice. Usually states are connected by transitions every which way.

9.3.2 Mealy Models and Moore Models

The finite state models used in this book are called **Mealy models** [MEAL55]. In a Mealy model, outputs are associated with transitions. The alternative model is called a

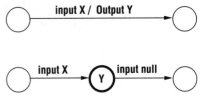

Moore model [MOOR56], in which the outputs are associated with states. The Moore model is easy to generate from the Mealy model by replacing every output code associated with a transition with an appropriate output state. Output states usually are denoted by a heavy border or a double border. In the example above, I replaced the transition with an extra state, the output state, in which the output action occurs. Note that I've also had to add a fake input (null) to show that the transition to the next state will occur without an further external input.

I favor Mealy models because:

1. **They contain fewer states** and therefore, have a simpler model. The complexity of a model is determined by the product of the number of input symbols and the number of states. If you increase the state count, you must increase the size of the model and therefore the complexity of the tests.

2. **They have stable states.** The Moore model always has transient states that don't sit still for us. That makes testing more difficult. In the Mealy model, you don't change states unless there's an input. In fairness, though, Mealy models also may have transient states if we allow null inputs, but the Mealy model usually has fewer such states.

3. **They are closer to implementation.** Programmers who do explicit finite-state implementations usually base them on Mealy rather than Moore models. If the test and design models differ, that's a source of test design bugs.

4. **They provide output repetition.** A given output, say **OPEN FILE**, can be associated with many different transitions. These would require a separate state for each instance and therefore another increase in the model's size.

5. **Table representation is easier.** Representing a finite-state model by a table is easier with Mealy than with Moore models.

The two models are theoretically equivalent. For every Moore model, there's a corresponding Mealy model and vice versa. Why the fuss? I've observed that when finite-state models are used in design, as in object-oriented programming, it is usually a Moore rather than a Mealy model. You should not mix the two model types. Pick one type (I urge Mealy) and stick to it.

Optional. Readers familiar with graph-theoretic models will see that I have a distinct preference for link-weighted rather than node-weighted models. The Moore model is, of course, a node-weighted model insofar as the outputs are concerned. The Moore model has advantages in describing sequential switching networks, especially asynchronous networks. Both models originated in support of automata and switching theory; but we are dealing with software here and not sequential switching networks.

It is easier, in general, to prove theorems about node-weighted models than link-weighted models and hence their prevalence in research papers; but when it comes to building practical tools, in which graphs are represented as linked lists, or in using the node-reduction algorithm (see BEIZ90), the link-weighted model is distinctly advantageous.

9.3.3 Transition Tables.

Models in graphical form are learning, rather than working, tools. You could use a linked-list representation as with any other graph, and indeed, we often see finite-state models presented that way in design documents. The other alternative is to use a tabular representation. We could have an n × n table (where n is the number of states) and, in each entry, put the input/output combination appropriate to that entry. We could, but we don't because the table (for typical software) would be mostly empty. Instead, we use a **state-transition table**—also called **state table** for short.

The state table has one row for every state and one column for every input. Actually, there are two tables, both with the same layout: the state-transition table and the **output table.** The entry in the state-transition table is the **NEXT STATE**. The entry in the output table is the appropriate output code (if any) for that transition. Sometimes it's convenient to combine the two tables by putting both the next state and output data into the cell, as in **next state/output code**. Here's the state table for the *Enterprise* drives.

STATE	r>r	r>n	n>n	n>r	n>d	d>d	d>n	r>d	d>r
RB	RB	NB							
RS	RB	NS							
RF	RS	NF							
NB			NB	RB	DB				
NS			NS	RS	DS				
NF			NF	RF	DF				
DB						DS	NB		
DS						DF	NS		
DF						DF	NF		

I marked the impossible cells (state-input combinations) by hatching; they are impossible, that is, in a properly implemented system. In this example, some transitions are impossible because that's the way physics work. Other inputs such as r>d and d>r are impossible because of the way the hardware works—the drive control. But see problems 2, 3, and 4 at the end of this chapter.

I haven't specified outputs. What might the outputs be for the *Enterprise* model? Perhaps activate fuel pump, ignition on. The difference between forward and reverse thrust might be which thruster fuel valve (bow or stern) is open. The fuel pumps and ignition must be activated for either thrust direction. So some output functions might apply to many different transitions. In state testing, we concentrate first on having the right states and transitions and then on outputs. For a less fanciful example, looking at the menu model, there are many places and menus in which we open and close files. We should test file opening and closing, of course. But once files are opened properly and we've gained confidence in that, it's not necessary to retest file opening in every context (i.e., every transition) in which it might take place.

9.3.4 Nested Machines

The table just shown is complicated: it has 81 entries (nine states and nine inputs). The desktop menu example is even more complicated. I counted 12 options on the menu bar and considering only those menu options that are activated by a normal key, 23 out of the 26 letters of the alphabet plus nine numerals or a total of 32 input codes were used. A single table to represent this would be 12 × 32 or 382 entries. We could build one big table, but we don't because:

1. Too many entries. Too many opportunities for test design bugs.

2. Too many blank entries. More bug opportunities.

3. Too many impossible state/input combinations.

4. There's a better way.

The better way is to use **nested machines.** That's what most people do intuitively. The control panel menu in Windows has three choices at the top level: the **control menu box**, **Settings**, and **Help**. We can build a four-state machine with one state for each of the three menus and one state in which no menu is active. We build a model for that level and explore all the ways we can switch from menu to menu, activate menus, deactivate menus, and so on, but

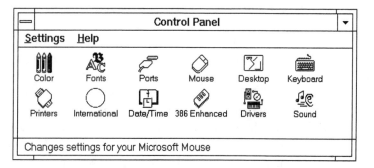

without doing or selecting anything in any of the menus. For each of the three menus, we create a separate finite-state model that explores how that menu works and how selections in it are made. Similarly for icon selection in the initial state (no menus showing) of the base model.

Continuing with our nested machine example, let's go to the **Settings** menu on the uppermost level. We now have a new model with the following choices: **C**olor, **F**onts, **P**orts, **M**ouse, **D**esktop, Keyboard, **P**rinters, **I**nternational, Date/**T**ime, **3**86-Enhanced, D**r**ivers, **S**ound, and E**x**it. The underlined letter indicates the key that must be tapped to select that item. So maneuvering around that menu requires another model. If we pick a choice, we typically activate yet another menu with its choices and therefore another model and so on.

Nested machines are the only practical way we have of dealing with complicated systems. If you look at typical design documents based on finite-state machines, you'll see that that's what good designers also do. They nest their design models. As a result, their implementation has the same nesting. Practically speaking, without supporting tools it's very difficult to deal with state tables that have more than a few hundred entries. That's not very big— 10 states and 20 input codes. Big machines with thousands of entries are routinely used in telephone exchange control software, but some of those tables took hundreds of work years to create, test, and debug.

9.3.5 Clean Up the Model

The possibility of errors in creating the model is high. In practice, state-machine models are big investments. You must distinguish between bugs in the model, in tests created by using the model, and in the system. It's cheaper to get rid of modeling bugs before you design tests than to find them during testing. Here are some of things to look for in the model and how to find them. The good news is that there's a theory of such models, algorithms based on those theories, and, in many cases, tools based on the algorithms. The bad news is that the theory is beyond the scope of this book and the algorithms, when implemented as tools, almost always apply to hardware and must be adapted for use in software models.

1. **Completeness and Consistency.** How many input symbols? How many states? The product of those two numbers (called the **state-symbol product**) is the number entries in the state table. There must be one and only one transition to the next state for *every* entry in the table: no more, no less. If any entry is missing, that's an ambiguity in the model. If any entry has more than one transition specified, that's a contradiction. The program cannot be either contradictory or incomplete. It will always do something in every state for every input, and only one thing. Seeming contradictions are nastier because they mean that your state machine is at least twice as big as you thought it was.

2. **Unique Input Encoding.** If the input encoding changes from state to state, you've got either a bug in your model or an awful design. That means that the state table's size isn't fixed. You can't practically analyze that stuff.

3. **Minimum Machines.** You create a model in which there are two sets of states that have different names but identical output actions and analogous transitions. Say you have two states, A and B, such that *every* input sequence that starts from A produces exactly the same output sequence if started from B. If so, there is no way an outsider can tell the two states apart. Despite differences in their names, the two states are equivalent and they can be merged. The same idea can apply to sets of states. You should clean up the model by merging all equivalent states. There are mechanical ways of doing this: see BEIZ90.

4. **Not Strongly Connected.** State models for software whose working states aren't strongly connected are almost always either a modeling error or a design bug. How do you feel about a program that has menus that can't be exited without shutting the system off? You can determine this manually for small models. For big models, there are algorithms beyond the scope of this book. Similarly, there are algorithms for finding unreachable states or sets of unreachable states. See BEIZ90, *partitioning algorithm.*

9.4 THE TECHNIQUE

9.4.1 General

The prescription for test design follows the pattern of the previous chapters.

1. **Identify Inputs.** What are the distinct input events you intend to model? Give each event a name and characterize it. Examples: specific incoming messages, belong to a specific input domain, a fixed sequence of inputs. Every input possibility does not belong in the model. Keep the distinct number of input events small (e.g., 10s and 20s).

2. **Define the Input Encoding.** You created the input encoding used in your model. It may or may not correspond to a comparable encoding used by the programmers. Don't include stuff that's done by software that you aren't testing. For example, if the operating system takes care of converting mouse position and clicks into menu item selection, don't include that in your model; assume the input comes to you encoded (by the operating system, say). You must test the input encoding process if that's part of the program's implementation.

3. **Identify States.** States often are created as a product of factors. If so, identify the factors and realize that there will be a unique state for every *combination* of factors—that product grows big very fast and nested models might be indicated. List the states you identify and give them systematic names. You should be dealing with dozens, not thousands, of states.

4. **Define the State Encoding.** If the designers are using a software implementation of a finite-state machine [BEIZ90], there may be an actual state encoding process and a state counter. If so, the state encoding process should be tested—but that could be very difficult in the context of pure behavioral testing. If there is no explicit finite-state design, then the state encoding is an aspect of your *model* and not necessarily part of the software. You still have to verify its correctness as a check of your model.

5. **Identify Output Events.** Only the simplest models have nice single output events that correspond directly to, say, outputting a single character. More likely, the output events consist of a sequence of actions. Identify such sequences. *In a nested model, the output event is the activation of the next model down in the model hierarchy.* Give each output event, whether simple or a sequence, a name.

6. **Define the Output Encoding.** If the design is an explicit finite-state design, then the programmers may have an output encoding for you to test; also difficult to do in the context of behavioral testing. Nevertheless, you must verify that your output encoding (which, after all, is only a model property) does indeed correspond to what actually happens.

7. **Build the State Table and Output Table and Clean Them Up.** This is the hardest part of the job, the most time-consuming and most error-prone.

8. **Design Your Tests.** You have three kinds of tests to design: (a) input encoding verification tests, (b) output encoding verification tests, and (c) state/transition verification tests. The first two are tests of your model. The last is a test of the software (and your model). These objectives and how to achieve them are discussed in section 9.4.2 below.

9. **Run the Tests.** Every test should start from the initial state, make a tour of various states to get to another state, and then return to the initial state.

10. **For Every Input Confirm: Transition, Output.** This may not be trivial. Usually some kind of design support is needed. See section 9.4.5 below.

Here are some tests for the *Enterprise:*

1. NS>NS. Always good to observe the system doing nothing.
2. NS>RS>NS
3. NS>DS>NS
4. NS>RS>RB>NB>DB>DS>NS
5. NS>DS>DF>NF>RF>RS>NS
6. NS>RS>RB>RB>NB>DB>DS>NS
7. NS>DS>DF>DF>NF>RF>RS>NS

Each test starts at the initial state, **NS**. From the initial state the test goes to a target state by the shortest route and returns by the shortest route back to the initial state—a tour. Tests are added as needed to assure link cover. Each test builds on previous, simpler tests. Once you've picked a set of covering tours, you have the input code needed for each transition. You also have the output code associated with each transition. You go backward through the input encoding to find the actual inputs and forward through the output encoding to find the details of the output action, if any. It may seem like a lot of work (and it can be), but there's nothing technically profound about it.

These tests are based on good experimentation rather than on an attempt to optimize the tests. Change as few things as you can from test to test and let each test be based on previous tests in which you already have confidence. This approach creates a lot of seeming redundancy in the tests, but it is warranted.

9.4.2 What to Verify

1. **Verify Input Encoding.** Does your model's notion of input encoding correspond to what's implemented? If they differ, which is wrong, the model or the software? How you verify that depends on what you're encoding. If the inputs are numerical, then you might use domain testing to verify input encoding. If character strings, then syntax testing, or for that matter, another state model. One way or the other you must confirm the correspondence between your model's notion of input events and the software's and explain all discrepancies.

2. **Verify Output Encoding.** There are (should be) relatively few distinct output events or action sequences. You've given each of them a name. If the coded output "A" means: "**open file, update file, close file, report back,**" then you must confirm that all that happens and that it happens in that order. You may have to examine intermediate computation steps, file activity logs, use a symbolic debugger . . . But however you do it, you must confirm that the actions of your output codes match the sequence of actions in the real software and explain any discrepancy if they don't.

3. **Are You in the Initial State?** The techniques discussed in this book assume that there is at least one initial state and that it is possible to get there. There could be several initial states in a complicated system. For example, the initial state for single-user operation is unlikely to be the same as for network operation. You can't begin to test unless you are in the initial state and know it. The software telling you that it is in the initial state isn't enough—after all, that could be the very bug for which we're looking. The initial state has properties such as which files are open, resource usages, programs active, and so on. Confirm these.

If there's an initial state set, such as a boot or load sequence, then you must confirm every state and transition in that set of states. This can be difficult if you don't have design support because such sequences often are automatic. A step mode is a very useful test aid.

4. **Can You Reach Every Exit State?** Typically there's not one but several exit states or a set of exit states: states that, once entered, will effectively take the processing out of your model. The obvious one is the state in which you close the program you're testing. But it isn't always that simple. For example, if I choose to close my word processor, I'm asked to confirm it. If I confirm that I want to exit and I have any open files that weren't previously stored, the program then asks me if I want to save the change. That's a nontrivial set of exit states.

5. **Verify State.** Are all the states that should be there present? The purpose of doing a tour to a target state is to show that the state exists and is reachable. You must, of course, have some positive means of knowing the state at all times. Usually this is possible in software testing, especially if there is an explicit state counter and if the designers have thought about testability. If you don't have a means to identify the state, testing is still possible, but it is much more difficult and beyond the scope of this book.

6. **Are There Extra States?** That's difficult to determine both theoretically and operationally. The heuristic prescription of section 9.4.3 below, however, usually finds extra states if they exist.

7. **Confirm Every Transition.** There is a potential output associated with every transition. More precisely, there is an *outcome* of every transition. The transition consists of two things: the new state and outputs if any. If there is a null "output" associated with a transition, that too must be confirmed. You defined a state encoding. That means you have detailed characteristics that will uniquely identify states. Confirm every component of the state encoding. But you could be fooled because of the possibility of extra states, discussed in the next section. Similarly, you must confirm every output action defined in your model's output encoding—especially null outputs. Make sure that nothing really happens for null outputs. If you end up in the correct state and had the right outputs (including null) for that transition, then it's a good bet that the transition was correct.

9.4.3 What About Extra States?

The general problem of how to discover extra states in a finite-state machine, say implemented as hardware, is difficult, advanced, and beyond the scope of this book. However, in software testing, we don't have to deal with the general problem but with a simpler one. For one thing, we can assume things that can't be assumed in the general case, such as knowing what state we're in. For another, the problem is simplified by the nature of state bugs in software.

When we have extra states in software, it's rarely one or two extra states, but more typically double the number of states we expect, or even 1,000 times the number of states expected. Extra states in software come about because of hidden finite-state behavior. One additional bit contributing to the state behavior doubles the number of states.

The next figure tells the story. The lower finite-state machine is the one we think we have. However, because of bugs or because our model was incomplete, there's another factor in place that we don't know about. At some point, because of a bug activated during one of our test tours, instead of making a transition from A to B, we actually make a transition from A to B' in the parallel universe of hyperspace. Incidentally, in software, it's rarely just one parallel universe but thousands or millions of them. If all those parallel universes are identical in *every* respect (save the factor that caused the creation of all those extra states), then it's unlikely that we'll discover it by any reasonable number of tests. But then, although there is a bug, it's harmless. However, if the alternate-universe state machine differs behaviorally even in small ways, we can find it.

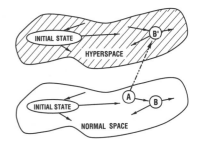

"Why bother?" you ask. "After all, it's only a small, harmless behavioral difference that we can easily tolerate." A good question deserving of an answer. As I just said, it's rarely one parallel universe but millions. In most of those universes, the small discrepancy is indeed harmless and tolerable; but in many universes the bug's symptoms are fatal. I have always been able to promote a tiny "harmless" behavioral difference into a fatal bug. You can't get developers excited about "harmless" symptoms. If you report that the screen flashed or that the mouse cursor moved when it shouldn't have, they'll shrug it off. But if you can promote such behavioral changes into a crash, and do it repeatedly, you'll get their attention. You promote bugs experimentally. Play with parameter values (e.g., file length, control codes, options, etc.) that should not affect the transition and see if you can increase the behavioral discrepancy—say getting the mouse cursor to move farther or getting the screen to blink twice. Probe along the lines that emphasize the behavioral differences and, before long, you'll have found the very precise set of circumstances that will cause a fatal symptom. A few hours of repeated testing and very careful observation on the typical PC application (say) will reward you with a crash or a shredded data base. (Be sure to have good backup and restoral facilities, though.)

The way to find the extra states in hyperspace is to repeat every test precisely. Make the tour from the initial state to the target state and back to the initial state (without using a RESET command if you can). You then compare all pertinent components of the state (say files open, resources in use, window state, etc.) after the test to before the test. The test is then repeated (precisely) and *every* outcome of *every* transition is compared to the previous run and *every*, repeat *every* change is noted.* *Any behavioral deviation whatsoever, even if harmless, tells you that you have extra states.*

This prescription does not, by any means, guarantee that you'll find the extra states if they exist, because, in general, such behavior can be discovered only by taking different paths from the initial state to the target state. Repeating the tests is not the *best* you *can* do, but the *least* you *must* do. If don't repeat the tests, it's unlikely that you'll discover the bug.

The idea of precisely repeating tests should not be restricted to tests based on finite-state behavior. Repeating every test this way is an excellent idea because bugs that cause unwanted finite-state behavior don't know what test technique we're using. **REPEAT THOSE TESTS:**

9.4.4 Coverage Hierarchy

As with all test techniques, there's a coverage hierarchy. Node cover alone tells us almost nothing. What's more, if this software already has been tested at a lower level (e.g., unit testing) by the designer, it's likely that node cover has been achieved. The central issue in finite-state testing is transitions. To test transitions, we also must confirm states (node cover). So we'll assume that as a minimum, as with most test techniques, we'll go for link (transition) cover. Is there anything beyond link cover? Lots: all beyond the scope of this book, but more important, beyond the needs of most testers using this technique.

There is a coverage hierarchy based on ever longer sequences of tests; where the length of a test sequence is measured by the number of transitions (or equivalently, input symbols). An entire literature of test methods for finite-state machines exists; it was developed originally for hardware logic testing. Although I won't tell you about those techniques (it would take an entire book), I can give you some insights into the circumstances that make such techniques essential. We've made three important assumptions in using finite-state testing methods for software.

1. We usually know the state we're in before and after each transition. In the general case, such as in testing the behavior of an integrated circuit, there's no way to know that except by observing behavior (e.g., the outputs). In some software testing situations, such as in testing a protocol

---

* This isn't as difficult as it seems. We have excellent tools for doing this comparison automatically, such as capture/playback tools. See Chapter 10.

in which you have no information about the internal state (of the system with which you're communicating, say), there is no way to know the internal state of the system under test.[*] If there's a problem with getting state information, then the basic techniques of this book won't suffice. The better approach is to design the software so that this information is available (see BEIZ90).

2. Output actions in hardware tend to be simple; such as a pulse output on a specific wire; but there are many valid transitions that could cause a pulse to be emitted on that wire. Therefore, it's not easy to tell that you have had a proper output—coincidental correctness is the rule, not the exception. In software, output actions are complex and often unique to the transition. Because they're complex, it's easy to tell one from the other. If they're the equivalent of pulses on a line, as might be the case for control software or for protocols, then the testing task is much more difficult and you may have hit the limits of the basic methods in this book.

3. Consider the nature of the bugs for which we're looking. We could be looking for a bug in the specifications. That's problematic and not peculiar to finite-state testing. If the developers have done a great job of implementing the wrong finite-state machine, then no testing technique will find it. Our assumption is that our model is correct and that the bugs are in the software implementation of that model. The likeliest bug in software is not a wrong state or a wrong transition here or there but gross effects, such as an entire parallel finite-state machines caused by hidden state variables. As a simple example, the program is designed to store recovery information every few seconds so that if there is a system crash it will recover by using the backup files. Say that the program fails to clear all of this data on a normal exit. It clears out the recovery files but leaves a crucial state variable unchanged. The next time the program is started, it attempts to recover (because it is told to do so), but the "required" recovery files aren't there—crash, crash, tinkle, tinkle. One wrong byte of data is 255 alternate universes: one 32-bit word is 4.3 billion of them. If you're meticulous about noting tiny behavioral differences, then you'll know in which universe you are.

9.4.5 Sensitization and Outcome Prediction

There's no sensitization or outcome prediction issue as such for finite-state testing. You "sensitize" by issuing the commands or inputs that cause the desired transition. You predict outcomes in doing your output encoding.

---

[*] Note that contemporary integrated circuit designers are installing a lot of additional circuitry to make that information available to production test machines.

Neither of these tasks is an insignificant amount of work, but it is straightforward and there are no special techniques involved. It must be done. The biggest error testers make in this respect is in not being meticulous enough. You really have to define everything in utmost detail. This is easy to do, however, with appropriate commercial tools, such as capture/playback tools discussed in Chapter 10.

The most important use of finite-state testing is not in the initial testing of software but in retesting software after changes during maintenance to confirm that things that shouldn't have changed didn't. In such cases, the previous run of the test provides both the inputs needed (sensitization) and the outcomes.

9.4.6 State Counting

The most important thing a tester can do, especially an independent tester, is to get an accurate count of the number of states and the number of input codes and, from that, the size of their product—the state-symbol product. Programmers who don't think about finite-state behavior implement implicit finite-state machines with trillions of states and billions of input codes. They can't be properly tested; not now, not ever. From the tester's perspective, such junk software is *so* very easy to break. Finite-state behavior based on several factors get big fast. See problem 6 for an eye-opener. As a one-time logic designer I learned that I had to do formal analysis of any finite-state machine with a state-symbol product bigger than 12—and even that was pushing the limits of my intuitive design ability. Getting a finite-state machine with a product in the hundreds right is a work of months unless there's a lot of regularity in the states and their transitions. Formal analysis (beyond the scope of this book) is mandatory. Machines with products in the thousands have labor investments measured in work years or centuries—not something you can do intuitively.

This sets the perspective of what is and isn't reasonable. You examine a system and determine that the state behavior is based on five factors, with 7, 13, 8, 4, and 3 possibilities for each respectively, and you determine that the possible inputs (after encoding) consist of 42 discrete actions. The product of these numbers is 366,912. As a tester, you should demand to see documentation for each and every one of those transitions. If it's not available, that software is untestable but very easy to break. The designers could have implemented nested machines, of course, and we hope that they did just that. If so, you have six much simpler machines to test.

Finding the value of the state-symbol product (for unnested machines) is the easiest and most productive thing you can do in finite-state testing. Doing so immediately tells you if this software isn't going to be tested adequately and therefore if it's going to be trivially easy to break.

9.4.7 Support Facilities and Testability

This is where programmers can and should earn their pay. I strongly urge programmers to use an explicit finite-state machine implementation (e.g., table-driven) if the state-symbol product is greater than 10 or so. See BEIZ90 for how to do this. If it's properly done, along with a good design that's been well analyzed (and therefore unlikely to be buggy), several features will aid testability significantly.

1. **Explicit State Counter.** There is a single, declared variable or memory location that defines the state at any time. It is accessible and can be recorded. The current state is always known.

2. **Reset, Master, and to Specified State.** There are various reset options, such as a master reset to the initial state. This may have options, such as: (a) a total reset (everything reinitialized), (b) a state-only reset (only the state counter changes, but not the status of files and such), (c) reset to a specified state. Reset could be fairly elaborate and have many parameters to dictate exactly what (besides the state counter) is to change. Good reset facilities are important in big state machines where to get to a specified state you might otherwise have to take a long tour through many other states.

3. **Step-Mode Operation.** This is the ability to step through the state graph one transition at a time, and for compound output actions one output event at a time. A pause is forced after every transition so that if the test is executed manually, the tester can confirm what happened; if the test is executed automatically, the tool can record the same.

4. **Transition Trace.** This is a trace record of every transition executed. That means the input code that initiated the transition, the current state, the state after the transition, the output code.

5. **Explicit Input Encoding Table.** An explicit input encoding mechanism exists. It's nicer if it's contained in a table. The input encoding is totally separated from subsequent processing.

6. **Explicit Output Encoding Table.** An explicit output encoding exists. This could be a table that defines what subroutines to call, or some other mechanism that is isolated from the rest of the processing.

7. **Explicit State Transition Table.** Explicit finite-state implementations always have an explicit transition table. The nice thing about such tables is that if a transition error is found, it's easy to fix.

These features are best built-in to the software from the beginning because they are difficult to retrofit. Obviously, such facilities need special operational modes and commands whose use should be prohibited to unauthorized users.

9.5 APPLICATION CONSIDERATIONS

9.5.1 Application Indicators [AVRI93, BAUE79, WILK77]

Here are some common situations that call for finite-state machine testing and/or applications in which this technique often is used.

1. **Menu-Driven Software.** Designers of commercial menu-driven software routinely use explicit finite-state machine designs for their menus. They also use finite-state testing to check the correctness of their menu structure.

2. **Object-Oriented Software.** The finite-state model is common to most object-oriented design paradigms. Proper testing of methods implies proper testing of state behavior; finite-state testing is obvious.

3. **Protocols.** A discussion of protocol testing is beyond the scope of this book. There is a big literature on the subject, all of which presumes a knowledge of finite-state testing methods [CHOW88, HOLZ87, SARI87, SIDH89].

4. **Device Drivers.** Most devices have finite-state behavior, and most drivers contain a finite-state machine.

5. **Former Hardware.** Tasks formerly done by hardware are increasingly done by software. That's not just electronics, but mechanical and electromechanical devices as well. An article in *Scientific American* [GIBB94] posits microprocessors (and software) in light switches, electric shavers (2 Kilobytes), automobiles power trains (30 K lines of code), TV (500 Kilobytes). A significant part of the behavior of such software translates directly into finite-state behavior.

6. **Installation Software.** Software installation and configuration software often exhibits finite-state behavior and can be tested productively that way.

7. **Backup and Recovery Software.** Backup and (especially) recovery software have a significant finite-state behavior. Increasingly, we have file or network servers with duplex processors. Such systems have been tested by finite-state models for a long time.

9.5.2 Bug Assumptions

It's not so much the assumptions we've made about bugs as it is the assumptions we've made about software that exhibits finite-state behavior.

1. **Ad-hoc Finite-State Machine.** The programmer doesn't realize that there's essential finite-state behavior in the program. As a consequence, there's no analysis, inadequate testing, and many, many, bugs.

2. **Encoding Bugs.** Of input codes, output codes, or state codes, whether explicit or implicit. If input encoding is implicit, then inconsistent encoding from state to state is very likely.

3. **Wrong Output.** This could be an output encoding error, or if there is no explicit output encoding, then a wrong subroutine call, say.

4. **Unsuspected State Behavior.** A vast proliferation of additional states caused by an unrecognized component of the state behavior.

5. **Crossing Nesting Boundaries.** 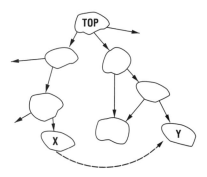 The implementation uses nested finite-state machines but because of bugs or ad-hoc bad design, the nesting boundaries are bypassed. The model on the right shows a nesting of several finite-state machines. Each blob is a set of states (e.g., a menu). If a we allow a transition from a state in X, say, to a state in Y, then the entire nesting has been corrupted, and, in fact, the total behavior is as if there were no nesting at all. There are other ways of accomplishing such nesting boundary crossings, but they must be implemented carefully. Crossing nesting boundaries like this is a common bug that usually can be found by finite-state testing. Have you ever used a menu-driven package, found yourself in a menu that you didn't select, and asked: "How did I get *here?*"

9.5.3 Limitations and Caveats

1. **Big State Graphs.** The techniques described in this book are intended for modest state graphs (state-symbol product in the hundreds). For big, unnested state graphs, such as those used in telephone exchange controls, with products measured in the thousands and tens of thousands, the types of transition tours described here are too expensive to conduct, even if the entire test design and execution is automated. That's the bad news. The good news is that people who deal routinely with such big machines have the tools and the expertise to use the more sophisticated techniques that are beyond the scope of this book. If you don't have the expertise and tools, you shouldn't be playing with such big finite-state machines.

2. **Nested Models Versus Nested Systems.** A rational model dictates the use of nested models, say, because an unnested implementation would have billions of states. You build a nice, nested model, but the actual software isn't nested. Your model captures only part of the actual behavior, and link covering the model by no means ensures link covering the finite-state behavior of the system. Your model is only a subset of the actual behavior, and a well-behaved subset at that. So, all of your tests are passed but the software is nevertheless buggy as all get out. A tool that tells you what actual states and transitions have been exercised is essential. Such tools are effectively impossible unless there's an explicit finite-state machine implementation, in which case you have only yourself to blame as a tester because you didn't look into the implementation to see if it was actually nested as in your model or if it wasn't.

3. **No Support.** The supporting facilities and testability aspects described in section 9.4.7 are intended to make testing reasonable and effective. The extent to which support like that exists is also a measure of how easy or how difficult it will be to conduct finite-state testing and how effective the tests will be at finding bugs.

9.5.4 Automation and Tools

As always, in the automation department, there is good news and bad news. The good news is that test design automation for finite-state machine testing has been studied for over 30 years and many effective algorithms have come out of those studies. The bad news is that almost all of the research has been aimed at hardware logic testing for which both the constraints and the bugs are different from testing software finite-state machines. The exception appears to be protocol testing, for which the hardware model is probably effective. Tools, such as they are, usually are integrated into broader LSI design systems and as such are not accessible to the software tester.

Commercial software-oriented test design tools do exist [POST94], but they are still rudimentary. Most software development organizations that have reason to do a lot of finite-state machine testing develop proprietary tools [MATT88]. Because these tools gives them a significant advantage, they neither publish the results nor make the tools available to outsiders.

9.6 SUMMARY

The finite-state machine model is a fundamental model of testing, applicable to many different kinds of software. It begins by defining a state-transition table that includes every state-input symbol combination. Typically, most models also will require an input and output encoding. Link (transition) cover is a minimum rational testing objective. With reasonable support facilities, such as explicit state counters and resets, simple tours will suffice to find most bugs. The most important thing the tester can do is to determine the state-symbol product and, from that, gauge whether testing is possible. The second most important thing a tester can do is to precisely repeat every test (not just finite-state tests, but every test) under a capture/replay system and to note even trivial behavioral changes in order to capture hidden finite-state behavior bugs.

9.7 SELF-EVALUATION QUIZ

1. **Define:** completely specified state graph, current state, exit state, finite-state machine, hidden finite state behavior, initial state, initial state set, input encoding, input event, input symbol, input symbol number, isolated state, menu-driven software, nested machines, null input, null output, number of states, output encoding, output event, output table, reachable state, reset, self-transition, state code, stable state, state counter, state-symbol product, state table, state transition, state transition table, strongly connected, tour, transient state, transition, unreachable state, working states.

2. Redo the *Enterprise* model under the assumption that the three drive controls are arranged in a triangle rather than in a line (because Klingon helmsmen prefer it that way—and Klingons usually get what they want). That is, the following additional inputs are possible: d>r, r>d. The laws of physics, however, do not change for Klingons. Design a new set of tests.

3a. Add warp drive (W) to the *Enterprise*. You can go into warp drive from any drive position (D, N, R), but the net effect is always to move in a forward direction. Warp drive does not obey Newton's laws, so if you were moving in reverse when warp drive was engaged, you can go directly into forward motion without stopping first. When warp drive is disengaged, you find yourself with the drive lever in the position it was in before warp drive was engaged, but moving forward. Do the model and design the tests.

3b. As with 3a, but for the Klingon flagship *Spklchutrgr Hrngrtch*.

4. LaForge improves the warp drive so that when it is disengaged, it resumes motion (forward, reverse, stop) as it was prior to engaging the warp drive. Do the model and design the tests.

5. If you're working in a window environment shell, do a model of the top level menus of that environment and run the tests you design.*

---

* In a formal course, I would use as many menu-driven examples as I could based on the computers and/or operating systems available to the students. The Enterprise and Toyota problems, however, are designed to illustrate gradually increasing modeling complexity.

6. My Toyota Tercel four-wheel-drive station wagon had the following gears on the main shift lever: R, N, SL, 1, 2, 3, 4, 5. There was another lever to switch from two-wheel to four-wheel drive and a clutch and brake. Here are some rules about driving this car:*

   a. You must go through neutral to shift gears, so the actual shift actions are: **N>N, N>R, N>SL, N>1, ... R>R, ... N>2, N>3, ... R>N, ... 5>N**. The drive selector has only two possibilities **2WD>4WD** and **4WD>2WD**. The clutch can be engaged (out) or disengaged (in); similarly for the brake. You can release the clutch if it's in or depress if it's out; ditto the brakes.

   b. You can shift from any gear except **SL** (Super Low) into neutral without using the clutch: **SL>N** needs the clutch.

   c. You must use the clutch to shift from neutral to any gear.

   d. You can't shift into **SL** unless you are in four-wheel drive.

   e. You can shift **2WD>4WD** or **4WD>2WD** without using the clutch, except if you are in **SL**, but you must be standing still or moving forward.

   f. Any gear shift (normal or drive selector) is possible with or without the clutch if you are stopped.

   g. If you are going backward and in **R** (reverse) gear, you can shift into first or second gear: that is, **R>N>1, R>N>2**.

   h. Shifting forward gears must be no more than two positions away in either direction. That is, the following shifts are possible: **N>1, 1>N>2, 1>N>3, 2>N>1, 2>N>3, 2>N>4, 3>N>1, 3>N>2, 3>N>4, 3>N>5, 4>N>2, 4>N>3, 4>N>5**, and so on. You always can shift from a gear to itself (including **R** and **SL**) with or without using the clutch, as long as you don't go to neutral; for example, **3>3**, but not **3>N>3**.

   i. Forbidden shift actions (e.g., **5>N>R**) should not be attempted. After all, we know that even the best transmission can be broken by abuse.

   j. You do only one thing at a time. That is, don't consider simultaneously moving the shift lever, the drive selector, the clutch, and the brake or any two of them simultaneously.

Define the input encoding scheme. Design the state table(s?), indicating all impossible transitions. Design a covering test set. Use some common sense in your test design, noting which tests are potentially dangerous and/or destructive to the car. The objective is to get a reasonably quick set of effective tests by making tours of the state without destroying transmis-

---

* I didn't make this up. This description is as close as I can get to a typical 2/4 WD transmission. My present car has 4WD, but it's an automatic. And I'm glad that automatic transmission designers use finite-state machine models and testing.

sions in the process. Don't try to design a truly minimal test set because that's a difficult theoretical problem. Here are some increasingly more difficult models to work on:

6.1 Two-wheel drive only, no super-low, only three forward gears.

6.2 As 6.1 with four forward gears.

6.3 As 6.1 with five forward gears.

6.4 Two/four-wheel drive, no super-low, three forward gears.

6.5 As 6.4 with four forward gears.

6.6 As 6.4 with five forward gears.

6.7 Two/four-wheel drive, super low, three forward gears.

6.8 As 6.7 with four forward gears.

6.9 As 6.9 with five forward gears.

6.10 Any of the above except that you can shift upward three gears away (e.g., **1>N>4**) but downward only to the next gear (e.g., **4>N>3**).

Hint: An input encoding need not correspond to a single input event but can denote a sequence of events, such as **4>3** denoting **4>N, N>3**. Nested machines, states, and/or inputs are what you make of them. Don't equate **G>G** with **G>N>G** (**G** is any gear); they're not the same.

10
Tools and Automation

10.1 SYNOPSIS

Arguments for you to use to convince people to invest in test tool automation. An overview of test tool features. The long-term prognosis for testing.

10.2 VOCABULARY

External Prerequisite Terms: by-product, cache memory, code, compiler, data, data corruption, debug package, dependability, edit, execution time, **FALSE**, formal methods, hot line, inspections, interpret, interrupt, keyboard, keypunch, hardware, initialize, maintenance, memory location, multitasking, network, object code, object oriented programming, operating system, optimizing compiler, paper tape, performance, pixel, platform, processing by-product, program, programmer, quality, random, residue, screen, **SMART-DRV**, software, source code, speculative execution, statement, text editor, throughput, **TRUE**, user, word processor.

Internal Prerequisite Terms: all-defs, all du-paths, all-paths, all-uses, assertion, behavioral testing, branch, bug, call tree, compound predicate, component, control flow, data flow, domain testing, environment, failure, feature interaction, input, instrumentation, integration testing, link, model, outcome, output, path, predicate, structural testing, syntax testing, system, test design bug, test script, tester, unit test, verify.

10.3 THE AUTOMATION IMPERATIVE [FREE88, HEND89, MILL86, NOMU87, PERE86, VOGE80]

My purpose in this section is not to convince *you*, dear reader, of the test automation imperative, because if you didn't believe in it you wouldn't be reading this book. My purpose is to help you articulate the arguments to use to justify an investment in test technology to corporate Ferrengies who are hostile to formal testing, never mind automated test tools.

One of the saddest sights to me has always been a human at a keyboard doing something by hand that could be automated. It's sad but hilarious. We're in the fifth decade of the computer industry and some of us are still forced to justify the use of computers—because that's what test automation is about. It's funny because a century ago, the steam locomotive reached its peak. Fifty years before that, intercity stagecoaches pulled by teams of horses had an outrider on the first horse to stabilize the team. Manual testing to me is like having such a rider at the front of a speeding locomotive: It's dangerous, degrading, and downright ridiculous.

If human dignity and the optimization of labor costs was what it was all about, then as so often in the past, the arguments for test automation would fall on deaf ears. Those are not the arguments to use to justify investment in automation, because creative accountants always can be found to tear our arguments apart. The argument to use is simple: Manual testing doesn't work. It never did work very well, it doesn't work now, and it won't work in the future. Manual testing is ill-contrived self-deception. It confuses sweat with accomplishment. And worst of all, it leads to false confidence. If false confidence is wanted, there are far cheaper (both legal and illegal) pharmacological ways to accomplish that.

1. **Manual Test Execution Doesn't Work.** The first myth to dispel is the belief that manual test execution works. We have excellent statistics on manual keystroke errors from the days of keypunching. Professional keypunchers averaged three errors per 1,000 keystrokes. This could be determined easily because initial keypunching was followed by rekeying during which a second operator verified the first operator. Comparison of the first keying with the second was fully automatic.

   The typical test case contains 250 characters. Testers who are not trained typists don't have the high accuracy of trained keypunch operators. Consequently, we should expect that most manually executed tests have at least one keystroke error. Furthermore, unlike the keypunch operator for whom verification was automated (more than 60 years ago), in manual testing verification is visual. This is an even more error-prone process than typing. People don't know how high the error rate of manual testing is because without execution automation, it's impractical to record how many execution attempts were made before a correct execution occurred, if ever. In my own experience, 20 years ago, it paid to use primitive execution automation tools such as paper tape and teletypes because manually executed tests were so unreliable as to be almost valueless.

2. **Manual Test Execution Leads to False Confidence.** Manual test execution is difficult, boring, brutal, and dehumanizing. Human nature, being what it is, especially in Western cultures, tends to equate effort with accomplishment: "We worked so hard we must have tested well." Bugs don't care about human struggle. In testing, the reward is in finding bugs, not in struggle. Extraordinary effort, however, needs justification. And the primary, false justification for manual testing is that it must be effective—why else would we work so hard? That's statistically unwarranted false confidence. False confidence is a warm feeling in the tummy. If that's what they want, it's far better not to test at all.

3. **Dependability Requirements Demands Automated Testing.** I execute 800,000 operations to my various disk drives on a typical day. It's easy to see that by just issuing a **SMARTDRV /s** command at the end of the day. There may be transient errors in some of those operations, but thankfully, between the hardware and operating system, I'm kept ignorant of them. I can't remember the last time I had recognizable software-induced data corruption. It is not unreasonable for me to expect that I should be able to use my system for the next 10 years without suffering data loss or corruption. It is also not unreasonable for me to want the same for the other 100 million PC users. If Microsoft wanted to provide statistically sound assurance (by current software reliability theories) that none of its platforms ever would suffer data loss or corruption as a result of disk activities, it would need 100 test engines running 24 hours a day, executing 1,000 tests per second, for approximately 3 million years.

Users demand very high dependability from us. All statistically valid methods of estimating software dependability are based on fully automatic test methods; and as you can see, even with automation the users' dependability needs can't be easily verified.

Humans can't execute the random test patterns needed to support all known software dependability assessments—because unless you're psychotic, you can't behave randomly. What can be inferred, then, about software's dependability from the kind of tests that can be executed manually? Nothing! Absolutely nothing! Nothing, nothing, nothing.* You can't confirm a 10^{-9} quality objective with a 10^{-1} test process. Period.

4. **How Many Times Is a Test Run?** Attempted justification for manual testing usually is based on a gross underestimate of the number of times tests will be run. By "gross" I mean an order of magnitude or more. If you believe that tests will be run just once, then test execution automation can't ever be justified. But why do people underestimate the number of times tests will be run? For one thing, they don't take into account test design errors. Testers are no more immune from bugs than programmers. If we have a good test—that is, a test that finds a bug—then it will be run dozens of times. At least three times to debug the test. At least three times to confirm that the bug is a hard, repeatable failure. Then again to demonstrate it to the programmer, who will likewise want to see it repeated—we're up to 10. Then two or three times more by the programmers as the fix is installed. Then two or three times more by the testers to confirm the fix. Twenty times is a low estimate, because we haven't taken into account all the managers who need convincing. If, as often happens in the

---

* But there's a lot to be inferred about the debilitating effects of manual testing and its error rates.

later stages of testing, the bug is not a simple bug that can be attributed to one component but results from an interaction between components, the count is easily tripled. If testing is effective (i.e., it finds lots of bugs), then the test rerun rate averaged over all tests (those that find bugs and those that don't) is very high—in the dozens.

There are no hard statistics on this because this isn't one of the metrics popularly recorded, but here's my experience. With primitive paper tape execution automation we had to use expensive Mylar tape (the tape itself cost 10 times the normal paper tape, and it also wore tape punches out much faster) because ordinary paper tape couldn't take the constant reruns. I don't know for sure, but it probably took 40 or 50 runs through the tape reader for ordinary paper tape to start showing wear. So ask yourself, were my testers merely incompetent, or is there a lesson here?

5. **It's a Maintenance World** [PIGO94]. The contemporary software development process isn't about creating and testing new code but about maintaining existing code. For most software products, about 80 percent of the effort is in maintenance, both **corrective maintenance** to fix discovered bugs and **progressive maintenance** to add enhancements and new features. Less than 5 percent of the code is modified in the typical maintenance cycle. However, that usually translates to requiring a complete, comprehensive **regression test** (i.e., a rerun of a major subset of the original test suite) [BURK88]. The almost universal experience with attempts at manual regression testing is that it doesn't actually happen. Either **progressive testing** (testing the new features) or **equivalency testing** (testing unchanged features) or both are sacrificed. This is a dangerous situation because as a product matures, the incidence of bugs caused by maintenance actions converges to the same bug rate as all other bugs combined. Maintenance programmers are no more immune from bugs than testers or original code programmers. Attempts at manual regression testing (because it doesn't really happen) take the incidence of maintenance bugs to unacceptably high levels.

6. **What Does Manual Testing Really Cost?** The cost of manual testing is almost impossible to determine because the information infrastructure needed to make accurate determinations exists only after test execution automation is in place. But we can determine total labor content by seeing how many individuals are testing. This must be done honestly, but it almost never is. You need total, end-to-end labor figures, especially including user service costs, hot line costs, and so on. If the total cost of software is honestly determined and properly allocated to various activities, then most organizations that make such determinations for the first time are shocked by the real cost of manual testing.

10.4 A BASIC TOOL KIT

10.4.1 General

This section is not intended to be a comprehensive review of test tools. That would take an entire book. For a review of current tools I recommend the following: FSTC83, GRAH91, GRAH93, DAIC93, MARC94, and SQET94. The tools business is evolving so rapidly that providing good guidance is impossible except by means of periodical publications.

The purpose of this section is to put tools in perspective and to discuss important technical features that you should look for in selecting commercial tools or in developing private ones. No tool exactly matches the features to be discussed; any given tool provides a mix of these features.

10.4.2 Coverage Tools

This book concerns behavioral testing. But ultimately what we test is a real piece of software, software with structure. How do we know that our testing has been good? Common sense dictates that at least every object-level instruction should be executed under test. Behavioral testing is based on a model of software, not on software, and models can be wrong; the model must be verified. The key part of that verification is that the model properly reflects the behavior embedded in the actual software. If we have tested all parts of our model but we haven't tested all the code, then our model is seriously deficient.

The purpose of **structural coverage** tools is to gives us an objective and quantitative measure of how much of the software we actually have executed by testing. It should be, *must be*, 100 percent. If we use behavioral testing methods, we still should check structural coverage because that's where reality lies. Every test technique implies a coverage metric that measures the extent to which that technique has been employed. Where a technique has a structural counterpart, you should use a corresponding structural coverage tool to confirm what was and wasn't actually covered. Where there is no obvious structural counterpart, you should record or otherwise determine the extent to which your tests provided coverage.

There are far too many sources of structural coverage tools of various kinds to list here or even to list references to them. For more information on commercial tools, I suggest the various tools guides in the bibliography: GRAH93, DAIC93, MARC94, and SQET94.

Here are the main categories of structural coverage tools.

1. **Control-flow Coverage.** The weakest form is **source code statement coverage**, which is, of course, mere node coverage and therefore almost useless. However, tools on the market provide measures of con-

trol-flow source statement coverage. That's obviously not enough; at least branch cover must be provided. In practice, especially with languages such as C that support compound predicates, it's long been known that mere branch (control-flow link) coverage is inadequate and that every predicate of a compound predicate must be tested at least once for TRUE and FALSE values. Many commercial tools provide all three coverage metrics: source code statement, source code branch, and source code predicate condition cover.

Control-flow coverage tools work (typically) by automatically modifying source code by adding instrumentation statements that then will be executed to record which paths and program segments actually have been executed under test.

All of these tools have some potentially serious limitations of which you should be aware.

a. **Different Compilers.** Coverage tools all embody a compiler or the equivalent. Because the test tool's compiler and the working compiler often are built by different organizations, there can be differences in the object code produced by each. For safety, tests run under a test tool should be repeated with the real compiler to confirm that the outcomes exactly match.

b. **Upper Limit on Size.** Coverage tools today are practically limited to code segments of at most 30,000 to 50,000 lines of source code. With increased size, not only does the execution time of the tests become objectionable, but there is an increased possibility of not properly catching every execution of every statement.

c. **Conditional Branch Handling.** Compilers use **lazy evaluation** in which predicate evaluation stops when the truth value of the predicate is determined. This means that it is possible to attempt to cover all predicate conditions (**TRUE/FALSE**) but not actually do so. With modern optimizing compilers, with further optimization done in the hardware, and with such hardware niceties as speculative execution and cache memories, *there is no assurance that a coverage tool tells the truth*. Predicates could be covered under test but not in practice, or vice versa. Caution is advised.

d. **Artificial Test Environment.** Test tools by nature impose an artificial environment. Proper behavior of interrupts, multitasking, cache memories, and many other operating system and hardware features either do not work as they do in reality or work differently. Again, rerun of all tests in the realistic environment is advised.

2. **Block Coverage (Profilers).** How can we measure object code coverage for a system consisting of several million bytes of instructions if the

unit test coverage tools are so limited? You can use **block coverage tools** or **profilers.** A profiler does not attempt to interpret the instructions executed (as does a normal coverage tool) but merely records if a given memory location (object-level instruction) has or has not been executed. From a practical point of view, that's as good as recording what source statement branches and predicates were executed. Profilers may provide this coverage data for individual bytes, individual object instructions, or blocks of bytes or instructions.

Object coverage can be done for every instruction execution, in which case the results are very precise but inaccurate because the system spends most of its time measuring itself. This mode is called **deterministic coverage.** The alternate mode is to sample instruction executions periodically. This is called **statistical coverage.** The advantage of statistical coverage is that the test environment is realistic and such impact as the coverage tool has can be corrected analytically. The disadvantage is that it may take thousands of test repetitions to get a statistically meaningful measure.

3. **Data-flow and Other Coverage Tools.** Although data-flow testing is defined here in terms of behavioral testing, there are corresponding structural concepts and associated coverage tools. There are tools that measure all-uses, all-definitions, all-du paths, and even all-paths [FRAN85, HORG92, KORE85, OSTR91]. None of these was commercially available in 1994. There are also (some commercial) coverage tools to record higher-level testing not discussed in this book, such as call-tree cover, which is essential to integration testing.

10.4.3 Test Execution Automation

First priority should be given to test execution automation because even modest test design automation generates vast numbers of tests, which without execution automation are useless. In most systems and software development environments, it is possible to automate test execution for 95 percent or more of all tests. One hundred percent execution automation probably is not desirable. It is certainly not desirable if the only way it can be done is to build complicated keypounding robots. If test execution automation is considered from the beginning and if it is a system design imperative, very high degrees of execution automation are possible—99 percent. The basic test execution automation tool is a **test driver.** The most popular form of test driver is the **capture/playback** tool.

1. **An Obvious But Bad First Approach.** The most common first approach to test execution automation is to write more code. A special-purpose program is written, within whose code are embedded all the

test data, the validation criteria, and all the rest. Well, who will test that code? Are we to have "test code testing" and "test test code testing testing," and if so, does this approach converge and how quickly? It's not the way to go. Once in a rare while it may pay to write specialized test software, but usually most testing needs can be met by using general-purpose test tools, such as drivers, in which test and validation data are treated as data rather than as code.

2. The **test driver** (and there are hundreds of them available, commercial, private, and freeware) is used to run tests automatically [CONK89, HOLT87, PANZ78]. A complete driver (but few of them are complete) should have all the following features. Use this as a checklist. Test driving proceeds in three distinct phases: **setup, execution,** and **postmortem.** Appropriate structural coverage tools can be (should be) part of the package.

   a. **Setup Phase.** Confirm the hardware/software configuration, because otherwise, how do you know you're running in the environment you think you're running? Loads and initializes prerequisite or corequisite components. Initializes other hardware and software elements as appropriate. Sets up access to data structures as required. Initializes instrumentation and coverage tools.

   b. **Execution Phase.** Reinitializes as appropriate for every test, without which the tool can't claim to be an execution automation tool. Loads and controls inputs for every test. Evaluates assertions. Captures outputs. Resets instrumentation for every test, as needed.

   c. **Postmortem Phase.** Employs proper test verification criteria. Reports test failures by exception. Compares actual to predicted outcomes, using **smart comparison** methods (e.g., allows you to specify what should and shouldn't be included in the comparison and with what tolerance). Passes execution data to coverage tool. Confirms path. Checks for residues and by-products. Passes control to debug package on test failure.

3. **Capture/Playback.** Also called **capture/replay** and **record/playback.** There are more commercial capture/playback tools on the market than any other test automation tool. I've put capture/playback both in test execution automation and test design automation because it serves in both capacities. It is a fundamental tool and is the most popular way to achieve a transition from manual to automated test execution. Capture/playback tools work in two phases, the capture phase and the playback phase. In the playback phase, it is just a test driver. I'll discuss the capture phase in the next section, Test Design Automation.

10.4.4 Test Design Automation [NAFT72]

The purpose of test design automation is to reduce the labor content of test creation. The extent to which there are or are not commercial tools associated with the various techniques discussed in this book was treated in the tools and automation sections of each chapter and will not be repeated here. It is enough to say that every technique discussed in this book can be aided by suitable tools or at least materially improved thereby.

1. **Capture/Playback.** The capture/playback tool is a test design automation tool because it captures significant events such as inputs, keystrokes, and so on, and software responses (e.g., outputs). It creates thereby a test script that can be run during the replay phase. Capture/playback tools can be simple or elaborate and can capture and replay everything from single keystrokes to pixel-by-pixel screen displays.

   The importance of capture/playback is that it often is the easiest way to transition from manual testing to automated testing. Capture/playback becomes an even more powerful design automation tool when used in conjunction with a text editor. Typically, if we look at a series of tests, we find that most of the characters or inputs are identical from test to test and there are only small variations in inputs and outcomes from test to test. Therefore, it is possible to run a single complicated scenario once and thereafter create the test variants by editing. If a test execution bug is discovered, the test is fixed by editing, so that we are assured that the testing bug will not recur on the next run. That's something that can't be done, never mind assured, for manually executed tests. A capture/playback tool is useless without a means of editing tests (e.g., a word processor).

2. **Multistrategy Generators.** As of 1994, there was only one commercial multistrategy test generator on the market—T [IDEI94]. Single-strategy generators based on heuristic domain testing, syntax testing, input combinations, random inputs, and other good and bad techniques exist. Such tools will continue to proliferate. Now that you understand the main behavioral test techniques, you can evaluate if the prospective test tool vendors understand the techniques or if they're just generating an unproven heuristic.

10.4.5 Hints for Test Vendor Selection

This isn't a lesson on tool evaluation and selection (yet another book?) but some important things to look for in evaluating tools and vendors.

1. **Eating Your Own Dog Food.** I first heard this from Microsoft's Roger Sherman. If you sell dog food, you should not hesitate to eat a bowl of your own product. You may not like the taste, but you know it's safe and

healthy. Ask the prospective tool vendor if he used his own product to test itself. If he hesitates, walk away because he doesn't have faith in his own product, and such faith is probably not warranted.

2. **How It Fits.** Test tools don't work alone. Until test tools are integrated into the broader software development environment and its associated tools and methodologies. You must consider not only the virtue of the tools but the ease with which you can integrate them into your environment. Good tools that can't fit with the rest of the toolkit are merely curiosities.

3. **Support.** Don't expect free support from tool vendors, but can you buy support at a fair price? Test tools, just like any other software development tool, can be complicated, especially if the tool is based on proprietary methods. I've seen vendors of excellent test tools thrown out of a commercial establishment because they were willing to sell the tool but not the support, without which the tool was dustware.

10.4.6 Don't Entrap Yourself

Here's a sad, common, but true scenario. An organization invests in test tools. There's a top-down commitment to quality at every level of the organization. The troops are willing and enthusiastic. Every developer and tester gets a licensed copy of the tool. A year later ask who's still using the tool. Despite the investment, initial enthusiasm, and all the rest, it's a paltry 5 percent. What went wrong? What so often does go wrong?

Everybody underestimated the time it would take to learn the tools and the underlying techniques and to achieve facility with it to the point that the tool and method were more productive than the old manual way.

You can learn the material in this book in a one-semester undergraduate course or in an intensive five-day seminar, but you will not be operationally adept unless you do the exercises and actually practice this stuff. Without practice, the methods won't be internalized and therefore will never become part of the way you work. In an undergraduate environment, that's automatic because there are exercises and a protracted time period over which to practice (and exams, of course, to ensure that the practice has been effective). There's no such mechanism in the typical industrial setting.

Both management and tester somehow expect to internalize these lessons by magic, without time for practice, and worst of all, they expect instant productivity improvements. How could that possibly be? A realistic expectation is to plan for a net productivity reduction and also quality reduction as the new methods are being learned. Mastering any one of the techniques in this book and getting to the point that you are more productive and effective with it, and learning how to use an associated tool should not take more than three to four weeks of full-time effort.

10.5 THE FUTURE OF TESTING

10.5.1 General

I don't believe in testing and I never have; but I won't fly in an aircraft whose software hasn't been tested properly. And I'm not contradicting myself. I believe in independent testing but not in independent test groups. And again, I'm not contradicting myself.

10.5.2 Why and How I Don't Believe In Testing

Testing is our last line of defense against bugs, not the first or only line of defense. When a bug is found by testing, it means that earlier phases of our software development process are wanting. A bug prevented is cheaper than a bug discovered. As testers we must strive to put ourselves out of business by promoting bug prevention methods and early bug discovery methods such as thorough analysis, prototypes, analytical models, formal methods (where effective), and inspections. Testing should be aimed at discovering the bugs that remain after the prior work has been done because those bugs don't yet succumb to design and analysis methods. Just as compilers eliminated syntax errors from the bug list, future tools will eliminate current bugs from the testers' domain. Object-oriented programming and improved operating systems promise to eliminate many currently common intercomponent interaction bugs. Formal methods may reduce or eliminate feature interaction bugs. I don't see testing actually disappearing because the remaining bugs (after process improvement) are always subtler and nastier. So I expect testing to get more technical, subtler, and more effective as time goes on.

10.5.3 Why and How I Don't Believe In Independent Testing

How about independent testing? The main purpose of independent testing is not what we thought it was 10 years ago. We believed then that independent testing was justified by objectivity: Only an independent test group could be objective. That's a bad argument that we don't see in other engineering fields: "We need an independent analysis of our building's structural design because our engineers can't be trusted to do a competent analysis." What a rotten basis for independent testing.

Historically, the main justification for independent testing was not objectivity (despite what we so vociferously affirmed) but tester survival and protection. The reason to have an independent test group is to protect the testers. If an organization is not quality-culture mature, then such protection is essential. In a mature organization in which the quality culture pervades, the immature reasons for independent testing do not apply. Developers can be trusted to be objective about evaluating their own work, and the testers don't need protection from developers. What then are some *good* reasons for an independent test group?

1. **To Protect the Testers and Provide Objectivity.** View this as a phase through which organizations must pass in order to achieve a quality culture. This is especially important if the quality imperative is imposed from above. It is, it is hoped, a passing phase. The independent test group can be dissolved and folded back into the development organization when quality has become everyone's business.

2. **Configuration Compatibility Testing.** Products that must work on many different platforms and in many different environments can benefit from an independent test organization. It's difficult for a developer to understand all the nuances of software and also all the problems specific to many widely variant configurations. An independent test group for configuration compatibility testing often is effective. Note, however, that this group runs different tests from those run by the developers.

3. **Performance and Throughput Testing.** For most software products, this is not a major issue today because throughput and performance are determined by things that are out of the developer's hands, such as the operating system. Where performance and throughput *are* important, this kind of testing generally is best left to specialists because heavy support in analytical modeling (e.g., queuing theory) is essential.

4. **Network Testing.** This is really a specialized form of the configuration testing problem. Software run over a network has additional complexities that require network knowledge, especially of the pertinent protocols. Here again, it is too much to ask for a developer to be both a product and a network expert, and independent test groups can be effective. It also is not unusual to have several levels of network testing that may or may not be done by different test organizations. Again, independent testers do different testing from developers.

5. **Localization.** The product appears in different versions for different languages, say, or to meet country-specific or industry-specific regulations and/or requirements. The group responsible for such localization effort often may conduct independent tests for that purpose.

6. **Risk Reduction and Life-Critical Software.** When human lives are at stake and/or there is a potential for extensive legal exposure as a result of failure, prudence (but not necessarily technical effectiveness) may dictate independent testing because of the widespread belief that this is the only way to ensure objectivity. It isn't really a wasted effort

because reducing legal exposure isn't a waste. However, this testing should not be a mere repetition of previous tests but should strive to explore potentially dangerous situations not previously tested.

10.5.4 The Future of Testing

Here are my hopes for testing.

1. That testing becomes a standard part of the software developer's undergraduate education. Not just as a one-time, optional course but a mandatory part of the programmer's education offered at at least three different levels in an undergraduate course of study: *Introductory Testing (Black-Box Testing)*, *Intermediate Testing (Integration and System Testing)*, *Advanced Testing (Testing Theory and Algorithms)*.

2. That it keeps pace with our ever-evolving software development process and apparently ever-increasing software complexity.

3. That the test tools industry disappears in its present form and takes its rightful place as an essential component of the broader software development tools industry.

4. That for most of us, testing ceases to be a profession but an inseparable aspect of what every conscientious developer routinely does.

10.6 Self-Evaluation Quiz

Define: capture/playback, configuration compatibility testing, corrective maintenance, coverage metric, coverage tool, deterministic profiler mode, driver execution phase, driver postmortem phase, driver set-up phase, eating your own dog food, equivalency testing, lazy evaluation, localization, maintenance, network testing, profiler, progressive maintenance, regression testing, smart comparison, statistical profiler mode, structural coverage, test driver, throughput testing.

APPENDIX A

Income Tax Forms

The forms in this appendix were produced by Turbo-Tax for Windows 1994® and have been reprinted by permission of INTUIT Inc.: all rights reserved. They are provided for reference and for your convenience in following the examples and working the exercises. Do not use them for any real income tax purposes whatsoever.

Form 1040

Department of the Treasury — Internal Revenue Service
U.S. Individual Income Tax Return **1994**

(99) IRS use only — Do not write or staple in this space.

For the year Jan 1 - Dec 31, 1994, or other tax year beginning ,1994, ending ,19

OMB No. 1545-0074

Label

Use the IRS label. Otherwise, please print or type.

Your first name	MI	Last name		Your Social Security No.
If a joint return, spouse's first name	MI	Last name		Spouse's Social Security No.
Home address (number and street). If you have a P.O. box, see instructions.			Apartment no.	For Privacy Act and Paperwork Reduction Act Notice, see instructions.
City, town or post office. If you have a foreign address, see instructions.		State ZIP Code		

Presidential Election Campaign

Do you want $3 to go to this fund? ....

► If a joint return, does your spouse want $3 to go to this fund ? ....

Yes No

Note: Checking 'Yes' will not change your tax or reduce your refund.

Filing Status

Check only one box.

1 ☐ Single
2 ☐ Married filing joint return (even if only one had income)
3 ☐ Married filing separate rtn. Enter spouse's SSN above & full name here...... ►
4 ☐ Head of household (with qualifying person). If the qualifying person is a child but not your dependent, enter this child's name here .... ►
5 ☐ Qualifying widow(er) with dependent child (year spouse died ► 19).

Exemptions

6a ☐ **Yourself.** If your parent (or someone else) can claim you as a dependent on his or her tax return, **do not** check box 6a. But be sure to check the box on ln 33b on pg 2.

No. of boxes checked on 6a and 6b .....

b ☐ **Spouse** ....

If more than 6 dependents, see instrs

c Dependents: (1) Name (first, initial, and last name)	(2) Ck if under age 1	(3) If age 1 or older, dependent's social security number	(4) Dependent's relationship to you	(5) Mos in your home

No. of your children on 6c who:
● lived with you ....
● didn't live with you due to divorce or separation
Dependents on 6c not entered above ....

d If your child didn't live with you but is claimed as your dependent under a pre-1985 agreement, ck here. .... ►
e Total number of exemptions claimed ....

Add numbers entered on lines above ►

Income

Attach Copy B of your Forms W-2, W-2G, & 1099-R here.

If you did not get a W-2, see instructions.

Enclose but do not attach any payment with your return.

7 Wages, salaries, tips, etc. Attach Form(s) W-2	7	
8a **Taxable** interest income. Attach Schedule B if over $400.	8a	
b **Tax-exempt** interest. **Don't** include on line 8a............... 8b		
9 Dividend income. Attach Schedule B if over $400.	9	
10 Taxable refunds, credits, or offsets of state and local income taxes..................	10	
11 Alimony received	11	
12 Business income or (loss). Attach Schedule C or C-EZ...................	12	
13 Capital gain or (loss). If required, Attach Schedule D...................	13	
14 Other gains or (losses). Attach Form 4797	14	
15a Total IRA distributions ...... 15a b Taxable amount	15b	
16a Tot pensions & annuities ... 16a b Taxable amount	16b	
17 Rental real estate, royalties, partnerships, S corporations, trusts, etc. Attach Sch E......	17	
18 Farm income or (loss). Attach Schedule F.	18	
19 Unemployment compensation.................................	19	
20a Social security benefits . 20a b Taxable amount	20b	
21 Other income.	21	
22 Add the amounts in the far right column for lines 7 - 21. This is your **total income**...... ►	22	

Adjustments to Income

Caution: See instructions .... ►

23a Your IRA deduction	23a	
b Spouse's IRA deduction	23b	
24 Moving expenses. Attach Form 3903 or 3903-F.............	24	
25 One-half of self-employment tax	25	
26 Self-employed health insurance deduction..................	26	
27 Keogh retirement plan and self-employed SEP deduction	27	
28 Penalty on early withdrawal of savings	28	
29 Alimony paid. Recipient's SSN ►	29	
30 Add lines 23a through 29. These are your **total adjustments** .... ►	30	

Adjusted Gross Income

31 Subtract line 30 from line 22. **This is your adjusted gross income.** *If less than $25,296 and a child lived with you (less than $9,000 if a child didn't live with you), see 'Earned Income Credit' in instructions.* .... ►

| 31 | |

D181

FDIA0112 11/15/94

Form **1040** (1994)

	32 Amount from line 31 (adjusted gross income)	**32**

Tax Computation

33a Ck if: ☐ **You** were 65/older, ☐ Blind; ☐ **Spouse** was 65/older, ☐ Blind

Add the number of boxes checked above and enter the total here .... ▶ **33a**

b If your parent (or someone else) can claim you as a dependent, ck here.... ▶ **33b**

c If you are married filing separately and your spouse itemizes deductions or you are a dual-status alien, see instructions and check here........... ▶ **33c** ☐

34 Enter the larger of your:

> **Itemized deductions** from Schedule A, line 29, **or**
> **Standard ded** shown below for your filing status. **But if you ckd**
> **any box on line 33a or b,** see instructions to find your standard
> ded. If you checked **box 33c,** your standard deduction is zero.

> • Single — $3,800   • Head of household — $5,600   • Married filing jointly
> or Qualifying widow(er) — $6,350   • Married filing separately — $3,175 **34**

35 Subtract line 34 from line 32 .... **35**

36 If ln 32 is $83,850 or less, multiply $2,450 by the total no. of exemptions claimed on ln 6e. If ln 32 is over $83,850, see the instructions for the amount to enter........... **36**

If you want the IRS to figure your tax, see instructions.

37 Taxable income. Subtract ln 36 from ln 35. If ln 36 is more than ln 35, enter -0-. **37**

38 Tax. Check if from **a** ☐ Tax Table, **b** ☐ Tax Rate Schedules, **c** ☐ Capital Gain Tax Worksheet, or, **d** ☐ Form 8615. Amount from Form(s) 8814.. ▶ **e** **38**

39 Additional taxes. Ck if from..... **a** ☐ Form 4970 **b** ☐ Form 4972 .... **39**

40 Add lines 38 and 39 .... ▶ **40**

Credits

41	Credit for child and dep care exp. Attach Form 2441	**41**	
42	Credit for the elderly or the disabled. Attach Sch R.	**42**	
43	Foreign tax credit. Attach Form 1116	**43**	
44	Other credits. Check if from **a** ☐ Form 3800 **b** ☐ Form 8396 **c** ☐ Form 8801 **d** ☐ Form (spec)	**44**	

45 Add lines 41 through 44 .... **45**

46 Subtract line 45 from line 40. If line 45 is more than line 40, enter -0-................. ▶ **46**

Other Taxes

47	Self-employment tax. Attach Schedule SE...........	**47**
48	Alternative minimum tax. Attach Form 6251	**48**
49	Recapture taxes. Ck if from **a** ☐ Form 4255 **b** ☐ Form 8611 **c** ☐ Form 8828	**49**
50	SS and Medicare tax on tip income not reported to employer. Attach Form 4137	**50**
51	Tax on qualified retirement plans, including IRAs. If required, att Frm 5329..............	**51**
52	Advance earned income credit payments from Form W-2	**52**
53	Add lns 46 - 52. This is your **total tax** .... ▶	**53**

Payments

Attach Forms W-2, W-2G, and 1099-R on page 1.

54	Federal income tax withheld. If any is from Form(s) 1099, ck ..... ▶	**54**	
55	1994 estimated tax payments and amount applied from 1993 return.................	**55**	
56	**Earned income credit.** If required, att Sch EIC. Nontaxable earned income: amount ▶ _____ and type ▶	**56**	
57	Amount paid with Form 4868 (extension request)............	**57**	
58	Excess social security and RRTA tax withheld..............	**58**	
59	Other payments. Check if from . **a** ☐ Form 2439 **b** ☐ Form 4136	**59**	
60	Add lns 54 - 59. These are your **total payments** ... ▶		**60**

Refund or Amount You Owe

61 If line 60 is more than line 53, subtract line 53 from line 60. This is the amount you **Overpaid** .... ▶ **61**

62 Amount of line 61 you want **Refunded to You**.......................... ▶ **62**

63 Amt of ln 61 you want **Applied to Your 1995 Est Tax** ...... ▶ **63**

64 If ln 53 is more than ln 60, subtract ln 60 from ln 53. This is the **Amount You Owe.** For details on how to pay, including what to write on your pmnt, see instructions.......... **64**

65 Estimated tax penalty. Also include on line 64 .... **65**

Sign Here

Keep a copy of this return for your records.

Under penalties of perjury, I declare that I have examined this return and accompanying schedules and statements, and to the best of my knowledge and belief, they are true, correct, and complete. Declaration of preparer (other than taxpayer) is based on all information of which preparer has any knowledge.

Your signature ▶	Date	Your occupation
Spouse's signature. If a joint return, BOTH must sign. ▶	Date	Spouse's occupation

Paid Preparer's Use Only

Preparer's signature ▶	Date	Check if self-employed ☐	Preparer's Social Security No.
Firm's name (or yours if self-employed) and address ▶		EIN	
		ZIP Code	

FDIA0112 12/14/94

Form **2106**

Department of the Treasury
Internal Revenue Service (99)

Employee Business Expense

► Attach to Form 1040.

OMB No. 1545-0139

1994

54

Your name	Social Security Number	Occupation in which expenses were incurred
		\<Untitled 1\>

Part I   **Employee Business Expenses and Reimbursements**

Step 1   Enter Your Expenses

			Column A Other than Meals and Entertainment	Column B Meals and Entertainment
1	Vehicle expense from line 22 or line 29......................................	1		
2	Parking fees, tolls, and transportation, including train, bus, etc, that **did not** involve overnight travel...	2		
3	Travel expense while away from home overnight, including lodging, airplane, car rental, etc. **Do not** include meals and entertainment.....................	3		
4	Business expenses not included on lines 1 through 3. **Do not** include meals and entertainment	4		
5	Meals and entertainment expenses...	5		
6	**Total expenses.** In column A, add lines 1 through 4 and enter the result. In column B, enter the amount from line 5...............................	6		

Note: If you were not reimbursed for any expenses in Step 1, skip line 7 and enter the amount from line 6 on line 8.

Step 2   Enter Amounts Your Employer Gave You for Expenses Listed in Step 1

7	Enter amounts your employer gave you that were **not** reported to you in box 1 of Form W-2. Include any amount reported under code 'L' in box 13 of your Form W-2...	7		

Step 3   Figure Expenses to Deduct on Schedule A (Form 1040)

8	Subtract line 7 from line 6..	8		
	Note: If both columns of line 8 are zero, stop here. If column A is less than zero, report the amount as income on Form 1040, line 7.			
9	In column A, enter the amount from line 8 (if zero or less, enter -0-). In column B, multiply the amount on line 8 by 50% (.50).....................	9		
10	Add the amounts on line 9 of both columns and enter the total here. **Also enter the total on Schedule A (Form 1040), line 20.** (Qualified performing artists and individuals with disabilities, see the instructions for special rules on where to enter the total.)............................... ►	10		

D181   **For Paperwork Reduction Act Notice, see instructions.**

Form **2106** (1994)

FDIA2712   11/22/94

Part II Vehicle Expenses (See instructions to find out which sections to complete.)

Section A — General Information

			(a) Vehicle 1	(b) Vehicle 2
11	Enter the date vehicle was placed in service	11		
12	Total miles vehicle was used during 1994	12	miles	miles
13	Business miles included on line 12	13	miles	miles
14	Percent of business use. Divide line 13 by line 12	14	%	%
15	Average daily round trip commuting distance....................	15	miles	miles
16	Commuting miles included on line 12..........................	16	miles	miles
17	Other personal miles. Add lines 13 and 16 and subtract the total from line 12	17	miles	miles

18 Do you (or your spouse) have another vehicle available for personal purposes?...................................... ☐ Yes ☐ No

19 If your employer provided you with a vehicle, is personal use during off duty hours permitted?.... ☐ Yes ☐ No ☐ Not applicable

20 Do you have evidence to support your deduction?... ☐ Yes ☐ No

21 If 'Yes,' is the evidence written?.. ☐ Yes ☐ No

Section B — Standard Mileage Rate (Use this section only if you own the vehicle.)

22	Multiply line 13 by 29 ¢ (.29). Enter the result here and on line 1. (Rural mail carriers, see instructions)......	22

Section C — Actual Expenses

			(a) Vehicle 1	(b) Vehicle 2
23	Gasoline, oil, repairs, vehicle insurance, etc	23		
24a	Vehicle rentals	24 a		
b	Inclusion amount	24 b		
c	Subtract line 24b from line 24a	24 c		
25	Value of employer-provided vehicle (applies only if 100% of annual lease value was included on Form W-2 — see instructions).....................	25		
26	Add lines 23, 24c, and 25	26		
27	Multiply line 26 by the percentage on line 14	27		
28	Depreciation. Enter amount from line 38 below....................	28		
29	Add lines 27 and 28. Enter total here and on line 1	29		

Section D — Depreciation of Vehicles (Use this section only if you own the vehicle.)

			(a) Vehicle 1	(b) Vehicle 2
30	Enter cost or other basis	30		
31	Enter amount of section 179 deduction	31		
32	Multiply line 30 by line 14 (see instructions if you elected the section 179 deduction)	32		
33	Enter depreciation method and percentage......................	33		
34	Multiply line 32 by the percentage on line 33...........................	34		
35	Add lines 31 and 34	35		
36	Enter the limitation amount from the table in the line 36 instructions	36		
37	Multiply line 36 by the percentage on line 14.............................	37		
38	Enter smaller of line 35 or line 37. Also enter this amount on line 28 above	38		

FDIA2712 10/18/94

Form **2210**

Department of the Treasury
Internal Revenue Service

**Underpayment of
Estimated Tax by Individuals, Estates and Trusts**

► **See separate instructions.**
► **Attach to Form 1040, Form 1040A, Form 1040NR, or Form 1041.**

OMB No. 1545-0140

1994

06

Name(s) shown on tax return

Identifying Number

Note: *In most cases, you do not need to file Form 2210. The IRS will figure any penalty you owe and send you a bill. File Form 2210 only if one or more boxes in Part I apply to you. If you do not need to file Form 2210, you still may use it to figure your penalty. Enter the amount from line 20 or line 36 on the penalty line of your return, but do not attach Form 2210.*

| Part I | **Reasons for Filing** — If 1a, b, or c below applies to you, you may be able to lower or eliminate your penalty. But you **must** check the boxes that apply and file Form 2210 with your tax return. If 1d below applies to you, check that box and file Form 2210 with your tax return. |

1 Check whichever boxes apply (if none apply, see the **Note** above):

a ☐ You request a **waiver**. In certain circumstances, the IRS will waive all or part of the penalty. See **Waiver of Penalty** in the instructions.

b ☐ You use the **annualized income installment method.** If your income varied during the year, this method may reduce the amount of one or more required installments. See the instructions.

c ☐ You had federal income tax withheld from wages and you treat it as paid for estimated tax purposes when it was **actually** withheld instead of in equal amounts on the payment due dates. See the instructions for line 22.

d ☐ Your required annual payment (line 13 below) is based on your 1993 tax and you filed or are filing a joint return for either 1993 or 1994 but not both years.

| Part II | **Required Annual Amount** |

2 Enter your 1994 tax after credits	**2**	
3 Other taxes	**3**	
4 Add lines 2 and 3	**4**	
5 Earned income credit	**5**	
6 Credit for federal tax paid on fuels	**6**	
7 Add lines 5 and 6	**7**	
8 Current year tax. Subtract line 7 from line 4	**8**	
9 Multiply line 8 by 90% (.90)	**9**	
10 Withholding taxes. **Do not** include any estimated tax payments on this line	**10**	
11 Subtract line 10 from line 8. If less than $500, stop here; **do not** complete or file this form. You do not owe the penalty	**11**	
12 Enter the tax shown on your 1993 tax return (110% of that amount if the adjusted gross income shown on that return is more than $150,000, or if married filing separately for 1994, more than $75,000). **Caution:** *See instructions*	**12**	
13 **Required annual payment.** Enter the **smaller** of line 9 or line 12	**13**	

Note: *If line 10 is equal to or more than line 13, stop here; you do not owe the penalty. Do not file Form 2210 unless you checked box 1d above.*

| Part III | **Short Method** (**Caution:** *Read the instructions to see if you can use the short method. If you checked box 1b or c in Part I, skip this part and go to Part IV.*) |

14 Enter the amount, if any, from line 10 above	**14**	
15 Enter the total amount, if any, of estimated tax payments you made	**15**	
16 Add lines 14 and 15	**16**	
17 **Total underpayment for year.** Subtract line 16 from line 13. If zero or less, stop here; you do not owe the penalty. Do not file Form 2210 unless you checked box 1d above	**17**	
18 Multiply line 17 by .05725	**18**	

19 ● If the amount on line 17 was paid **on or after** 4/15/95, enter -0-.

● If the amount on line 17 was paid **before** 4/15/95, make the following computation to find the amount to enter on line 19.

| Amount on line 17 | x | Number of days paid before 4/15/95 | x | .00025 | **19** | |

20 **Penalty.** Subtract line 19 from line 18. Enter the result here and on Form 1040, line 65; Form 1040A, line 33; Form 1040NR, line 66; or Form 1041, line 26 ► **20**

D181   For Paperwork Reduction Act Notice, see instructions.

Form **2210** (1994)

FDIZ0312 11/22/94

Part IV	**Regular Method** (See the instructions if you are filing Form 1040NR.)

		Payment Due Dates			
Section A – Figure Your Underpayment		**(a)** 4/15/94	**(b)** 6/15/94	**(c)** 9/15/94	**(d)** 1/15/95
21 Required installments. If box 1b applies, enter the amounts from Schedule AI, line 26. Otherwise, enter 1/4 of line 13, Form 2210, in each column	21				
22 Estimated tax paid and tax withheld. For column (a) only, also enter the amount from line 22 on line 26. If line 22 is equal to or more than line 21 for all payment periods, stop here; you do not owe the penalty. Do not file Form 2210 unless you checked a box in Part I	22				
Complete lines 23 through 29 of one column before going to the next column.					
23 Enter amount, if any, from line 29 of previous column	23				
24 Add lines 22 and 23	24				
25 Add amounts on lines 27 and 28 of the previous column	25				
26 Subtract line 25 from line 24. If zero or less, enter -0-. For column (a) only, enter the amount from line 22	26				
27 If the amount on line 26 is zero, subtract line 24 from line 25. Otherwise, enter -0-	27				
28 Underpayment. If line 21 is equal to or more than line 26, subtract line 26 from line 21. Then go to line 23 of next column. Otherwise, go to line 29 .... ▶	28				
29 Overpayment. If line 26 is more than line 21, subtract line 21 from line 26. Then go to line 23 of next column	29				

Section B – Figure the Penalty (Complete lines 30 through 35 of one column before going to the next column.)

April 16, 1994 – June 30, 1994 **Rate Period 1**		4/15/94 Days:	6/15/94 Days:		
30 Number of days **from** the date shown above line 30 **to** the date the amount on line 28 was paid **or** 6/30/94, whichever is earlier	30				
31 Underpayment on line 28 × (Number of days on line 30 / 365) × .07 ▶	31	$	$		
July 1, 1994 – September 30, 1994 **Rate Period 2**		6/30/94 Days:	6/30/94 Days:	9/15/94 Days:	
32 Number of days **from** the date shown above line 32 **to** the date the amount on line 28 was paid **or** 9/30/94, whichever is earlier	32				
33 Underpayment on line 28 × (Number of days on line 32 / 365) × .08 ▶	33	$	$	$	
October 1, 1994 – April 15, 1995 **Rate Period 3**		9/30/94 Days:	9/30/94 Days:	9/30/94 Days:	1/15/95 Days:
34 Number of days **from** the date shown above line 34 **to** the date the amount on line 28 was paid **or** 4/15/95, whichever is earlier	34				
35 Underpayment on line 28 × (Number of days on line 34 / 365) × .09 ▶	35	$	$	$	$

36 Penalty. Add all the amounts on lines 31, 33, and 35 in all columns. Enter the total here and on Form 1040, line 65; Form 1040A, line 33; Form 1040NR, line 66; or Form 1041, line 26 .... ▶	36	$

FDIZ0312 12/15/94

Form **2688**

Department of the Treasury
Internal Revenue Service (99)

Application for Additional Extension of Time to File
U.S. Individual Income Tax Return

► See Instructions.
► You Must complete all items that apply to you.

OMB No. 1545-0066

1994

59

Please type or print.

File the original and one copy by the due date for filing your return.

Your first name	MI	Last name		Your Social Security Number

If a joint return, spouse's first name	MI	Last name		Spouse's Social Security Number

Home address (number, street, and apartment number or rural route). If you have a P.O. box, see the instructions.

City, town or post office	State	ZIP Code

1 I request an extension of time until _____, 19 ___, to file Form 1040EZ, Form 1040A, or Form 1040 for the calendar year 1994, or other tax year ending_____, 19 ___.

2 Have you filed Form 4868 to request an extension of time to file for this tax year?.................................... ☐ Yes ☐ No
If you checked 'No,' we will grant your extension only for undue hardship. Fully explain the hardship on line 3.

3 Explain why you need an extension ► _____
_____
_____
_____
_____

If you expect to owe gift or generation-skipping transfer (GST) tax, complete line 4.

4 If you or your spouse plan to file a gift tax return (Form 709 or 709-A) for 1994, generally due by April 17, 1995, see the instructions and check here .... ⎰ **Yourself** .... ► ☐
⎱ **Spouse** .... ► ☐

Signature and Verification

Under penalties of perjury, I declare that I have examined this form, including accompanying schedules and statements, and to the best of my knowledge and belief, it is true, correct, and complete; and, if prepared by someone other than the taxpayer that I am authorized to prepare this form.

Signature of taxpayer ► _____ Date ► _____

Signature of spouse ► _____ Date ► _____
(If filing jointly, BOTH must sign even if only one had income)

Signature of preparer other than taxpayer ► _____ Date ► _____

File original and one copy. The IRS will show below whether or not your application is approved and will return the copy.

Notice to Applicant — To Be Completed by the IRS

☐ We **have** approved your application. Please attach this form to your return.

☐ We **have not** approved your application. Please attach this form to your return. However, because of your reasons stated above, we have granted a 10-day grace period from the date shown below or due date of your return, whichever is later. This grace period is considered to be a valid extension of time for elections otherwise required to be made on returns filed on time.

☐ We **have not** approved your application. After considering your reasons stated above, we cannot grant your request for an extension of time to file. We are not granting the 10-day grace period.

☐ We cannot consider your application because it was filed after the due date of your return.

☐ We **have not** approved your application. The maximum extension of time allowed by law is 6 months.

☐ Other _____

_____ Director

_____ By _____
Date

	Name

P L E A S E **T Y P E** **O R** **P R I N T**

Number and street (include suite, room, or apt no.) or P.O. box number if mail is not delivered to street address	If you want the copy of this form returned to you at an address other than that shown above or to an agent acting for you, enter the name of the agent and/or the address where the copy should be sent.

City, town or post office	State	ZIP Code	

D181 **For Paperwork Reduction Act Notice, see Instructions.**

Form **2688** (1994)

FDIA3401 10/18/94

Form **3903**	**Moving Expenses**	OMB No. 1545-0062

Form **3903**

Department of the Treasury
Internal Revenue Service

Moving Expenses

► **Attach to Form 1040.**

► **See separate instructions.**

OMB No. 1545-0062

1994

62

Name(s) shown on Form 1040	Your Social Security Number

Part I   Moving Expenses Incurred in 1994

Caution: *If you are a member of the armed forces, see the instructions before completing this part.*

1 Enter the number of miles from your **old home** to your **new workplace** .... **1** ____ miles

2 Enter the number of miles from your **old home** to your **old workplace** .... **2** ____ miles

3 Subtract line 2 from line 1. Enter the result but not less than zero .... **3** ____ miles

Is line 3 at least 50 miles?

Yes ►   Go to line 4. Also, see **Time Test** in the instructions.

No ►   You **cannot** deduct your moving expenses incurred in 1994. Do not complete the rest of this part. See the **Note** below if you also incurred moving expenses before 1994.

4 Transportation and storage of household goods and personal effects .... **4** ____

5 Travel and lodging expenses of moving from your old home to your new home. **Do not** include meals .... **5** ____

6 Add lines 4 and 5 .... **6** ____

7 Enter the total amount your employer paid for your move (including the value of services furnished in kind) that is **not** included in the wages box (box 1) of your W-2 form. This amount should be identified with code **P** in box 13 of your W-2 form .... **7** ____

Is line 6 more than line 7?

Yes ►   Go to line 8.

No ►   You **cannot** deduct your moving expenses incurred in 1994. If line 6 is less than line 7, subtract line 6 from line 7 and include the result in income on Form 1040, line 7.

8 Subtract line 7 from line 6. Enter the result here and on Form 1040, line 24. This is your **moving expense deduction for expenses incurred in 1994** .... **8** ____

Note: *If you incurred moving expenses before 1994 and you did not deduct those expenses on a prior year's tax return, complete Parts II and III on page 2 to figure the amount, if any, you may deduct on Schedule A, Itemized Deductions.*

For Paperwork Reduction Act Notice, see separate instructions.   Form **3903** (1994)

FDIA3712 10/05/94

Self-Employment Tax

► See Instructions for Schedule SE (Form 1040).
► Attach to Form 1040.

OMB No. 1545-0074

1994

17

Name of person with **self-employment** income (as shown on Form 1040)

Social security number of person with **self-employment** income ►

Who Must File Schedule SE

You must file Schedule SE if:

- You had net earnings from self-employment from other than church employee income (line 4 of Short Schedule SE or line 4c of Long Schedule SE) of $400 or more, **or**

- You had church employee income of $108.28 or more. Income from services you performed as a minister or a member of a religious order **is not** church employee income.

Note: *Even if you have a loss or a small amount of income from self-employment, it may be to your benefit to file Schedule SE and use either 'optional method' in Part II of Long Schedule SE.*

Exception: If your only self-employment income was from earnings as a minister, member of a religious order, or Christian Science practitioner, **and** you filed Form 4361 and received IRS approval not to be taxed on those earnings, **do not** file Schedule SE. Instead, write 'Exempt—Form 4361' on Form 1040, line 47.

May I use Short Schedule SE or MUST I use Long Schedule SE?

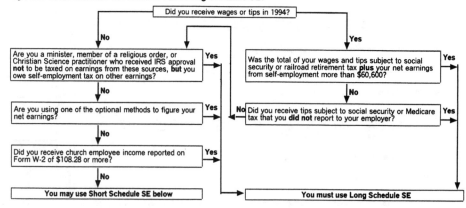

Section A — Short Schedule SE. Caution: *Read above to see if you can use Short Schedule SE.*

1	Net farm profit or (loss) from Schedule F, line 36, and farm partnerships, Schedule K-1 (Form 1065), line 15a	**1**	
2	Net profit or (loss) from Schedule C, line 31; Schedule C-EZ, line 3; and Schedule K-1 (Form 1065), line 15a (other than farming). Ministers and members of religious orders see instructions for amounts to report on this line. See instructions for other income to report	**2**	
3	Combine lines 1 and 2	**3**	
4	**Net earnings from self-employment.** Multiply line 3 by 92.35% (.9235). If less than $400, **do not** file this schedule; you do not owe self-employment tax .... ►	**4**	
5	**Self-employment tax.** If the amount on line 4 is: • $60,600 or less, multiply line 4 by 15.3% (.153). Enter the result here and on **Form 1040, line 47.** • More than $60,600, multiply line 4 by 2.9% (.029). Then, add $7,514.40 to the result. Enter the total here and on **Form 1040, line 47.**	**5**	
6	**Deduction for one-half of self-employment tax.** Multiply line 5 by 50% (.5). Enter the result here and on **Form 1040, line 25** **6**		

D181 **For Paperwork Reduction Act Notice, see Form 1040 instructions.**

Schedule **SE** (Form 1040) 1994

FDIA1101   10/19/94

State and Local Tax Refund Worksheet   1994

► Keep for your records

Name(s) shown on return	Social Security Number

1 Enter state or local income tax refund, from Form(s) 1099-G (or
   similar statement) .... 1 _____

2 Enter your total allowable itemized deductions from your 1993 Schedule A,
   line 26 .... 2 _____

Filing status on your 1993 Form 1040
☐ Single
☐ Married filing jointly or qualifying widow(er)
☐ Married filing separately
☐ Married filing separately and your spouse itemized deductions
☐ Head of household

*Note: If the filing status on your 1993 Form 1040 was married filing separately and your spouse
itemized deductions in 1993, skip lines 3 through 5 and enter the amount from line 2 on line 6.*

3 Enter the amount shown below for the filing status claimed on your 1993
   Form 1040:
   ● Single, enter $3,700 ....
   ● Married filing jointly or qualifying widow(er), enter $6,200 .... 3 _____
   ● Married filing separately, enter $3,100 ....
   ● Head of household, enter $5,450 ....

4a Enter the number from your 1993 Form 1040, line 33a .... 4a_____

4b Multiply line 4a by $700 ($900 if your filing status was single or head
   of household) .... 4b_____

5 Add lines 3 and 4b .... 5 _____

6 Subtract line 5 from line 2. If zero or less, enter -0- .... 6 _____

7 Taxable refund. Enter the smaller of line 1 or line 6 here and on Form 1040,
   line 10 .... 7 _____

Form 1040
Line 20

Social Security Income Worksheet

► Keep for your records

1994

Name(s) shown on return	Social Security Number

		Taxpayer	Spouse
A	Enter the total amount from Box 5 of **all** your Forms SSA-1099		
B	Enter the total amount from Box 5 of **all** your Forms RRB-1099		

1 Add amounts from line A and line B .... _____
2 Enter one-half of line 1 .... _____
3 Add the amounts on Form 1040, lines 7, 8a (before U.S. savings bond interest
exclusion), 8b, 9 through 14, 15b, 16b, 17 through 19, and line 21 .... _____
4 Foreign earned income exclusion, foreign housing exclusion, exclusion of income
from U.S. possessions, or exclusions of income from Puerto Rico by bona fide
residents of Puerto Rico that you claimed .... _____
5 Add lines 2, 3, and 4 .... _____
6 Amount from Form 1040, lines 23 through 29, plus any write-in amounts on line 30
(other than foreign housing deduction) .... _____
7 Subtract line 6 from line 5 .... _____
8 Enter $25,000 ($32,000 if married filing jointly; $0 if married filing separately
and you lived with your spouse at any time in 1994). .... _____
9 Subtract line 8 from line 7, If zero or less, enter -0- .... _____

If line 9 is zero, stop; none of your social security benefits are taxable. Do not
enter any amounts on Form 1040, lines 20a or 20b or Form 1040A, lines 13a or 13b.
But if you are married filing separately and you **lived apart** from your spouse
for all of 1994, enter -0- on Form 1040, line 20b or Form 1040A, line 13b. Be sure
to enter "D" to the left of Form 1040, line 20b or Form 1040A, line 13b.

If line 9 is more than zero, go to line 10.

10 Enter $9,000 ($12,000 if married filing jointly; $0 if married filing separately
and you lived with your spouse at any time in 1994 .... _____
11 Subtract line 10 from line 9. If zero or less, enter -0- .... _____
12 Enter the **smaller** of line 9 or line 10 .... _____
13 Enter one-half of line 12 .... _____
14 Enter the smaller of line 2 or line 13 .... _____
15 Multiply line 11 by 85% (.85) If line 11 is zero, enter -0- .... _____
16 Add lines 14 and 15 .... _____
17 Multiply line 1 by 85% (.85) .... _____
18 **Taxable social security benefits.** Enter the **smaller** of line 16 or line 17 .... _____

• Enter the amount from line 1 on Form 1040, line 20a, or Form 1040A, line 13a.
• Enter the amount from line 18 on Form 1040, line 20b or Form 1040A, line 13b.

Form 1040   **Self-Employed Health Insurance Deduction Worksheet**   **1994**
Line 26   ► Keep for your records

Name	Social Security Number

Note: If you have more than one source of income subject to self-employment tax, or you file Form 2555, **enter your payments on the first line of this worksheet, then use the worksheet in Publication 535 to compute your deduction, and override line 5 below.**

A Enter total payments made for health insurance coverage for you,
your spouse, and dependents .... **A** _____

B Medical care insurance expense from Schedule K-1 Partnership Worksheets .... **B** _____

1 Total payments made for health insurance coverage for you, your spouse,
and dependents. .... **1** _____

2 Percentage used to figure the deduction .... **2** ____ x .25

3 Multiply line 1 by the percentage on line 2 .... **3** _____

C Net profit from your trade or business... **C** _____

D If you are a statutory employee **and** are considered self-employed for
the purposes of the health insurance deduction, enter your net
profit from the business .... **D** _____

E Enter your wages from an S Corporation in which you are a more than
2% shareholder... **E** _____

4 Net profit and any other earned income from business under which the insurance
plan is established, minus any deductions you claim on Form 1040, lines 25 & 27 .. **4** _____

5 **Self-employed health insurance deduction.** Enter the **smaller** of line 3 or line 4
here and on Form 1040, line 26. (**Do not** include this amount in figuring any
medical expense deduction on Schedule A (Form 1040)) .... **5** _____

Standard Deduction Worksheet for Dependents   1994

Use this worksheet **only** if someone can claim you as a dependent.

► Keep for your records

Name(s) shown on return	Social Security Number

1 Enter your **earned income** (defined below). If none, enter -0- .... **1** _____

2 Minimum amount .... **2** _____

3 Enter the **larger** of line 1 or line 2 .... **3** _____

4 Enter on line 4 the amount shown below for your filing status:
   - Single, enter $3,800
   - Married filing separately, enter $3,175
   - Married filing jointly or Qualified widow(er) enter $6,350 .... **4** _____
   - Head of Household, enter $5,600

5 **Standard deduction.**

   a Enter the **smaller** of line 3 or line 4. If under 65 and not blind, stop here and enter this amount on Form 1040, line 34; or Form 1040A, line 19. Otherwise, go to line 5b .... **5a** _____

   b If 65 or older or blind, multiply $950 ($750 if married filing jointly or separately, or qualified widow(er)) by the number on Form 1040, line 33a; or Form 1040A, line 18a. **5b** _____

   c Add lines 5a and 5b. Enter the total here and on Form 1040, line 34; or Form 1040A, line 19. .... **5c** _____

Earned income *includes wages, salaries, tips, professional fees, and other compensation received for personal services you performed. It also includes any amount received as a scholarship that you must include in your income. Generally, your earned income is the total of the amount(s) you reported on Form 1040, lines 7, 12, and 18, minus the amount, if any, on line 25; or on Form 1040A, line 7.*

Itemized Deductions Worksheet

1994

► Keep for your records

Name(s) shown on return	Social Security Number

1 Add the amounts on Schedule A, lines 4, 9, 14, 18, 19, 26, 27 and 28 . . . . **1** _____

2 Add the amounts on Schedule A, lines 4, 13, and 19, plus any gambling
losses included on line 28 . . . . **2** _____

    Caution: *Be sure your total gambling losses are identified on the Miscellaneous
Itemized Deductions Statement.*

3 Subtract line 2 from line 1. If the result is zero, **Stop Here;**
enter the amount from line 1 above on Schedule A, line 29 . . . . **3** _____

4 Multiply line 3 above by 80% (.80) . . . . **4** _____

5 Enter the amount from Form 1040, line 32 . . . . **5** _____

6 Enter $111,800 ($55,900 if married filing separately) . . . . **6** _____

7 Subtract line 6 from line 5. If the result is zero or less,
Stop Here; enter the amount from line 1 above on
Schedule A, line 29 . . . . **7** _____

8 Multiply line 7 above by 3% (.03) . . . . **8** _____

9 Enter the **smaller** of line 4 or line 8 . . . . **9** _____

10 **Total itemized deductions.** Subtract line 9 from line 1. Enter the result here
and on Schedule A, line 29 . . . . **10** _____

Individual Retirement Account Worksheet 1   1994

► Keep for your records

Name(s) shown on return		Social Security Number

		(a) Your IRA	(b) Working Spouse's IRA
1 Enter IRA contributions made for 1994, but do not enter more than $2,000	**1**		
2 Enter your wages and other earned income	**2**		
3 Enter the smaller of line 1 or line 2. Enter on Form 1040, line 23a or 23b (Form 1040A, line 15a or 15b)	**3**		
Nonworking spouse's IRA			
4 Enter the smaller of line 2 or $2,250	**4**		
5 Enter the amount from line 3	**5**		
6 Subtract line 5 from line 4	**6**		
7 Enter IRA contributions made for 1994 for the nonworking spouse but not more than $2,000	**7**		
8 Enter the smaller of line 6 or line 7. Enter on Form 1040, line 23a or 23b (Form 1040A, line 15a or 15b)	**8**		

Cited References and Bibliography

AFIF90   Afifi, F.H., and White, L.J. "Testing for Linear Errors in Nonlinear computer Programs." Technical Report CES-90-03, Department of Computer Science, Case Western Reserve University, March 1990.

AFIF92   Afifi, F.H., White, L.J., and Zeil, S.J. "Testing for Linear Errors in Nonlinear Computer Programs." *Proceedings of the 14th International Conference on Software Engineeing*, Australia, pp. 81–91.

ALLE72   Allen, F.E., and Cocke, J. "Graph Theoretic Constructs for Program Control Flow Analysis." *IBM Research Report* RC3923. Yorktown Heights, N Y: T.J. Watson Research Center, 1972.

ANDE79   Anderson, R.B. *Proving Programs Correct.* New York: John Wiley & Sons, 1979.

ANDR81   Andrews, D.M., and Benson, J.P. "An Automated Program Testing Method and Its Implementation." Fifth International Conference on Software Engineering, San Diego, CA, March 9–12, 1981. Use of assertions in testing.

ANSI94   *ANSI/IEEE Standard P1044–1994. Standard Classification for Software Anomalies.* New York: American National Standards Institute, 1994.

AVRI93   Avritzer, Alberto, and Larson, Brian. "Load Testing Software Using Deterministic State Testing." *Proceedings of the 1993 International Symposium on Software Testing and Analysis*, Cambridge, MA, June 28–30, 1993. pp. 82–88.

BABE94   Baber, Robert L. "Proofs of Correctness." In MARC94, pp. 925–930.

BACK59   Backus, J. "The Syntax and the Semantics of the Proposed International Algebraic Language." *Proceedings of the ACM-GAMM Conference.* Paris, France: Information Processing, 1959.

BALC89   Balcer, Marc J., Hasling, William M., and Ostrand, Thomas J. "Automatic Generation of Test Scripts from Formal Test Specifications." *Proceedings of the ACM SIGSOFT '89.* Third Symposium on Software Testing, Analysis, and Verification. Key West, FL, December 13–15, 1989. pp. 210–218. Automatic behavioral test generation based on the proprietary TSL specification language.

BARN72   Barnes, B.H. "A Programmer's View of Automata." *Computing Surveys* 4 (1972): 222–239. Introduction to state graphs and related automata theory topics from a software-application perspective.

BASI87   Basili, V.R., and Selby, R.W. "Comparing the Effectiveness of Software Testing Strategies." *IEEE Transactions on Software Engineering* 13, #12 (1987): 1278–1296. A (rare) attempted controlled experiment to explore the relative effectiveness of behavioral versus structural testing, coverage metrics, professional versus student programmers.

BAUE79   Bauer, J.A., and Finger, A.B. "Test Plan Generation Using Formal Grammars." Fourth International Conference on Software Engineering, Munich, Germany, September 17–19, 1979. Use of state-graph model for automated test case generation. Application to telephony.

BEIZ84   Beizer, B. *Software System Testing and Quality Assurance*. New York: Van Nostrand Reinhold, 1984. Test and QA management, integration testing, system testing. Organization of testing, behavioral testing, formal-acceptance testing, stress testing, software reliability, bug-prediction methods, software metrics, test teams, adversary teams, design reviews, walkthroughs, etc.

BEIZ90   Beizer, B. *Software Testing Techniques*, 2nd ed. New York: Van Nostrand Reinhold, 1990. The testing book to read after this one. Structural test techniques, behavioral test techniques in more detail, interaction of software design and testability, algorithms for tool builders.

BEIZ96   Beizer, B. *Integration and System Testing* (in preparation). Integration testing strategies, reintegration, system testing techniques. Application of test techniques to system testing. *Black-Box Testing* is a prerequisite.

BELF76   Belford, P.C., and Taylor, D.S. "Specification Verification—A Key to Improving Software Reliability." In *Proceedings of the PIB Symposium on Computer Software Engineering*. New York: Polytechnic Institute of New York, 1976. Verification of specifications, use of specification languages, and related subjects.

BEND70   Bender, R.A., and Pottorff, E.L. *Basic Testing: A Data Flow Analysis Technique*. IBM System Development Division,

Poughkeepsie Laboratory, TR-00.2108, October 9, 1970. Earliest known description of data-flow testing.

BEND85   Bender, R.A., and Becker, P. *Code Analysis.* Larkspur, CA: Bender and Associates, P.O. Box 849, 94939. Proprietary software development and test methodology that features use of data flow testing techniques.

BERA94   Berard, Edward V. "Object Oriented Design." In MARC94, pp. 721–729.

BERL94   Berlack, H. Ronald. "Configuration Management." In MARC94, pp. 180–206. Detailed overview of software configuration control and management practices.

BISW87   Biswas, S., and Rajaraman, V. "An Algorithm to Decide Feasibility of Linear Integer Constraints Occurring in Decision Tables." *IEEE Transactions on Software Engineering* SE–13, #12 (December 1987), pp. 1340–1347.

BOEH81   Boehm, Barry W. *Software Engineering Economics.* Englewood Cliffs, N J: Prentice-Hall, 1981. Source book for all aspects of software economics.

BOEH86   Boehm, Barry W. "A Spiral Model of Software Development and Enhancements." *ACM Software Engineering Notes* 11, (4), (1986): 22–42.

BOWD77   Bowditch, N. *American Practical Navigator,* 70th ed. Washington, DC: Defense Mapping Agency Hydrographic Center, 1977. The oldest book in continuous publication except for the Bible. What our discipline should strive to be when it grows up.

BRIT85   Britcher, R.H., and Gaffney, J.E. "Reliable Size Estimates for Software Systems Decomposed as State Machines." Ninth International Computer Software and Applications Conference, Chicago, IL, October 9–11, 1985. Representation of program as finite-state machine relates state-machine size to program size.

BRZO62   Brzozowski, J.A. "A Survey of Regular Expressions and Their Application." *IRE Transactions on Electronic Computers* 11 (1962): 324–335. Survey of regular expression theory and relation to finite-state machines.

BRZO63   Brzozowski, J.A., and McCluskey, E.J., Jr. "Signal Flow Graph Techniques for Sequential Circuit State Diagrams." *IEEE Transactions on Electronic Computers* 12 (1963): 67–76. Basic paper that applies flow graphs to regular expressions and state-graphs of finite-state automata.

BURK88   Burke, R. Black-Box Regression Testing—An Automated Approach. Fifth International Conference on Testing Computer Software, Washington, DC, June 13–16, 1988.

BUTL89   Butler, R.W., Mejia, J.D., Brooks, P.A., and Hewson, J.E. "Automated Testing for Real-Time Systems." Sixth International Conference on Testing Computer Software, Washington, DC, May 22–25, 1989.

CHEN78   Chen, W.T., Ho, J.P., and Wen, C.h. "Dynamic Validation of Programs Using Assertion Checking Facilities." Second Computer Software and Applications Conference, Chicago, IL, November 1978.

CHOW78   Chow, T.S. "Testing Software Design Modeled by Finite State Machines." *IEEE Transactions on Software Engineering* 4 (1978): 78–186. Testing software modeled by state graphs with examples from telephony. Categorizes types of state-graph errors and shows relation between type of coverage and the kind of errors that can and can't be caught.

CHOW88   Chow, C.H., and Lam, S.S. "Prospec: An Interactive Programming Environment for Designing and Verifying Communication Protocols." *IEEE Transactions on Software Engineering* 14 (1988): 327–338.

CLAR76   Clarke, Lori A. "A System to Generate Test Data and Symbolically Execute Programs." *IEEE Transactions on Software Engineering* 2 (1976): 215–222. Although aimed at structural testing, the method and tools could be applied just as easily to behavioral control flow and data flow models.

CLAR82   Clarke, Lori A., Hassel, J., and Richardson, D.J. "A Close Look at Domain Testing." *IEEE Transactions on Software Engineering* 8 (1982): 380–390. Good survey and critique; exposition of error types and what does and doesn't work to catch them and why.

CLAR89   Clarke, Lori A., Podgurski, Andy, Richardson, Debra J., and Zeil, Steven J. "A Formal Evaluation of Data Flow Path Selection Criteria." *IEEE Transactions on Software Engineering* 15 (1989): 1318–1332.

COHE78   Cohen, E.I. *A Finite Domain-Testing Strategy for Computer Program Testing.* Ph.D. diss., Ohio State University, June 1978.

CONK89   Conklin, J. "Automated Repetitive Testing." Sixth International Conference on Testing Computer Software, Washington, DC, May 22–25, 1989.

COOP81   Cooper, Robert B. *Introduction to Queuing Theory.* New York: Elsevier North Holland, 1981.

CROS92   CrossTalk Communications. *CASL Programmer's Guide.* Rosswell, GA: Digital Communications Associates, 1992.

DAIC93   Daich, Greg, and Price, Gordon. *Test Preparation Execution, & Evaluation Software Technologies Report.* Software Technology Support Center, Hill AFB, Ogden, UT. Customer Service 801–777–7703. Free periodical guide to test tools and technology approved for use in U.S. government. Also, *Reengineering Tools Report, Source Code Static Analysis Technologies Report*, vols. 1 and 2. Your tax dollars at work.

DAVI88   Davis, A.M. "A Comparison of Techniques for the Specification of External System Behavior." *Communications of the ACM* 31, #9 (1988): 1098–1115. Survey of state graphs, state tables, decision tables, decision trees, program design languages, Petri nets, requirement languages, and specification languages in developing requirements and tests from them.

DEON74   Deo, N. *Graph Theory with Applications to Engineering and Computer Science.* Englewood Cliffs, N J: Prentice-Hall, 1974.

EBER94   Ebert, Jurgen and Engels, Gregor. "Design Representations." In MARC94, pp. 382–394. Survey of popular design models and representations, all of which can be used as a basis for test design.

ELME73   Elmendorf, W.R. *Cause-Effect Graphs in Functional Testing.* TR-00.2487, IBM Systems Development Division, Poughkeepsie, NY, 1973.

FAGA76   Fagan, M.E. "Design and Code Inspections to Reduce Errors in Program Development." *IBM Systems Journal* 3 (1976): 182–211. Still one of the best expositions on inspections ever written.

FENT91   Fenton, Norman E. *Software Metrics: A Rigorous Approach.* London: Chapman and Hall, 1991. A rigorous but very accessible book on software metrics, suitable for a first course.

FRAN85   Frankl, P.S., Weiss, S.N. and Weyuker, E.J. "Asset—A System to Select and Evaluate Tests." *Proceedings of the IEEE Conference on Software Tools* (April 1985): 72–79.

FRAN88   Frankl, P.G., and Weyuker, E.J. "An Applicable Family of Data Flow Testing Criteria." *IEEE Transactions on Software Engineering* 14, #10 (1988): 1483–1498.

FREE88   Freeman, P.A., and Hunt, H.S. "Software Quality Improvement Through Automated Testing." Fifth International Conference on Testing Computer Software, Washington, DC, June 13–16, 1988.

FSTC83   Federal Software Testing Center. *Software Tools Survey.* Office of Software Development report #OSD/FSTC-83/015, 1983. Survey of 100 software development tools, language, source.

FUJI94   Fujii, Roger U. "Independent Verification and Validation." In MARC94, pp. 568–572. What an independent test group is all about.

FURG89   Furgerson, Donald F., Coutu, John P., Reinemann, Jeffrey K., and Novakovich, Michael R. "Automated Testing of a Real-Time Microprocessor Operating System." Sixth International Conference on Testing Computer Software, Washington, DC, May 23–25, 1989. Description of application of CrossTalk CASL scripting language to test script design and to construction of a testing environment.

GERH88   Gerhart, Susan L. "A Broad Spectrum Toolset for Upstream Testing, Verification, and Analysis." Second Workshop on Software Testing, Verification, and Analysis, Banff, Canada, July 19–21, 1988.

GIBB94   Gibbs, Wayt. "Software's Chronic Crisis." *Scientific American*, 71, #3 (1994): 86–95.

GILB93   Gilb, Tom, and Graham, Dorothy. *Software Inspections.* Menlo Park, CA: Addison-Wesley, 1993. As good and as readable text on inspections as you're likely to find.

GOOD75   Goodenough, J.B., and Gerhart, S.A. "Toward a Theory of Test Data Selection." *IEEE Transactions on Software Engineering* 1 (1975): 156–173. The beginning of testing theory; historical interest.

GRAD87   Grady, Robert B., and Caswell, D.L. *Software Metrics: Establishing a Company-Wide Program.* Englewood Cliffs, NJ: Prentice-Hall, 1987. A practical guide to implementing a total metrics program based on experience in a supportive, sophisticated, software development organization.

GRAD92   Grady, Robert B. *Practical Software Metrics for Project Management and Process Improvement*. Englewood Cliffs, NJ: Prentice-Hall, 1992. Yet another practical guide to metrics in an industrial setting, courtesy of Hewlett-Packard.

GRAH91   Graham, Dorothy R. "Software Testing Tools: A New Classification Scheme." *Journal of Software Testing, Verification, and Reliability* 1, #3 (October–December 1991): 17–34. An overview and rational taxonomy for test tools.

GRAH93   Graham, Dorothy R., and Herzlich, Paul. *CAST Report: Computer Aided Software Testing*. London: Cambridge Market Intelligence, 1993. Periodical report on test tools for mostly European platforms.

GRAH94   Graham, Dorothy R. "Testing" In MARC94, pp. 1330–1353. Testing with a software development process perspective.

HAML88   Hamlet, R., and Taylor, R. "Partition Testing Does Not Inspire Confidence." Second Workshop on Software Testing, Verification, and Analysis, Banff, Canada, July 19–21, 1988. Shows that partition testing methods cannot be used to obtain statistically meaningful software reliability measures.

HAML94   Hamlet, Richard. "Random Testing." In MARC94, pp. 970–978.

HANF70   Hanford, K.V. "Automatic Generation of Test Cases." *IBM System Journal* 9 (1979): 242–257. Use of BNF to generate syntactically valid test cases for testing a PL/I compiler.

HANT76   Hantler, S.A., and King, J.C. "An Introduction to Proving the Correctness of Programs." *ACM Computing Surveys* 8, 3 (1976): 331–353.

HARR89   Harrold, M.J., and Soffa, M.L. "An Incremental Data Flow Testing Tool." Sixth International Conference on Testing Computer Software, Washington, DC, May 22–25, 1989.

HEND89   Henderson, B.M. "Big Brother—Automated Test Controller." Sixth International Conference on Testing Computer Software, Washington, DC, May 22–25, 1989.

HERA88   Herath, J., Yamaguchi, Y., Saito, N., and Yuba, T. "Dataflow Computing Models, Languages, and Machines for Intelligence Computations." *IEEE Transactions on Software Engineering* 14, 12 (1988): 1805–1828. Although the paper is aimed at intelligence processing, the overview and tutorial is one of the best around.

HERM76   Herman, P.M. "A Data Flow Analysis Approach to Program Testing." *Australian Computer Journal* (November 1976): 92–96. Earliest known published discussion of heuristic data flow testing.

HOLT87   Holt, D. "A General Purpose Driver for UNIX." Fourth International Conference on Testing Computer Software, Bethesda, MD, June 15–18, 1987.

HOLZ87   Holzman, G.J. "Automated Protocol Validation in Argos: Assertion Proving and Scatter Searching." *IEEE Transactions on Software Engineering* 13 (1987): 683–696. Experience in automatically generated state machine-based testing cases as applied to protocol verification. Application and strategies for systems with on the order of 1024 states.

HORG92   Horgan, J.R., and London, S.A. "A Dataflow Coverage Testing Tool for C." *Proceedings Symposium on Assesment of Quality Software Developement Tools.* Los Alamitos, CA: IEEE CS Press, 1992, pp. 2–10. Description of the ATAC public domain C dataflow test tool.

HORG94   Horgan, J.R., London, S.A., and Lyu, M,R. "Achieving Software Quality with Testing Coverage Measures." *IEEE Computer* 7, #9 (Sept. 1994): 60–70.

HOWD76   Howden, W.E. "Reliability of the Path Analysis Testing Strategy." *IEEE Transactions on Software Engineering* 2 (1976): 208–215. Proof that the automatic generation of a finite test set that is sufficient to test a routine is not a computable problem. Formal definition of computation error, path error, and other kinds of errors.

HOWD80   Howden, W.E. "An Evaluation of the Effectiveness of Symbolic Testing." *IEEE Transactions on Software Engineering* 6 (1980): 162–169.

HOWD86   Howden, William E. "A Functional Approach to Program Testing and Analysis." *IEEE Transactions on Software Engineering* 12 (1986): 997–1005.

HOWD87   Howden, William E. *Functional Program Testing and Analysis.* New York: McGraw-Hill, 1987.

HOWD89   Howden, William E. "Validating Programs Without Specifications." *Proceedings of the ACM SIGSOFT '89,* Third Symposium on Software Testing, Analysis, and Verification.

Key West, FL, December 13–15, 1989, pp. 2–9. Exposition of error-based testing.

IDEI94   IDE, Inc. *Stp/T User's Guide*. Iselin, NJ: Interactive Development Environments, 1994.

IEEE94   *IEEE Software Engineering Standards*. New York: IEEE, 1994. Collection of ANSI/IEEE standards on software engineering.

JENG89   Jeng, B., and Weyuker, E.J. "Some Observations on Partition Testing." *Proceedings of the ACM SIGSOFT '89*, Third Symposium on Software Testing, Analysis, and Verification. Key West, FL, December 13–15, 1989.

JENG94   Jeng, B.C., and Weyuker, E.J. " A Simplified Domain-Testing Strategy." *ACM Transactions on Software Engineering and Methodology* 3 (July 1994): 254–270.

KAVI87   Kavi, K.M., Buckles, B.P., and Bhat, N.U. "Isomorphism Between Petri Nets and Dataflow Graphs." *IEEE Transactions on Software Engineering* 13 (1987): 1127–1134. Relation between Petri Nets and data-flow models.

KEMM85   Kemmerer, R.A. "Testing Formal Specifications to Detect Design Errors." *IEEE Transactions on Software Engineering* 11,#1 (1985): 32–43.

KOLM88   Kolman, B. *Introductory Linear Algebra with Applications*, 4th ed. New York: Macmillan and Company, 1988. Introductory text used in computer sciences curricula.

KORE85   Korel, Bogdan, and Laski, Janusz. "A Tool for Data Flow Oriented Program Testing." Second Conference on Software Development Tools, Techniques, and Alternatives, San Francisco, CA, December 2–5, 1985.

KORE88   Korel, Bogdan, and Laski, Janusz. "STAD—A System for Testing and Debugging: User Perspective." Second Workshop on Software Testing, Verification, and Analysis. Banff, Canada, July 19–21, 1988, pp.13–20.

KRAU73   Krause, K.W., Smith, R.W., and Goodwin, M.A. "Optimal Software Test Planning Through Automated Network Analysis." IEEE Symposium on Computer Software Reliability, 1973. Early example of path testing, graph models, coverage, and automated generation of paths.

LASK90   Laski, J. "Data Flow Testing in STAD." *Journal for Systems and Software* 12 (1990): 3–14.

LAYC92   Laycock, Gilbert. "Formal Specification and Testing: A Case Study." *Journal of Software Testing, Verification, and Reliability* 2, #1 (May 1992): 7–23. Category-partition model and test generation based on the Z specification language.

LEMP89   Lemppenau, W.W. "Hybrid Load and Behavioral Testing of SPC-PABX Software for Analog or Digital Subscribers and Trunk Lines." Sixth International Conference on Testing Computer Software, Washington, DC, May 22-25, 1989.

MARC94   Marciniak, John (editor-in-chief). *Encyclopedia of Software Engineering.* New York: John Wiley & Sons, 1994. *The* essential reference book that no serious software engineer or aspirant thereto should be without. Any technical term or concept used in this book that you do not know you can probably learn from MARC94. Get the CD-ROM version when it comes out.

MASO90   Mason, T., and Brown, D. *Lex and yacc.* Sebastapol, CA: O'Reilly and Associates, 1990.

MATT88   Matthews, R.S., Muralidhar, K.H., and Sparks, S. "MAP 2.1 Conformance Testing Tool." *IEEE Transactions on Software Engineering* 14, #3 (1988): 363–374.

MCNA60   McNaughton, R., and Yamada, H. "Regular Expressions and State Graphs for Automata." *IRE Transactions on Electronic Computers* EC-9 (1960): 39–47. Survey of the theory of regular expressions as applied to finite state automata. Proof of fundamental theorems.

MEAL55   Mealy, G.H. "A Method for Synthesizing Sequential Circuits." *Bell System Technical Journal* 34 (1955): 1045–1079.

MILL66   Miller R.E. *Switching Theory.* New York: John Wiley & Sons, 1966. Basic reference on switching and automata theory.

MILL75   Miller, E.F., and Melton, R.A. "Automated Generation of Test Case Data Sets." International Conference on Reliable Software, Los Angeles, CA, April 1975.

MILL78   Miller, E.F., and Howden, W.E. eds. *Tutorial: Software Testing and Validation Techniques,* 2nd ed. New York: IEEE Computer Society, 1981. A bargain resource for pre-1981 literature; huge bibliography up to and including 1981.

MILL86   Miller, E.F. "Mechanizing Software Testing." TOCG Meeting, Westlake Village, CA, April 15, 1986. San Francisco: Software Research Associates.

MOLL93   Moller, K.H., and Paulish, D.J. *Software Metrics*. London: Chapman and Hall, 1993. Metrics from an industrial viewpoint.

MOOR56   Moore, E.F. "Gedanken Experiments on Sequential Machines." In *Automata Studies. Annals of Mathematical Studies #34*. Princeton, NJ: Princeton University Press, 1956.

MORE90   Morell, Larry J. "A Theory of Fault-Based Testing." *IEEE Transactions on Software Engineering* 16, #8 (August 1990): 844–857.

MURA89   Murata, T. "Petri Nets: Properties, Analysis And Applications." *Proceedings of the IEEE* 77, #4 (1989): 541–580. In-depth tutorial, huge bibliography.

MUSA90   Musa, John D., Iannino, Anthony, and Okumoto, Kazuhira. *Software Reliability: Professional Edition*. New York: McGraw-Hill, 1990.

MYER79   Myers, G.J. *The Art of Software Testing*. New York: John Wiley & Sons, 1979. A golden oldie.

NAFT72   Naftaly, S.M., and Cohen, M.C. "Test Data Generators and Debugging Systems...Workable Quality Control." *Data Processing Digest* 18 (1972). Survey of automatic test data generation tools.

NOMU87   Nomura, T. "Use of Software Engineering Tools in Japan." Ninth International Conference on Software Engineering, Monterey, CA, March 30–April 2, 1987. Survey of 200 Japanese software development groups rates test tools as having the highest productivity return; ahead of a standard process, programming and design tools, and reviews.

NORT94   Northrup, Linda M. "Object-Oriented Development." In MARC94, pp. 729–737.

NTAF88   Ntafos, Simeon C. "A Comparison of Some Structural Testing Strategies." *IEEE Transactions on Software Engineering* 14, # 6 (June 1988): 868–874. Excellent survey of structural test techniques.

ONOM87   Onoma, A.K., Yamura, T., and Kobayashi, Y. "Practical Approaches to Domain Testing: Improvement and Generalization."

Proceedings of the Computer Software and Applications Conference, Tokyo, Japan, October 7–9, 1987, pp. 291–297.

OSTR86   Ostrand, T.J., Sigal, R., and Weyuker, E. "Design for a Tool to Manage Specification-Based Testing." Workshop on Software Testing, Banff, Canada, July 15–17, 1986.

OSTR88   Ostrand, T.J., and Balcer, M.J. "The Category-Partition Method for Specifying and Generating Functional Tests." *Communications of the ACM* 31, #6 (1988): 676–686.

OSTR91   Ostrand, Thomas J., and Weyuker, Elaine J. "Data Flow-Based Test Adequacy Analysis for Languages with Pointers." ACM Sigsoft Symposium on Software Testing, Analysis, and Verification, October 8–10, 1991, Victoria, BC, Canada.

OSTR94   Ostrand, Thomas J. "Categories of Testing." In MARC94, pp. 90–93. Overview of different types of testing and where and how used.

PANZ78   Panzl, D.J. "Automatic Software Test Drivers." *IEEE Computer* 11 (1978): 44–50.

PATR88   Patrick, D.P. "Certification of Automated Test Suites with Embedded Software." National Institute for Software and Productivity Conference, Washington, DC, April 20–22, 1988.

PERE85   Perera, I.A., and White, L.J. "Selecting Test Data For the Domain Testing Strategy." Technical report TR-85-5, Department of Computer Science, University of Alberta, Edmonton, Alberta, Canada, 1985.

PERE86   Perelmuter, I.M. "Directions of Automation in Software Testing." Third Conference on Testing Computer Software, Washington, DC, September 29–October 1, 1986.

PETE76   Peters, L.J., and Tripp, L.L. "Software Design Representation Schemes." PIB Symposium on Computer Software Reliability, Polytechnic Institute of New York, April 1976. Survey of software models, including HIPO charts, activity charts, structure charts, control graphs, decision tables, flowcharts, transaction diagrams, and others.

PETE81   Petersen, J.L. *Petri Net Theory and the Modeling of Systems.* Englewood Cliffs, NJ: Prentice-Hall, 1981. Basic text on Petri nets.

PIGO94   Pigoski, Thomas M. "Maintenance." In MARC94, pp. 619–636.

POST94   Poston, Robert M. "Test Generators." In MARC94, pp. 1327–1330.

POWE82   Powell, P.B. ed. *Software Validation, Verification, and Testing Techniques and Tool Reference Guide*. National Bureau of Standards Special Publication 500-93, 1982. Survey of testing, verification, validation, tools, and techniques with comments on effectiveness and supporting and resources needed for each.

RAPP82   Rapps, S., and Weyuker, E.J. "Data Flow Analysis Techniques for Test Data Selection." Sixth International Conference on Software Engineering, Tokyo, Japan, September 13–16, Long Beach, CA: 1982, pp. 272–278.

RAPP85   Rapps, S., and Weyuker, E.J. "Selecting Software Test Data Using Data Flow Information." *IEEE Transactions on Software Engineering* 11 (1985): 367–375.

RICH81   Richardson, D.J., and Clarke, L.A. "A Partition Analysis Method to Increase Program Reliability." Fifth International Conference on Software Engineering, San Diego, CA, March 9–12, 1981. Partition analysis testing; behavioral/structural hybrid based on domain testing.

RICH85   Richardson, D.J., and Clarke, L.A. "Partition Analysis: A Method Combining Testing and Verification." *IEEE Transactions on Software Engineering* 11 (1985): 1477–1490. Early look at behavioral domain testing.

RICH89   Richardson, Debra J., O'Malley, O. and Tittle, Cindy. "Approaches to Specification-Based Testing." *Proceedings of the ACM SIGSOFT '89*, Third Symposium on Software Testing, Analysis, and Verification. Key West, FL, December 13–15, New York, NY: 1989, pp. 86–96. Behavioral testing based on formal specification languages, Anna and Larch.

ROPE93   Roper, Marc, and Rashid, Ab Bin Ab Rahim. "Software Testing Using Analysis and Design Based Techniques." *Journal of Software Testing, Verification, and Reliability* 3, #3–4 (September–December 1993): 166–179. Behavioral data flow models used as a basis for test design.

ROYC70   Royce, W.W. "Managing the Development of Large Software Systems." *Proceedings IEEE WESCON* (August 1970): 1–9.

RUGG79   Ruggiero, W., Estrin, G., Fenchel, R., Razouk, R., Schwabe, D., and Vernon, M. "Analysis of Data Flow Models Using the Sara Graph Model of Behavior." *Proceedings of the 1979 National Computer Conference.* Montvale, NJ: AFIPS Press, 1979. A more elaborate data flow behavioral model than presented here.

SARI87   Sarikaya, Behcet, Bochmann, Gregor V., and Cerny, Eduard. "A Test Design Methodology for Protocol Testing." *IEEE Transactions on Software Engineering,* SE–13, #5 (May 1987): 518–531.

SCAC94   Scachi, Walt. "Process Maturity Models." In MARC94, pp. 851–869.

SCHI69   Schiller, H. "Using MEMMAP to Measure the Extent of Program Testing." IBM Systems Development Division, Poughkeepsie, NY, Report TR 00.1836, February 10, 1969. Description of the use of an early software statement/branch coverage analyzer.

SCHL70   Schlender, Paul, J. Path Analysis Techniques. Memo, IBM System Development Division, Poughkeepsie, NY, April 27, 1970. Early discussion of data flow testing (all definitions); notes (without proof) that branch coverage is included in all definitions.

SIDH89   Sidhu, Deepinder P., and Leung, Tink-Kau. "Formal Methods for Protocol Testing: A Detailed Study." *IEEE Transactions on Software Engineering* 15, #4 (April 1989): 413–423. Automatic test generation for protocol testing from finite-state model.

SNEE86   Sneed, H.M. "Data Coverage Measurement in Program Testing." Workshop on Software Testing, Banff, Canada, July 15–17, Washington, DC: 1986, pp. 34–40. Reports experience with use of data-flow coverage metrics; tools, comparison of effectiveness with control-flow coverage.

SOFT88   Software Research, Inc. *SPECTEST™ Description, METATEST™ Description.* San Francisco, CA: Author, 1988.

SQET94   Software Quality Engineering. *Tools Guide.* Jacksonville, FL: Author, 1994. Periodical tools guide specific to software testing.

STAK89   Staknis, M.E. "The Use of Software Prototypes in Software Testing." Sixth International Conference on Testing Computer Software, Washington, DC, May 22–25, 1989.

THEV93   Thevenod-Fosse, Pascale, and Waeselynck, Helene. "STATE-MATE Applied to Statistical Software Testing." *Proceedings of the 1993 International Symposium on Software Testing and Analysis.* Cambridge, MA, New York, NY: ACM Press, June 28–30, 1993, pp. 99–109.

TRIP88   Tripp, Leonard L. "A Survey of Graphical Notations for Program Design—An Update." *ACM SIGSOFT, Software Engineering Notes* 13, #4 (October 1988): 39–44. Concise survey.

TSAI90   Tsai, W.T., Volovik, Dmitry, and Keefe, Thomas, F. "Automated Test Case Generation for Programs Specified by Relational Algebra Queries." *IEEE Transactions on Software Engineering* 16, #3 (March 1990): 316–324. Automated test generation based on domain models.

VOGE80   Voges, U., Gmeiner, L., and von Mayrhauser, A. A. "Sadat—An Automated Test Tool." *IEEE Transactions on Software Engineering* 6, #3 (May 1980): 286–290.

VOGE93   Vogel, Peter A. "An Integrated General Purpose Automated Test Environment." *Proceedings of the 1993 International Symposium on Software Testing and Analysis.* Cambridge, MA, June 28–30, New York, NY: ACM Press, 1993, pp. 61–69.

WALL94   Wallace, Dolores R. "Verification and Validation." In MARC94, pp. 1410–1433.

WARN64   Warner, C.D., Jr. *Evaluation of Program Testing.* Poughkeepsie, NY: IBM Data Systems Division Development Laboratories, TR 00.1173, July 28, 1964. Earliest known use of a hardware instruction coverage monitor: COBOL and FORTRAN source.

WEIN90   Weinberg, Gerald M., and Freedman, D.P., *Handbook of Walkthroughs, Inspections and Technical Reviews.* New York: Dorset House, 1990.

WEIS81   Weiser, Mark D. "Program Slicing." Proceedings of the Fifth International Conference on Software Engineering (439–449) March 1981.

WEIS84   Weiser, Mark D. "Program Slicing." *IEEE Transactions on Software Engineering* SE-10 (1984): 352–357.

WEIS85   Weiser, Mark D., Gannon, John D., and McMullin, Paul R. "Comparison of Structural Test Coverage Metrics." *IEEE Software* (March 1985), 80–85.

WEIS91   Weiss, Stewart N. and Frankl, Phyllis G. "Comparison of All-Uses and All-Edges: Design, Data, and Analysis." Hunter College, New York, Dept. of Computer Science, Technical Report CS-TR 91-04.

WEYU90   Weyuker, Elaine. J. "The Cost of Data Flow Testing—An Empirical Study." *IEEE Transactions on Software Engineering* 16 (February 1990).

WEYU94A   Weyuker, Elaine J. "Data Flow Testing". In MARC94, pp. 247–249. Key theoretical concepts and definitions for structural data flow testing.

WEYU94B   Weyuker, Elaine J., Goradia, Tarak, and Singh, Ashutosh. "Automatically Generating Test Data from a Boolean Specification." *IEEE Transactions on Software Engineering* 20, #5 (May 1994): 353–363.

WHIT78   White, Lee J., Cohen, E.I., and Chandrasekaran, B. "A Domain Strategy for Computer Program Testing." Columbus, OH: Computer and Information Science Research Center, Ohio State University, Technical Report OSU-CISRC-TR-78-4, August 1978.

WHIT80   White, Lee J., and Cohen, E.I. "A Domain Strategy for Computer Program Testing." *IEEE Transactions on Software Engineering* 6 (1980): 247–257. Use of linear predicates and associated inequalities to establish test cases, boundary choices, etc. Generalization to n-dimensional problems.

WHIT85   White, Lee J., and Sahay, P.N. "A Computer System for Generating Test Data Using the Domain Strategy." IEEE SOFTFAIR Conference II, San Francisco, CA, December 2–5, 1985.

WHIT87   White, Lee J. "Software Testing and Verification." In *Advances in Computers*, vol. 26, pp. 335–391. New York: Academic Press, 1987. Superior tutorial and overview of theory.

WHIT94   White, Lee J., and Leung, Hareton K. N. "Integration Testing." In MARC94, pp. 573–577.

WHIT95   White, Lee J. "Consistency and Completeness Checking of Domain Specifications." 12th International Conference on Testing Computer Software. Washington, DC, June 12–15, 1995.

WILK77   Wilkens, E.J. "Finite State Techniques in Software Engineering." (First) Computer Software and Applications

Conference, Chicago, IL, November 1977. Application of finite-state machine models to software design.

WING94   Wing, Jeannette, M. "Formal Methods." In MARC94, pp. 504–517. p. 12.

WILS82   Wilson, C., and Osterweill, L.J. "A Data Flow Analysis Tool for the C Programming Language." Sixth Computer Software and Applications Conference, Chicago, IL, November 8–12, 1982.

YERH80   Yeh, R.T., and Zave, P. "Specifying Software Requirements." *IEEE Proceedings* 68 (1980): 1077–1085. Examines specifications as a source of program bugs and suggests methodology for specification design.

YOSH87   Yoshizawa, Y., Kubo T., Satoh, T., Totsuka, K., Haraguchi, M., and Moriyama, H. "Test and Debugging Environment for Large Scale Operating Systems." Eleventh International Computer Software and Applications Conference, Tokyo, Japan, October 7–9, 1987.

ZEIL83   Zeil, S.J. "Testing for Perturbations of Program Statements." *IEEE Transactions on Software Engineering* SE-9, 3 (May 1983): 335–346.

ZEIL89   Zeil, S.J. "Perturbation Techniques for Detecting Domain Errors." *IEEE Transactions on Software Engineering* 15, 8 (June 1989): 737–746.

ZUSE90   Zuse, Horst. *Software Complexity. Measures and Methods.* New York: Walter de Gruyter, 1990. Encyclopedic book on metrics.

ZUSE94   Zuse, Horst. "Complexity Metrics/Analysis." In MARC94, pp. 131–165. Excellent survey of the theory and practice of software metrics.

ZWEB92   Zweben, Stuart H., Heym, Wayne D., and Kimmich, J. "Systematic Testing of Data Abstractions Based on Software Specifications." *Journal of Software Testing, Verification, and Reliability* 1, #4 (January– March, 1992), pps. 39–55. Use of control–flow and data-flow models based on specifications and application of analogous structural test techniques. Experimental results shows relative technique strengths and effectiveness similar to that obtained for structural testing.

SUBJECT INDEX

bug, **6**
data, 140
test, 5, 12
SEI maturity model, xvii, 274
selector node, **41,** 45, 99, 107, 113–114, 135
selector predicate, **38,** 109
self–:
  deception, 233
  loop, **28**
  testing, 12, 13
  transition, **205,** 209
semantic analysis, **180**
semantic error, 189
specification: *See also* requirements., 187
sensitization, 45, 54, **57**-59, 63, 65, 67, 113–114
  algebraic sensitization, 59
  logic sensitization, 57, 58
  path, **45**
  state testing sensitization, 221–222
  transaction flow sensitization, 139–140
sequencing, 94, 98
  convenient sequencing, 98
  essential sequencing, **98–99**
  nonessential sequencing, 98
server discipline, queue, **127,** 137–139
service cost, 235
shared data, 5, 88
side effect, 4, 9, 115
simple:
  path, 101, 105
  predicate, **43**–45
  queue, **127**
simulator , code, 5
simultaneous equations, 60
single–server queue, **127**
slice, **103, 107,** 117, **132,** 275
  cover, 132
  data–flow slice, **103, 107–108**
  selection, 107
  transaction–flow slice, **132**
  superslice, **135**
smart comparison, **239**
software, 2, 6, 9, 16, 63, 72, 73, 96
  bad software, 190
  complexity, 13
  cost, 235
  dependability, 234

development, 9-17, 241, 263
  economics, 263
  engineering, 270
  good software, 93
  life–critical software, 166
  mature software, 9
  menu–driven software, 25, **28, 196,** 204, **207,** 224
  reliability, 5, 11, 234, 267, 271
  untestable software, 222
sort test, 137, 138
sorting, 100
source code, 8
space character, **178–179**
spanning link, **32**
special value testing, 160
specification, **3,** 7, 27, 28, 45, 46, 50, 64, 66, 73, 102, 157
  bug, 57, 62, 221, 277
  domain specification, 157
  formal specification, 186, 269
  language, 262, 270, 273
  natural–language, 50
  numerical specification, 173
  semantic specification, 187
  writer, 157
split:
  bug, 141
  node, **123**
  transaction, 135
spreadsheet, 63, 115, 116
STAD, 269, 270
star operator, BNF, **181**
state, **2, 204**
  code, **204–205**
  counter, **205,** 218, 223
  counting, 205, **214,** 222, 227
  cover, 220–221
  current state, **205**
  encoding, **204–205,** 216, 218
  exit set, **207**
  extra state, 218-220
  final state, **2,** 3
  graph, 20, **25,** 205, 209, 225, 265
    strongly connected state
    graph, **206**
  hidden state, 219
  initial state, **2**-4, **205,** 209, 217–218
  isolated state, **206**
  model, 25, 99, 130, 207-209,

226, 276
number of states, 205, **214**, 222, 227
output table, **212**
reachable state, **206**
set, initial, **206**
stable state, 211
–symbol product, 205, **214**, 222, 227
table, **212,** 213, 216, 223, 226, 265
tour, initial, **207**
transaction state, **122**
transient state, 211
transition, **205**
unreachable state, **206,** 215
working initial state set, **207**
working state, **206**
state machine, 82, **205,** 263
ad–hoc state machine, 225
completely specified machine, **207**
link, 208, 209
minimal machine, 215
nested machine, **213**–214, 225, 226
node, 208
strongly connected machine, 215
table representation, 211
state testing, 196, 216, 261, 262, 264 , 268, 274
application, 224
automation, 226
bug assumption, 224–225
limitations, 225–226
sensitization, 221–222
statement cover, **236**
statement label, 21
statistical cover, **238**
statistical testing, 11
status request transaction, 130
step–mode operation, 223
stepwise refinement, 15
storage management test, 5
storage node, **88,** 89
strategic mores, 16
strictly ordered graph, **190**
string, **179**
beginning, **180**
behead, **181**
concatenate, **181**
curtail, **181**

end, **181**
field, **179**
head, **180**
name, **179**
set, **179**
tail, **181**
strong domain testing, 171–172
strongly connected:
finite–state machine, 215
graph, 35, 82, 83
state graph, **206**
structural:
cover, **236**
data flow test criteria, 103
test(ing), xi, xiv, **8,** 11, 103, 271
structured:
construct, 50
language, 65, 73, 75, 76
model, 98
programming, 72
subdomain, **153**
subgraph, **103**
submodel, **126**
subprogram, **6**
subroutine, 4
call, 5
substring , 180, **181**
subsystem, **6**
subtest, **3**
superslice, **135**
symbolic:
constant, 93
debugger, 115
substitution, 59, 156
symmetric relation, **22, 27–28,** 33, 35
symptom, **4,** 7
synchronization test, **99, 127**–128, 136–137
syntax, **179**
analysis, **180**
context dependent syntax, 195–196
cover, 190
errors, 13, 189
graph, 70, 187
incomplete syntax, 198
inconsistent syntax, 198
/semantics mismatch, 198
syntax test(ing), 72, 194, 217, 267
application, 196-198
automation, 199

CITATION INDEX